There Will Always Be Boxing

BOOKS BY THOMAS HAUSER

GENERAL NON-FICTION

Missing
The Trial of Patrolman Thomas Shea
For Our Children (with Frank
Macchiarola)
The Family Legal Companion
Final Warning: The Legacy of Chernobyl
(with Dr. Robert Gale)
Arnold Palmer: A Personal Journey
Confronting America's Moral Crisis (with
Frank Macchiarola)
Healing: A Journal of Tolerance and
Understanding
With This Ring (with Frank Macchiarola)
Thomas Hauser on Sports
Reflections

BOXING NON-FICTION

The Black Lights: Inside the World of
Professional Boxing
Muhammad Ali: His Life and Times
Muhammad Ali: Memories
Muhammad Ali: In Perspective
Muhammad Ali & Company
A Beautiful Sickness
A Year at the Fights
Brutal Artistry
The View from Ringside
Chaos, Corruption, Courage, and Glory
I Don't Believe It, But It's True
Knockout (with Vikki LaMotta)
The Greatest Sport of All

The Boxing Scene
An Unforgiving Sport
Boxing Is . . .
Box: The Face of Boxing
The Legend of Muhammad Ali (with
Bart Barry)
Winks and Daggers
And the New . . .
Straight Writes and Jabs
Thomas Hauser on Boxing
A Hurting Sport
A Hard World
Muhammad Ali: A Tribute to the Greatest
There Will Always Be Boxing

FICTION

Ashworth & Palmer
Agatha's Friends
The Beethoven Conspiracy
Hanneman's War
The Fantasy
Dear Hannah
The Hawthorne Group
Mark Twain Remembers
Finding The Princess
Waiting for Carver Boyd
The Final Recollections of Charles
Dickens
The Baker's Tale

FOR CHILDREN

Martin Bear & Friends

There Will Always Be Boxing

Another Year Inside the Sweet Science

By Thomas Hauser

The University of Arkansas Press
Fayetteville
2017

ISBN: 978-1-68226-041-8
e-ISBN: 978-1-61075-621-1

21 20 19 18 17   5 4 3 2 1

∞The paper used in this publication meets the minimum requirements of the
American National Standard for Permanence of Paper for Printed Library
Materials Z39.48-1984.

Library of Congress Control Number: 2017947016

For boxing fans everywhere.
Thank you.

Contents

Author's Note

There Will Always Be Boxing contains the articles about professional boxing that I authored in 2016. The articles I wrote about the sweet science prior to that date have been published in *Muhammad Ali & Company*; *A Beautiful Sickness*; *A Year at the Fights*; *The View from Ringside*; *Chaos, Corruption, Courage, and Glory*; *I Don't Believe It, But It's True*; *The Greatest Sport of All*; *The Boxing Scene*; *An Unforgiving Sport*; *Boxing Is*; *Winks and Daggers*; *And the New*; *Straight Writes and Jabs*; *Thomas Hauser on Boxing*; *A Hurting Sport*; *Muhammad Ali: A Tribute to the Greatest*; and *A Hard World*.

Fighters and Fights

Andre Ward fights like Bernard Hopkins in a young body.

Reflections on Sergey Kovalev vs. Andre Ward

2016 has been a disappointing year for boxing fans. Few of the fights that we wanted to see actually happened. Instead, we saw Canelo Alvarez running away from Gennady Golovkin; Tyson Fury taking a knee; the decline of Premier Boxing Champions; and the ruination of boxing in New York. The sport was hungry for a big fight that would showcase the best fighting the best. Within that framework, the November 19 match-up between Andre Ward and Sergey Kovalev loomed as the most important fight of the year.

Ward had a storied amateur career. He started boxing at age nine with Virgil Hunter as his trainer and lost his first bout. He fought 124 more times as an amateur and lost only four of those fights.

"I remember vividly the last time I lost a fight and the emotions I felt before and after," Andre recently told this writer. "I was thirteen, almost fourteen years old and fighting a guy from Baton Rouge, Louisiana, named John Revish in the finals of the National Silver Gloves. I knew he was good. I knew he was a puncher. And I allowed myself to be beaten before the fight started. Fear plays a large role in boxing. It's how you use the fear that counts. Fear can motivate you. But if it goes to the dark side, you can be paralyzed by fear. That's what happened to me in that fight, and I promised myself I'd never let it happen again."

Ward won a gold medal in the 178-pound division at the 2004 Athens Olympics and is the only American male to have captured a gold medal in boxing since 1996. The high point of his professional career to date has been an undefeated run in Showtime's 168-pound "Super-Six" tournament that saw him vanquish Mikkel Kessler, Arthur Abraham, and Carl Froch. Andre emerged from the tournament as a hot property. Gracious, well spoken, twenty-seven years old, he was grouped with Floyd Mayweather and Manny Pacquiao at the top of most pound-for-pound lists. Nine months later, he knocked out Chad Dawson. Dawson was dead at the weight, but it was still a pretty good win.

Then things soured. Promotional problems, nagging injuries, and a disinclination to go in tough led Ward to four fights in four years against less than stellar opposition (Edwin Rodriguez, Paul Smith, Sullivan Barrera, and Alexander Brand). Three of those four bouts went the distance. And Roc Nation Sports (Andre's new promoter) was unable to build the Ward brand to the extent that it wanted to.

Kovalev, now thirty-three, was born in the factory town of Kopeysk, Russia. By his own admission, he participated in more than a few street robberies when he was young. At age eleven, he walked into a boxing gym for the first time.

"When I was in the amateurs," Kovalev says, "I never thought that someday I would turn pro. For me, professional boxing was crazy. I thought pro boxing was just beating the whole brain out of your head. It's very dangerous. In the amateurs, it was enough with injuries and some hard fights. I felt like I would never be able to do twelve rounds. My wife pushed me to turn pro. [A friend of Kovalev's current manager, Egis Klimas] found me in Russia and met with me in Moscow and we started to talk about professional boxing. I started to think about it, but it was a maybe. Finally, I made my decision after the 2008 Russian championships, when I won the final fight and the victory was given to my opponent."

Kovalev began his pro career in the United States in 2009 under the tutelage of trainer Don Turner. He now lives in Florida and, like Ward, entered the ring on November 19 undefeated as a pro. Sergey was also the reigning IBF, WBA, and WBO 175-pound champion and widely regarded as the best light-heavyweight in the world. John David Jackson is his current trainer, but Turner is still in the corner on fight night.

One of the remarkable things about Kovalev is his growing fluency in English.

"Sergey couldn't speak English when he came to America," Ellen Haley, director of publicity for Main Events (Kovalev's promoter) says. "It's remarkable how much he has learned. If we say something he doesn't understand, he'll ask what it means and repeat it with us several times."

As for boxing, John David Jackson observes, "Sergey's biggest advantage is his punching power. Power like his is God-given. You either have it or you don't, and he has it. His second biggest advantage is he's a better boxer than most people give him credit for. Sergey is a very good boxer. He's a very good technician. He knows how to box. He has better boxing skills than people realize."

Kovalev doesn't just knock people down; he hurts them.

"You never know when and how life will punch you," Sergey says.

Virtually all fighters come from hard origins. When they start boxing, they substitute one kind of hard life for another. Like Kovalev, Andre Ward personifies that truth.

Ward was born in San Francisco to a black mother and white father. Both of his parents were addicts. His father's curse was heroin; his mother's, cocaine. Andre's mother was largely absent during his childhood. Frank Ward tried to be a good father and provide for his two sons. But several stints in rehab spoke to the trouble he had staying clean.

Virgil Hunter took Andre and his brother in to live with his own family when Andre was twelve. Frank Ward died when Andre was sixteen. After that, Andre, by his own admission, went through a period of drinking and hanging out with the wrong crowd. With Hunter's help, he got back on track and qualified for the 2004 Olympics.

Looking back on it all, Ward says, "I got my values from my dad. He had his demons, but he died clean and sober. He's been gone for over a decade now. If I could have him back for a day, I'd tell him how much I miss him and love him. I'd tell him about where I am in my career; the gold medal and everything that's happened since then. And I'd want him to see my family."

Religion and boxing have given Ward's life structure.

"My relationship with God is my foundation," Andre states. "It's the reason I'm able to be a good husband, a good father, and a good friend."

Ward and his wife, Tiffany, live in a gated community in Oakland with their four children (three sons and a daughter). Virgil Hunter looks at Andre's life today and says, "Andre knows who he is. He knows what he wants. And he has made enough money now to be okay with his past."

Brin-Jonathan Butler in an article for *Undefeated* described the experience of meeting Ward for the first time: "There's charm in his smile and warm handshake. But something changes when you feel the first chill from the cool breeze of his intelligence and power of observation. He has the poised glance of a masterfully composed croupier, giving away nothing while reflexively sizing up and processing all available data."

Ward is articulate and thoughtful. There's a dignity and pride about him that are sometimes mistaken for arrogance. He's guarded and protects himself at all times. One gets the impression that, in all public situations, whether it's in or out of the ring, Andre's first instinct is to do a risk-reward calculation. Whatever situation he's in, he wants to be in control. He also takes great care in how he presents himself to the world.

"I don't do a lot of interviews," Ward acknowledges. "I love speaking to the media if someone is really interested in listening. But too often, someone comes in. They already have a point of view, and all they want is to take a few quotes out of everything I say that they can use to validate the way they've already decided they want to portray me."

Here, it should be noted that, after a long one-on-one interview with Andre several weeks ago, I compared my notes with some of the quotes in Butler's article. In many instances, the wording was virtually identical. To repeat: Ward takes great care in how he presents himself to the world.

"I don't want my story to be reduced to just another cliché; rags to riches, kid from the ghetto, and all that," Ward told Butler. "I know I'm very guarded. How do you think I survived? Guarded is what got me by. But I want people to know what I've come through and overcome because maybe that can inspire somebody."

Among other personal thoughts Ward has shared are:

★ "I know what it is to be bi-racial, when both sides don't accept you and you have that confusion of not feeling accepted. You're left asking, 'Who am I?'"

★ "I'm aware of some of the things that people say about me. I'm boring. I don't have a personality. I don't do this; I don't do that. I don't engulf myself in it anymore the way I used to. I'm more secure now in who I am."

★ "They always say you change after you get famous. They don't tell you that, really, it's everyone else around you that changes."

★ "I'm not chasing fame. I'm fine with going places and no one knowing who I am."

"I don't know Andre Ward," Hall-of-Fame matchmaker Bruce Trampler says. "Without knowing much about his promotional situation,

I don't like the way he left Dan Goossen [Andre's previous promoter]. But in addition to his being a very good fighter, there's one other thing that impressed me about him. I was in Reno in 2010 for a Top Rank card to celebrate the one hundredth anniversary of Jack Johnson against Jim Jeffries. It was the day of the fight. I was in a hamburger place called Johnny Rocket's that was in the hotel. Ward was there with his wife and children, sitting about twenty feet away from me. I didn't know him on a personal level and I didn't want to intrude on his time with his family, so I didn't go over to say hello. But I did watch him. And I was very impressed by the way he interacted with his family and the way he treated people who came over to him to say hello. I said to myself, 'This guy has class. He's a nice guy.'"

Ward is a consummate professional. He always comes prepared to fight. At the kick-off press conference for Kovalev-Ward, he told the media, "You don't prepare for these moments in eight to ten weeks. I've been preparing for this moment since I was a kid. You guys only see us once or twice a year. Imagine what's going on when you're not around."

The fact that Ward won an Olympic gold medal at 178 pounds, dropped down to 168 pounds when he turned pro, and stayed in the super-middleweight division until 2015 shows considerable discipline on his part. As for his ring craftsmanship, Hamilton Nolan writes, "Watching him for a round or two does not always reveal the depth of his talent. His speed is not blinding and his power is not overwhelming. His greatest gift is decision-making. At any given moment, he is always making the right choice. This starts as almost imperceptible and, over the course of a fight, adds up to domination. Every tiny mistake an opponent makes pulls Ward closer to victory. To an even greater degree than Mayweather, Ward is the thinking man's champ."

"I find a way to win," Ward states. "That's what I specialize in. I find a way. Half the battle is getting in the ring. Either you're courageous or crazy to do it, but I get there." Then he adds, "A fighter needs a mean streak. I wouldn't want to be in the sport without one. I have a heart. I don't want my opponent to be hurt badly. But during the fight, I'm not thinking about it."

Ward's hero is Roy Jones. "Roy is something special to me," Andre says.

Suppose Ward got in the ring, and Roy Jones in his prime was in the opposite corner?

"That's a tough one," Andre answers. "Roy is the guy. He'll always be the guy in my mind. Part of it would be the mental part of fighting someone I've always looked up to. Like all fighters—all athletes, really—I have a switch. I'd have to turn the switch like Larry Holmes did with Ali and say, 'We're not friends right now. It's not teacher and student. I'm your equal.' And once I did that, Roy was such a great fighter. He's a guy I'd really have problems with. I'd go with a heavy dose of fundamentals. From time to time, I'd try to show him a bit of himself, lead left hooks and things like that. But mostly fundamentals."

Boxing has taken a toll on Ward over the years.

"You don't feel most of the punches," he says. "They're just reminders. But I really don't like to get hit. I feel violated every time I get hit. And 125 amateur fights, thirty professional fights, all that training. I've taken a lot of punishment. You might not see it. I might not be lying on the canvas, unconscious. But my wife sees me when I have trouble getting out of bed and I'm in pain for days after a fight."

"Andre doesn't want to be great," HBO blow-by-blow commentator Jim Lampley says. "He wants to be perfect."

★ ★ ★

Kovalev-Ward shaped up as the biggest ring challenge either man had faced to date. It was a toss-up fight between two elite boxers. And unlike situations where an aging champion is challenged by a considerably younger opponent, age wouldn't be a factor. Kovalev is only ten months older than Ward.

There was a hint of controversy at the September 6 kick-off press conference in New York.

"When I see Andre Ward [in the hotel] this morning," Kovalev advised the media, "I say 'hi.' He didn't even say 'hi.' Nothing. Fuck him."

"We're getting ready to fight," Ward responded. "We're not friends. We're not buddies. We passed in the hallway. I gave him a head nod. I don't know what he was looking for. If he's using that to motivate himself, that's cool."

Kovalev-Ward was Andre's first fight in Las Vegas. Sergey had fought there twice before but never in a major bout. It was the first pay-per-view fight for either man. And it was a legacy fight for both of them.

The contest also had huge implications for Roc Nation Sports (Ward's promoter) and Main Events (which promotes Kovalev).

Boxing has been a money-losing venture for Roc Nation Sports. Its flagship fighters (Ward and Miguel Cotto) have huge contractual guarantees. And after two years, the rest of its boxing program has yet to develop. The sweet science has been a cash drain for Roc Nation founder, rap impressario Shawn Carter a/k/a Jay Z. But he can afford it.

Main Events, by contrast, is a boxing promotional company that has to make ends meet based on its revenue flow from the sweet science. At present, its primary revenue stream is generated by Kovalev.

Kovalev-Ward never rose in magnitude as an event to the level of its merit as a fight. The November 8 presidential election dominated the pre-fight news, and the Chicago Cubs' World Series triumph all but eliminated boxing from the sports media. Boxing still suffers from the fan resentment that followed the May 5, 2015, encounter between Floyd Mayweather and Manny Pacquiao. Pacquiao's November 5, 2016, fight against Jesse Vargas siphoned off some pay-per-view dollars that might otherwise have gone to Kovalev-Ward. UFC's November 12 card at Madison Square Garden (which marked the return of MMA to New York) was another distraction. During fight week, there was more talk in the general sports media about the possibility of Floyd Mayweather versus Conor McGregor and Mayweather-Pacquiao II than there was about Kovalev-Ward.

Kovalev's partisans noted that it had been a long time since Ward went in tough. Moreover, Andre's primary opponents in the "Super-Six" tournament—Carl Froch, Mikkel Kessler, and Arthur Abraham—were good fighters but not great ones. Kovalev would have been heavily favored to beat any of them. Sergey's November 2014 victory over Bernard Hopkins was also seen as a factor. The mental pressure, mind games, and tactical measures that went into fighting Hopkins were expected to serve Kovalev well against Ward.

"The same thing that happened to Hopkins will happen to Ward," John David Jackson said.

Jackson also said the following:

★ "A lot of so-called experts say that Ward is the smarter fight. Ward is smart at what he does, but a lot of what he does is not fighting. It's surviving and making his opponent frustrated with the tactics that he uses. Sergey can fight against any style. He's very intelligent in the ring. He knows how to solve other fighters' defensive mechanisms."

★ "Ward is crafty and patient. But you can't be that patient and crafty when you got a guy who has bombs in both hands. You don't have time to dictate the pace of the fight and jab here and hold there when you have a guy coming at you with power in both hands. He's not going to be able to do all of the things that he wants to do. This fight here, he has to fight. Then he's rolling the dice. If Ward engages, he'll make himself vulnerable and leave himself open to counterpunches."

★ "Sergey is a pure all-around fighter. He doesn't come into the ring trying to be a one punch knockout artist. He looks to break down his opponents systematically. He does want a knockout, but he's learned how to build up to the knockout. He knows how to cut the ring off and break guys down to the body."

★ "If Sergey hits him flush, Ward will go down like a ton of bricks. If Ward tries to prove that he has power, that would work to our advantage because it means he'll have to stand there and try to engage with Sergey. Ward has a handgun; he's fighting against a tank; and the tank is smart."

"You can be a technician," Don Turner added. "You can be this; you can be that. But when you get hit by Kovalev, everything changes."

Could Kovalev win a decision against Ward?

"The judges gave Sergey every round against Hopkins," Turner noted.

But those who thought Ward would win voiced equal confidence. Good defense beats good offense in most sports. Andre had risen to the occasion at the Olympics and the Super-Six tournament. Bart Barry spoke for many of his sportswriting brethren when he opined, "Ward has approximately twice Kovalev's craft and can fight effectively while moving in three times as many directions as Kovalev, who does incredibly well while moving forward and moving forward."

Kovalev's signature wins had been against Hopkins (a tough out, but forty-nine years old at the time) and Jean Pascal (who had lost to both Hopkins and Carl Froch).

"I'm not Bernard Hopkins," Ward declared. "And no disrespect to Bernard, I'm not forty-nine years old, almost fifty, which is what Bernard was when he fought Kovalev."

"One way to beat Kovalev is to get off first," Virgil Hunter said. "Hit him just hard enough to keep him off balance and force Sergey to reset. Bernard Hopkins knew that. But at age forty-nine, he couldn't do it."

"Andre hits hard enough to get Kovalev's attention," Hunter continued. "And his punches are sharp enough to cut. If Andre gets Kovalev's attention early, if Kovalev says to himself, 'This guy hits harder than I thought,' it changes the flow of the fight. Can Andre knock Kovalev out with one shot? No. But he can hit Kovalev often enough and hard enough to knock him out."

Ward also had his say on the matter:

★ "I don't have a style. I'm formless. I'm unpredictable. People can't put their finger on my style. I can't put my finger on my style. My greatest asset is my mind and the fact that people underestimate me. They look at me and say, 'He's good; he can box.' But I'm more than that. I do what I have to do to win. I am what I need to be."

★ "Kovalev is not just a big puncher. He's a boxer. He's a thinker. He understands range, positioning, and things like that. He comes from a good boxing background. He's technically sound. He can do multiple things in the ring. We're not ignorant of that. There's a lot more to him than just being a big puncher. But most European fighters like range. They aren't trained to fight on the inside. Obviously, that's something we'll try to take advantage of. It's all about execution."

★ "At the end of the day, many people make the same mistake with me. They call me a great boxer or a great neutralizer, but there's so much more going on with me than that. If I was just about defense and neutralizing, then a lot of these big punchers would walk through me. And there's a reason they don't."

★ "However Kovalev wants to bring it, we've got our game plan. It's about making constant adjustments, the ebbs and flows. You got to find ways to make adjustments to get the job done in those big moments. That's what's going to separate the guy who gets his hand raised at the end of the fight from the guy who doesn't."

Lennox Lewis visited the media center at the MGM Grand in Las Vegas one day before Kovalev-Ward and reminisced about being at ringside with Andre in Montreal for the January 30, 2016, Kovalev-Pascal fight.

"Andre was there to check out Kovalev," Lennox recalled. "And after a few rounds, he told me, 'I've seen what I have to see. He doesn't know enough.'"

That said, both sides understood that the outcome of Kovalev-Ward was very much in doubt.

Sergey Kovalev: "This fight is a huge test for me. He's a great boxer. He's a great champion. He's undefeated. This fight is fifty-fifty who will win. Underdog, favorite; it does not matter."

Andre Ward: "Sergey is good. To be honest with you, I expected Kovalev-Hopkins to be more competitive than it was. But I've been in these situations before. So has Kovalev. He's got to get it done. I've got to get it done."

John David Jackson: "Ward is a very smart fighter. He has been able to be evasive and avoid the big shots. He does that very well. He suffocates his opponents so they can't punch. He is able to deflect a lot of your strengths while exposing a lot of your weaknesses. There's been a lot of talk on both sides. Come Saturday, that's all over with and it will be about who's the best man in the ring."

Virgil Hunter: "We're in with a dangerous fighter. We know that. I want the best Andre Ward and the best Sergey Kovalev in the ring on fight night. Then we'll see who's the better fighter."

Just prior to each fighter weighing in at the division limit of 175 pounds, Don Turner was asked, "What's going to happen in this fight?"

"Who knows?" Turner answered.

★ ★ ★

Prior to Kovalev-Ward, Andre Ward had spent approximately ten hours in the ring in actual combat over the course of thirty professional fights. Sergey Kovalev had logged roughly four hours in thirty-one bouts. For thirty-six minutes of combat, they were at war with each other.

When I'm at ringside for a major fight, I watch the action closely for three minutes of every round. Most of the notes I take are written down on an 8-½ by 11-inch pad in the one-minute rest period between rounds.

Occasionally, I scrawl a note during a round without looking down at my pad. I also score each round.

The notes I wrote while sitting in the press section during Kovalev-Ward are below. Some of these comments were cumulative and reflected what I'd seen in earlier rounds.

Round 1—Each man boxing cautiously . . . Ward coming in with his head down . . . Kovalev rocks Ward with a hard stiff jab . . . Ward holding on . . . Robert Byrd breaks them while Kovalev is pumping rights to the body.

Round 2—Kovalev stalking . . . His jab is effective . . . Drops Ward with a straight right hand . . . Ward seems a bit shaken . . . They both threw right hands and Kovalev's landed.

Round 3—Ward leading with his head . . . Throwing elbows . . . Wrestling . . . Did fighting Hopkins prepare Kovalev for this?

Round 4—Ward making defensive adjustments . . . Kovalev not scoring cleanly, but ineffective aggression is better than no aggression at all.

Round 5—Very few clean punches landing . . . Lead left hook is Ward's best weapon, but he hasn't done much with it so far.

Round 6—Ward wrestling, elbowing. The more he sees what Robert Byrd is letting him get away with, the more he does it.

Round 7—Ward finding a better distance . . . Few solid punches landing. Stiff jabs elicit "oohs" from the crowd.

Round 8—Kovalev stalking, Ward pot-shotting.

Round 9—Kovalev seems to be tiring a bit . . . There are times when this resembles Greco-Roman wrestling.

Round 10—Robert Byrd has been out of position too often in this fight. And he has given Ward license to do pretty much what he wants.

Round 11—Ward seems a bit tired . . . Finally, Byrd warns Ward. Was it for lacing or a forearm to the throat. He did both . . . Several more low blows from Ward.

Round 12—Ward comes out more aggressively . . . It was a good fight; not a great one.

It was a difficult fight to score. There were a lot of close rounds. According to CompuBox, Kovalev outlanded Ward by a 126-to-116 margin. Also, Sergey landed the harder blows. But take away round two and the statistics were roughly even.

Sitting at ringside, I scored the bout 115-113 (6-5-1 in rounds) for Kovalev. Most, but not all, of the media at ringside thought that Sergey had won. Harold Lederman of HBO scored the bout 116-111 for Kovalev. ESPN had it 115-112 for Kovalev.

All three judges—Burt Clements, Glenn Trowbridge, and John McKaie—scored the fight 114-113 in Ward's favor. Watching a video replay several days later, I felt that 114-113 for Ward was within the realm of reason. But as Frank Lotierzo wrote afterward, "It's easier to make the case for Kovalev winning than it is for Ward."

Kovalev was more direct in his post-fight comments. "It is the wrong decision," Sergey said. "The witnesses are here. They saw it. It is the USA, and all the judges were from the USA. It is a sport. Don't make it politics. It is a sport, and I won the fight."

Robert Byrd's refereeing was more problematic than the judging. Byrd let Ward lead with his head and grapple for much of the fight. He overlooked Andre's low blows, elbows, and forearms to the throat, and seemed more prone to break clinches when Kovalev had a free hand and was pumping blows to Ward's body. Byrd was also out of position for much of the fight. His performance was disappointing and surprising since, in the past, he has usually positioned himself well and refused to tolerate excessive holding and other inappropriate tactics.

I don't blame Ward for fighting the way he did. He did what he had to do to win. As long as Byrd let him get away with it, so be it. But Byrd is seventy-four years old. And men in their seventies have lost a step. Trust me; I'm seventy years old. I know.

Bob Bennett (executive director of the Nevada State Athletic Commission) has defended Byrd's refereeing of Kovalev-Ward.

"Robert was consistent," Bennett said several days after the bout. "He didn't want to dictate the flow of the fight. I don't think his age was a factor. I think he did a good job."

A contrary view was expressed by Larry Merchant. I had breakfast with Merchant at the airport on the morning after Kovalev-Ward. "I didn't like the way Robert Byrd handled himself," Merchant said. "It wasn't a level playing field. There have been times when I've been really troubled by what I saw a referee do during a fight. I was troubled by Richard Steele at Chavez-Taylor. I was troubled by the way the referee [Eddie Cotton] handled Lewis-Tyson. I didn't like the refereeing job [by Joe Cortez] at Mayweather-Hatton. And I was troubled by Robert Byrd last night. There was an aroma to it."

A source close to the Nevada State Athletic Commission says that Byrd underwent back surgery last year. After refereeing Ishe Smith vs. Tommy Rainone in Las Vegas on December 18, 2015, he was out of action for nine months. That surgery should have been disclosed to each fighter's camp before Kovalev-Ward. Had there been disclosure, it's likely that the Kovalev camp would have pressed for a different referee.

Because of Byrd's stewardship and controversy over the judges' decision, Kovalev-Ward was not a fully satisfying night. Of course, Ward had predicted as much. "There always seems to be a 'but' in the equation when people talk about me," Andre said earlier this month. "After I beat Kovalev, some people will give me my due and others will say that all I did was outbox him."

Give Ward credit. He got off the canvas, fought to win, and won.

As for the future; the Kovalev camp says that it has an airtight clause that guarantees an immediate rematch. Roc Nation seems less than enthusiastic about that prospect.

Early indications are that the pay-per-view numbers for Kovalev-Ward will be disappointing. The announced attendance of 13,310 was far short of a sellout, and thousands of tickets were given away through Tidal (a global music and entertainment platform). Roc Nation had guaranteed Ward a reported $5 million to fight Kovalev. And Andre's contract with his promoter would seem to indicate more red ink for Jay Z and company if Ward-Kovalev II happens.

Meanwhile, it makes sense to step back and take a long look at Ward. Only in America could a boxer win an Olympic gold medal; be thoughtful, articulate, and a good family man; live his life free of scandal; emerge victorious from a legitimate "Super-Six" tournament; triumph over Sergey Kovalev; be recognized as one of the best fighters in the world pound-for-pound; and be largely ignored by the mainstream sports media.

How good a fighter is Ward?

"That's not for me to say," Andre answers. "But I know I'm a really good fighter. I've never cheated the sport. I've played my part in the amateurs and the pros. I've always given my all. Greatness is being able to repeat a great performance again and again and again. I think I've done that."

"But boxing is just a season for me," Ward continues. "It's what I do. It isn't who I am. I won't be doing this forever. No one does. What I want is to walk away from boxing on my own terms. Right now, I have laser focus on finishing strong. Then I'll look forward to whatever comes next. I'll have a life after boxing. I just don't know yet what it will be. And I hope that, after I leave the sport, boxing will be a little better because I was in it."

It will be.

Deontay Wilder believes in himself. But as of this writing, his team has done its best to avoid putting him in the ring against tough opponents.

Heavyweights at Barclays Center

January 16, 2016, marked the sixteenth fight card at Barclays Center in Brooklyn. The show was billed as featuring two world heavyweight championship fights, which is a little like saying there will be two Olympic gold-medal races in the 100-meter dash on the same afternoon with different participants in each race. But that's what boxing is like these days.

The four combatants—Deontay Wilder, Artur Szpilka, Vyacheslav Glazkov, and Charles Martin—had a composite ring record of 98 wins, 1 loss, and 2 draws between them. But of those wins, only one (Wilder's 2015 decision over Bermane Stiverne) was against an opponent who could be considered "world class" at the time the fight took place. Most of the opponents were on the order of Kertson Manswell, who was knocked out by Wilder, Glazkov, and Martin, and probably would have been knocked out by Szpilka had they fought.

Lennox Lewis and Mike Tyson were among the 12,668 fans at Barclays Center on fight night to remind people of what a heavyweight champion used to be.

The first "championship" bout of the evening matched Vyacheslav Glazkov (21-0-1, 13 KOs) against Charles Martin (22-0-1, 20 KOs) for the IBF title, which the sanctioning body declared vacated when Tyson Fury signed for a rematch against Wladimir Klitschko rather than fight a "mandatory" defense against Glazkov.

Glazkov came out of the Ukrainian amateur system and won a bronze medal in the super-heavyweight division at the 2008 Beijing Olympics. But he has struggled as a professional, fighting to a draw against Malik Scott and eking out controversial decisions over Derrik Rossy and Steve Cunningham.

Martin, a southpaw, is one of the heavyweights that promoter Michael King was trying to develop before his untimely death last year. He has been fighting professionally for less than forty months and had never fought a world-class opponent. Indeed, an argument could be made that Martin had never fought a good club fighter. He can punch a bit and outweighed Glazkov by 31 pounds (249 to 218). But the assumption was that the more technically proficient Glazkov would outbox him.

Round one of Glazkov-Martin was a feeling-out stanza. Martin brings his jab back slowly and low, but at least he was throwing something (which Glazkov wasn't). To outbox an opponent, which Vyacheslav was expected to do, a fighter has to throw punches.

Round two saw more inaction. Then, forty-eight seconds into round three, Martin stepped with his lead foot (the right) onto Glazkov's lead foot (the left), and Vyacheslav went down awkwardly. As soon as the action resumed, Showtime commentator Al Bernstein observed, "Something bothered Glazkov during that slip. His demeanor as a fighter has changed." Seconds later, as Glazkov was throwing a right to the body, he tumbled to the canvas and rose, limping badly.

"He was hurt from before," Bernstein said.

At that point, without a meaningful punch having been landed, referee Earl Brown had no choice but to stop the fight. A subsequent examination by New York State Athletic Commission ring doctor Gerard Varlotta led to the pronouncement that Glazkov's anterior cruciate ligament (ACL) had been torn clean through.

Martin was declared the winner on a third-round TKO. But it's likely that Glazkov tore his ACL when the fighters' feet got tangled and he went down for the first time. Thus, an argument can be made that the decision should be changed to "no contest." Should that happen, it would remove the loss from Glazkov's record and vacate the IBF title.

Meanwhile, for the time being at least, Martin has a "world championship" belt. It's hard to imagine the heavyweight title being more devalued than it has been in recent years. But this fight did just that.

The second "heavyweight championship" contest on the card saw Deontay Wilder (35-0, 34 KOs) put his WBC strap on the line against Artur Szpilka (20-1, 15 KOs).

Wilder was a nineteen-year-old community college student in Alabama when his daughter, Naieya (who is now ten), was born with spina bifida. At that point, he dropped out of college to support her. He began going to a boxing gym in 2005 and won a bronze medal at the 2008 Beijing Olympics.

Deontay's nickname ("The Bronze Bomber") references his Olympic medal and is a nod toward another Alabama-born heavyweight champion, Joe Louis ("The Brown Bomber").

Wilder is trained by Mark Breland. The two men make an odd couple. Breland is quiet and introspective. Deontay is out there and loves to talk. "He's a little quieter in camp than he is in public," Breland notes. "But not much. He likes to clown around a lot."

With regard to Wilder's ring skills, Breland says, "There's a lot of room for improvement. But he's doing everything we tell him to do."

At a media sitdown in December 2015 Wilder declared, "I ain't scared to fight nobody."

Whether his matchmakers share that confidence is another matter. Deontay has been protected. He's no longer a novice. He has been fighting professionally for seven years. But his resume is short on credible opponents.

Szpilka was within Team Wilder's comfort range. Artur was obliterated by Bryant Jennings and was on the canvas three times in two fights against Mike Mollo. And he isn't a big puncher.

Mike Tyson put matters in perspective when asked about Wilder by Showtime's Jim Gray before the fight:

> Tyson: I don't know the guy he's fighting.
> Gray: Szpilka.
> Tyson: Spilky? I have no idea who he is.

Here it might be noted that Szpilka's curriculum vitae includes an eighteen-month stint in prison in his native Poland for brawling as a "soccer hooligan." Wilder had his own run-in with the law when he was arrested in 2013 after an incident in a Las Vegas hotel room and charged with domestic battery by strangulation. According to a police report, the woman in question had a possible broken nose, swelling around her eyes, a cut lip, and red marks on her neck. Wilder's attorney later said that Deontay was apologetic and had mistakenly thought the woman was planning to rob him. The matter was settled out of court.

Wilder, at 6 feet 7 inches tall, towered over Szpilka, although Artur outweighed him by four pounds. Deontay was a 15-to-1 betting favorite.

As for the fight; Szpilka fought as well as he could, which is to say that he fought gamely and with the ring craftsmanship of a soccer hooligan. Wilder seemed uncertain as to how to fight a southpaw and failed to jab effectively, which would have made it an easier fight. Neither guy went to the body.

As round nine neared an end, Szpilka repeated one of the many fundamental mistakes he'd been making throughout the fight. To wit, he squared up and leaned in with his head as he was throwing a wide over-hand left. Wilder beat him to the punch with a perfectly thrown straight right that landed flush on Artur's jaw and rendered Szpilka unconscious. It was a dramatic end to a sloppy fight.

After the bout, Tyson Fury (who holds the WBA and WBO heavy-weight belts by virtue of his recent victory over Wladimir Klitschko) clamored into the ring and carried on like he was at a WWE spectacle.

Fury-Wilder might happen at some point in the future. Meanwhile, Deontay keeps talking Klitschko-Fury-Povetkin and keeps fighting Molina-Duhaupas-Szpilka.

Three Months Later—More on the Heavyweights

At the moment (April 11, 2016), there are more "world champions" from the United Kingdom (eleven) than from the United States (nine). More significantly, England is becoming the nexus for heavyweight championship boxing.

Three of the four major sanctioning body belts are now in English hands. Tyson Fury of Cheshire holds the WBA and WBO titles by virtue of his November 2015 victory over Wladimir Klitschko. And Hertfordshire's Anthony Joshua separated Charles Martin from his senses in London on April 9 to claim the IBF crown.

Let's put Joshua vs. Martin in perspective.

Martin, age twenty-nine, is the product of a venture undertaken by the late Michael King, an American media mogul who poured an enor-mous amount of money into taking a group of large, athletically gifted young men with no boxing experience and training them to be fighters. Charles was maneuvered to a January 16, 2016, fight against Vyacheslav Glazkov for the vacant IBF heavyweight belt and emerged with the strap when Glazkov tore his anterior cruciate ligament and was unable to continue. But given the mediocre nature of the competition that Martin had faced, virtually no one took him seriously as a "champion."

Joshua, age twenty-six, won a gold medal in the super-heavyweight division at the 2012 London Olympics and had been carefully matched en route to a 15-0 (15 KOs) record. Prior to fighting Martin, he'd competed for a mere 4,446 seconds as a professional fighter. That's fewer than twenty-five rounds.

In the past, Joshua would have been considered a year or two away from a title opportunity. But in the past, Martin wouldn't have been a champion. Charles was a good opponent for Anthony to test his skills against. Realistically speaking, Joshua had fought better opponents in the amateurs than Martin (with the exception of Glazkov) had fought in his entire pro career.

Joshua acknowledged as much during a pre-fight media conference call when he noted, "I think that, when the red carpet's been laid out for you, you can only walk down it with the amount of experience that you have. At the end of the day, let's strip away the heavyweight title and look at the opponent I'm facing."

Martin, by contrast, seemed borderline delusional with regard to the task at hand. His pre-fight declarations included:

★ "I'm not going to go in there respecting anybody's power. I don't care what he's bringing to the table."

★ "I can't be stopped. I'm like Lamon Brewster versus Wladimir Klitschko when he [Klitschko] unloaded all those shots until he couldn't throw any more punches. And then what did Lamon Brewster do? Knock him the fuck out. Just that will to win, man. You can throw whatever you want, but I'll walk through fire to get you."

★ "He doesn't have any footwork. He can't box. He can't move. The only thing he's relying on is his power, and I got more tools than that. If he thinks he's going to be able to land hard punches on me and stuff like that, he's got another think coming. I'm very elusive. I'm a technician."

★ "When I get in there and start doing the things that I do in there, he's gone. Everybody thinks that he's a superstar, and I know that he's not ready."

Martin weighed in at 245 pounds, Joshua at 244.

Joshua was a 9-to-2 betting favorite.

It didn't last long.

Martin fights like a guy who has learned to box by the numbers. Very little about the sweet science is second nature to him. In round one, he seemed tentative to the point of being passive. He also stood straight up, rarely moved his head, and (as is his wont) brought his jab back slowly and low.

Joshua scored points in the first stanza with his jab and an occasional straight right hand. Then, a minute into round two, he countered Martin's jab with a straight right that put the American on the canvas. Seconds later, that scenario repeated itself. This time, referee Jean-Pierre Van Imschoot counted Martin out, and Joshua had an IBF heavyweight championship belt to go with his Olympic gold medal.

The count might have been a trifle fast. But if the bout had gone on, Joshua would simply have knocked Martin down again.

Joshua is a work in progress. He now has a championship belt and a great deal of potential. But is he the next great heavyweight? Right now, whether he's even ready to fight top-echelon heavyweights is an open issue.

And Three Months After That

It used to be fun to watch Chris Arreola fight. Now it's sad; a view that was reinforced when WBC heavyweight titleholder Deontay Wilder knocked out the shell of what Arreola once was on July 16, 2016.

Arreola made his mark as a hit-me-and-I'll-hit-you-back brawler. But he had a pretty good amateur pedigree and reasonably good ring skills when he chose to utilize them. Once upon a time, he was the #1 heavyweight in America. He got a big push from HBO, but showed an aversion to training properly and ate his way out of serious contention. That led Henry Ramirez (Chris's longtime trainer) to observe, "Sometimes I don't think he gives us the best chance to win. Sometimes he comes in a little too far out of shape."

Wilder was scheduled to make a mandatory defense of his WBC title against Alexander Povetkin in Russia on May 21 of this year. But Povetkin tested positive for meldonium (a substance that was added by the World Anti-Doping Agency to its banned substance list effective January 1, 2016), at which point the WBC ordered that the bout be postponed. Thereafter, Wilder opted for Arreola as his next opponent.

This was Arreola's third opportunity to fight for a heavyweight belt. His two earlier efforts (against Vitali Klitschko and Bermane Stiverne) ended in "KO by." Now thirty-five, he entered the ring to face Wilder with a 36-4-1 (31 KOs) ledger. But Chris had never beaten a world-class opponent. And over the previous fifty-three months, his record revealed two wins, two losses, a draw, and one no contest. In his four most recent outings, he'd been knocked out by Stiverne and struggled against Curtis Harper, Fred Kassi, and Travis Kauffman. His best days are long behind him.

Worse, Arreola had broken his ankle in March of this year, which negated any inclination he might otherwise have had to train during what became his recovery period. And Henry Ramirez acknowledged that he and Chris weren't told that Wilder-Arreola was on until the last weekend in May.

Arreola has long been popular among boxing fans for his engaging personality and refreshing candor. Asked if he thought that, given his recent ring performances, he deserved another title opportunity, Chris replied, "Let's be honest, man. Do I deserve it? Come on. No. But when a title shot comes knocking, you don't turn it down."

Wilder was in accord, saying, "Does he deserve the title shot? No, he doesn't. He knows it. But is Chris Arreola the perfect guy for this fight? Of course he is."

Wilder was a 20-to-1 betting favorite.

As for the fight, there was a time when Arreola would have posed problems for Wilder. But that was when a British pound was worth $1.71 in US currency. The pound might make a successful comeback someday. Arreola won't.

Wilder-Arreola resembled an aging bull being torn apart by a sadistic matador.

Arreola entered the ring looking like a heavily tattooed blob. His strategy seemed to be to wait for Wilder to make a stupid mistake and then turn the tide with one big punch. The problem with that strategy was, in addition to having lost his reflexes and timing, Arreola appears to have lost his punch.

"Arreola" and "elusive" are rarely seen in the same sentence unless "not" appears between them. Chris has never been hard to hit. And while boxing aficionados have long questioned Wilder's skills, stamina, and (most of all) his chin, Deontay's power has never been suspect.

For most of the night, Arreola plodded forward in an attempt to get to Wilder's body, his own body jiggling as his tattoos took on the look of images in an amusement park fun-house mirror.

Wilder controlled the proceedings with his jab, mocking Arreola from time to time by gyrating his hips in clinches. Chris was cut on the bridge of the nose in round two and knocked down in round four. By the middle stanzas, his left eye was swollen shut and his right eye was closing. After eight ugly rounds, Henry Ramirez stopped the carnage.

It never should have started.

Unlike many professional athletes, Gerry Cooney has been happier after his days in the spotlight ended than he was before.

Gerry Cooney: Then and Now

On January 16, 2016, Barclays Center in Brooklyn hosted Deontay Wilder vs. Artur Szpilka and Vyacheslav Glazkov vs. Charles Martin: two bouts that were advertised as "world heavyweight championship" fights. I was sitting in the press section next to a man who knows what it's like to fight for the real heavyweight championship of the world.

Gerry Cooney turned pro in 1977 and, after Muhammad Ali's retirement, became the hottest commodity in boxing. He was big, WHITE, good looking, and he could PUNCH. By 1982, Cooney had a 25-and-0 record highlighted by crushing knockout victories over Jimmy Young, Ron Lyle, and Ken Norton. Cooney-Norton was a scary fifty-four-second blowout that left Norton unconscious with his eyes open, staring unseeing into space.

Thirteen months after Cooney-Norton, on June 11, 1982, Cooney challenged Larry Holmes for the heavyweight championship of the world. It was a massive event, one of the most heavily promoted, intensely watched fights in the history of boxing.

Holmes-Cooney was up for grabs on the judges' scorecards when Larry knocked Gerry out in the thirteenth round. Cooney had five fights in the eight years that followed, winning three and coming up short against Michael Spinks and George Foreman. He retired in 1990 at age thirty-three. But his career really ended after Holmes-Cooney. And arguably, before that: after Cooney-Norton.

"The truth is," Gerry told me at Barclays Center, "the good part of my career ended the night I knocked out Norton. I'd already started hurting myself with drinking. And that night, after the fight, I tried cocaine for the first time. That's when I needed someone to take me aside and say. 'Let's get focused, not just with boxing but with life.' But I had too many enablers around me, and they weren't going to challenge what was working for them."

Years of substance abuse followed.

"I got sober on April 21, 1988," Gerry said, recounting a crucial turning point in his life. "For a long time after that, it embarrassed me that I never reached my full potential as a boxer. It still bothers me a little. I could have done so much more . . . If I'd taken better care of myself . . . If I'd had a little more experience before I fought Holmes . . ."

"The way it is for an athlete," Cooney continued, "when things are right, you're in a zone. For a batter in baseball, the ball comes in like it's in slow motion. For me in boxing when things were right, it was like I had tunnel vision and could slow time down. There's nothing like being in that zone. It's the greatest feeling in the world. I could create an opening in the moment I needed it and land that big shot."

The undercard at Barclays Center was mediocre. Cooney's thoughts turned to the great heavyweights of his lifetime.

"Ali was the best. I would have loved the challenge of fighting him when he was young. George Foreman was a devastating puncher. Lennox Lewis was a talented guy. He fought a little scared, which isn't necessarily a bad thing. Riddick Bowe had good all-around skills. The young Mike Tyson—the good Mike Tyson—is on my short list. Joe Frazier and Evander Holyfield had all the heart in the world. Holmes was good enough to beat me and a lot of other guys. All those guys had their gifts."

As for the heavyweights of the new millennium, Cooney opined, "The Klitschkos had good size and they could fight. Vitali had more guts and was the tougher of the two. He was a better fighter than Wladimir. Tyson Fury is soft, and he's not a big puncher. I'm a fan of Deontay Wilder, but he still hasn't learned how to fight. And his chin might not be good, which is why they're keeping him away from punchers. Anthony Joshua is green. He needs more rounds against better opponents, but he has potential."

Vyacheslav Glazkov vs. Charles Martin was a dreary affair, cut short when Glazkov tore his anterior cruciate ligament in the third round and was unable to continue, making Martin the new IBF "world heavyweight champion."

Wally Matthews, who covered boxing for *Newsday* and the *New York Post* decades ago, came over to say hello. Cooney greeted him warmly.

"I've got a question for you. Do you ever get the feeling that you were born thirty years too late?" Matthews asked rhetorically.

Cooney laughed.

After Matthews had gone, Gerry reflected further on his years in the sweet science.

"Boxing was good to me," he said. "It helped me deal with a lot of anger that I had inside from when I was growing up. And I made good money. Not as much as I should have, because there were people I trusted who stole from me. But I came out of boxing okay."

"I've got a great life now," Cooney continued. "I'm the happiest guy in the world. I've got a great wife. I've got great kids. I love the way things turned out for me. If I'd beaten Holmes, the way my head was back then, who knows what would have happened. I wish I'd won. But life was so fast for me back then. If I'd won, I might not be alive today."

Jerry Izenberg, the dean of American sportswriters, has followed Cooney from the fighter's early ring career to the present day.

"One of the things I've learned over time," Izenberg says, "is that very few people really change. They might do a few things differently as they get older. Maybe they get a bit more polished. But they're still the same person inside. Gerry Cooney has changed. He put his demons behind him and went from being a jerk at times to being a great guy. And he's been a great guy for a long time now."

Gerry Cooney is not just a boxing success story. He's a success story.

Terence Crawford has a good grasp of recent boxing history. "I used to watch a lot of old fights," he says. "Pernell Whitaker, Sugar Ray Leonard, Meldrick Taylor, Shane Mosley, guys like that, until I got older and developed my own style."

Terence Crawford Comes to New York

Elite fighters look different from good ones when they're in action. They have a glow.

WBO 140-pound champion Terence Crawford has a glow. Fight fans had the opportunity to witness him in the ring on February 27, 2016, when he dismantled Hank Lundy in five rounds. But they might not be aware of how unlikely Crawford's rise has been.

Crawford comes from Nebraska, a largely rural state better known for cornfields and meat slaughterhouses than boxing. Max Baer was born in Nebraska in 1909 but moved to California at an early age. That's it for Nebraska's previous boxing royalty.

Bob Boozer is the only person born in Nebraska to have averaged more than 5.4 points per game over the course of a National Basketball Association career. Boozer was born in 1937.

Nebraska-born Major League Baseball players include Sam Crawford (1880), Grover Alexander (1887), Richie Ashburn (1927), Bob Gibson (1935), and Wade Boggs (1958). That's five Hall of Famers since professional baseball was inaugurated 140 years ago.

Malcolm X, Gerald Ford, Dick Cheney, Marlon Brando, Fred Astaire, Henry Fonda, and Warren Buffet round out the list of the most famous Nebraska-born notables. Of that group, only Buffet chose to spend his adult years in the Cornhusker State.

"In the amateurs," Terence Crawford notes, "people would look at where I was from and say, 'Nebraska. That's an easy win.'"

Crawford started boxing when he was seven. "I was always the littlest guy with the biggest heart," he says. "I never liked school. I was on the streets a lot. I got into trouble. I can't say where I'd be now without boxing."

Terence turned pro on March 14, 2008, and, after four consecutive wins, found more trouble. As recounted by British boxing writer Steve Lillis, "Crawford's life changed in September 2008 after a wild day that started when he was attacked by bouncers with Mace spray and a night stick after trouble at a party. He had rowed with his mother earlier because he should have been in the gym. So he didn't bother going home and went to play the dice game that almost cost him his life. While Crawford sat in a car with his loot, a gunman fired the bullet that hit him in the head behind his right ear."

"That's when I sat down and just thought about life," Crawford told Lillis. "You're supposed to be in the house getting ready for a fight, and you're out shooting dice and getting shot. You hang with those types of people, that's what happens. The only reason that [the bullet] didn't go through my skull was because the window slowed it down. Ever since then, I've got a purpose. I didn't want my son growing up with his dad in jail, dead, or him seeing me do negative things. I just stopped everything to be a better role model for my son."

"Wrong place, wrong time, wrong people," Crawford says today. "I was doing stupid things where I shouldn't have been when I should have been home sleeping. But it taught me a lesson. I look on life now like I don't take anything for granted."

On March 1, 2014, Crawford journeyed to Scotland and captured the WBO lightweight crown with a twelve-round decision over Ricky Burns. Next came a star-making performance in Crawford's hometown of Omaha: a ninth-round stoppage of Yuriorkis Gamboa. Victories over Raymundo Beltran (a workmanlike decision), Thomas Dulorme (KO 6 for the WBO 140-pound title), and Dierry Jean (KO 10) followed. That left the twenty-eight-year-old Crawford with a 27-and-0 (19 KOs) record.

British promoter Frank Warren recently called Crawford "the most talented of the American boxers now that Floyd Mayweather claims to have retired" and added, "Crawford is a slick, clinically punching fighter much in the mold of the early Mayweather but without the egotistical baggage. He is also more exciting, with fast switch-hitting hands and well-honed technique."

On a personal level, Crawford has a likable manner, answers questions in a direct thoughtful way, and seems comfortable with who he is. He and his live-in girlfriend have had three children together and also live with her child from a previous relationship. Apart from boxing, his passion is fishing.

"I'm not into fancy things," Terence says. "Me showing off money is making sure my family is okay and buying my mom a new car."

Crawford-Lundy was contested in The Theater (the small arena) at Madison Square Garden. Everyone knew Terence could sell out a venue in Omaha. The question was, what could he do in New York?

Lundy (26-5-1, 13 KOs) was a heavy underdog. The thirty-two-year-old challenger had lost to Thomas Dulorme, Raymundo Beltran, Mauricio Herrera, Viktor Postol, and John Molina Jr. Equally telling, his only victory since May 2014 had been against Carlos Winston Velasquez (who had lost twenty of his previous thirty-two fights). As earlier noted, Crawford had beaten both Dulorme and Beltran.

Crawford and Lundy engaged in a spirited verbal battle in the build-up to their encounter:

* Lundy: "I'm on your ass. This is real. It's war. Fight night, I'm gonna break your will. I'm gonna beat your ass. It's gonna be bad."

* Crawford: "You're always woofin'. 'I'm gonna do this; I'm gonna do that.' That's talking, boy. You ain't gonna do shit. We know about you. You can talk all you want. I'm for real. I'm gonna hit you in the mouth."

* Lundy: "Everything I hit you with, you're gonna feel my pain and struggle."

* Crawford: "Hank Lundy is a big-mouthed guy that runs around saying everybody's scared of him. He says he's willing to die in the ring to beat me. That's him getting hit in the head too much. I'm not willing to die in the ring. I got four young kids. So I'm going in and coming out alive with the victory."

"Lundy isn't an easy mark," Brad Goodman (a matchmaker for Top Rank, which promoted the bout) said. "Lundy can fight. But Crawford can fight better."

When fight night came, the arena was sold out. A vocal contingent of Crawford fans who had flown from Nebraska to New York was in attendance.

Lundy was there to win. But so was Crawford.

Terence (as he often does) turned southpaw in the first minute of the bout. He's a patient fighter, who takes his time breaking down an opponent. Once he'd adjusted to Lundy's rhythm, it was just a matter of time.

In round four, Lundy switched to a southpaw stance in a futile effort to blunt Crawford's attack.

Midway through round five, Crawford landed a hard straight left to the temple followed by a chopping left hand up top that staggered the challenger. A barrage of punches highlighted by a brutal right to the body and another straight left put Lundy on the canvas. He rose on unsteady legs and was pinned in a corner with punches raining down upon him when referee Steve Willis stopped the assault at the 2:09 mark.

Crawford is a very good fighter. Now he needs the inquisitors who will tell us whether or not he's great. Terence thinks that, ultimately, the answer to that question will be "yes."

"The boxing game is wide open," Crawford says. "Mayweather, Pacquiao, Cotto; they're all leaving. It's time for us young fighters to take over the sport. I wouldn't be in boxing if I didn't believe I'm the best. I was that little kid who loved to fight. If I won the lottery, I'd still box. I can't leave boxing until I finish what I'm building."

Adrien Broner likes to brag that he has won "championships" in four weight divisions. Given the boxing politics involved, that's a little like a guy going to a brothel four times and saying that he "scored with four beautiful women."

Broner-Theophane:
April Fool's Day in Washington, DC

It's hard to believe that Washington, DC, could become more dys-functional than it already is in this bizarre election year. But Adrien Broner and the District of Columbia Boxing and Wrestling Commission are doing their best to achieve that end.

On April 1, 2016 (a/k/a April Fool's Day), Broner (now 32-2, 24 KOs) entered the ring to face Ashley Theophane (39-7-1, 11 KOs). Broner is well known to fight fans. Theophane is a limited boxer with zero notable wins on his ledger. Each time Ashley has stepped up to the world-class level, he has lost.

Broner brands himself as "AB" and says that the initials stand for "about billions." A recent video posted online shows him throwing his change (bills, not coins) in the air as he leaves a Walmart check-out counter and declaring of the cashier, "He must not know. I'm AB. I don't need no change."

This was one of Broner's more socially acceptable postings. Previous postings include inter alia (1) Broner having intercourse with two women and no condom, and (2) Broner, half-dressed while purportedly defecat-ing into a toilet in Popeye's and then wiping himself with United States currency. The video was posted on YouTube with the title "Adrien Broner takes a shit in Popeye's."

But back to those "AB" initials. At the moment, "aggravated battery" seems more accurate than "about billions."

As first reported by TMZ, Broner has been indicted on charges of felony assault and aggravated robbery in conjunction with an incident that occurred in his hometown of Cincinnati in the early morning hours of January 21, 2016. More specifically, it's alleged that Broner and an acquaintance named Christopher Carson were engaged in a series of high-stakes bowling games during which Broner lost $14,000 ($8,000 in cash and $6,000 in credit). As the bowling alley was readying to close, Broner asked Carson for one last bet, this one for $6,000 in the hope of clearing his credit. Carson refused and, as he left the alley at 3:00 a.m., was confronted by Broner.

Jake Donovan of BoxingScene.com reported what is alleged to have happened next: "Broner was accompanied by eight unnamed individuals. A violent argument ensued with the boxer demanding that his acquaintance give him back the $8,000 in cash. Carson claims that his refusal to do so prompted Broner to punch him in the neck/chin area, splitting Carson's chin as well as a tooth. From there, Broner went to a vehicle and retrieved a 9mm handgun, at which point the gathered crowd in the parking lot scattered. Carson attempted to plead his way out of the incident, raising his arms in surrender mode, only to allegedly have been struck a second time by Broner, knocking him unconscious. The existing lawsuit alleges that Broner then reached into Carson's pockets, extracting $10,000 in cash—the $8,000 he lost plus another $2,000 in the victim's possession. Upon regaining consciousness, Carson discovered he had been robbed and injured, opting to head to the emergency room for treatment of such injuries in lieu of reporting the incident to the local authorities. The matter made its way to law enforcement—thus presenting grounds for an arrest warrant—once proof was allegedly offered in the form of video evidence as well as what the warrant described as a detailed account of events provided by credible witnesses."

On February 6, Carson filed a civil lawsuit against Broner. Meanwhile, Adrien had relocated to Washington, DC, where he was training in preparation for the Theophane fight. The warrant issued for his arrest had not yet been acted upon by the authorities. Then, strangely, the warrant was downgraded from being subject to nationwide service to being actionable only in Ohio. The downgrade was confirmed to Mitch Abramson of "The Ring" by Julie Wilson (chief assistant prosecutor and public information officer for the Hamilton County, Ohio, prosecutor's office).

Chris Finney (Carson's attorney) told Abramson, "I think it's interesting that locally, who amended the arrest warrant and why? Why did this rich guy get special treatment? Somebody pulled the plug and screwed things up."

Then, to further complicate matters, Broner weighed in for the Theophane fight four-tenths of a pound over the 140-pound "championship" limit, refused to shed the extra ounces, and surrendered his bogus WBA belt on the scales. The incident was reminiscent of a June 21, 2012, bout against Vicente Escobedo, when Adrien weighed in for a 130-pound WBO title fight at 133.5 pounds and was stripped of his bauble.

Broner-Theophane was televised by Spike as part of a three-bout telecast. Dana Jacobson served as host. Scott Hanson, Jimmy Smith, and two-time PED-loser Antonio Tarver provided commentary. Hanson distinguished himself early in the going by advising viewers, "President Obama and his wife [are] obviously watching live on Spike Sports." One assumes the remark was intended as a joke. But it's hard to know with certainty since Floyd Mayweather once assured a national television audience that Barack Obama would carry his belt to the ring if Floyd fought Manny Pacquiao.

As for the fight itself, referee Luis Pabon stopped the contest in round nine with Theophane still on his feet but taking too many punches, the most noteworthy of which was a clearly low blow. Kudos to the Spike production team for its post-fight highlighting of the low blow, which all three Spike commentators missed.

After the fight, Broner bemoaned the fact that—in his words—"I've been going through a lot this week" (as if it were someone else's fault) and called out Floyd Mayweather. He sounded like a WWE villain without the charm.

Also, it's worth noting that the incident for which Broner was indicted occurred on January 21, 2016. The lawsuit against him was filed on behalf of the alleged victim on February 6. The story didn't become news until it was reported by TMZ on March 24. That's how much Adrien Broner matters in the larger scheme of things.

Broner-Theophane was embarrassing for boxing on multiple levels. The epidemic of fighters blowing off weight cheats fans and opponents. And Broner's legal situation tarnishes the sport.

Broner, like all criminal defendants, is entitled to the presumption of innocence unless and until proven guilty insofar as the criminal justice system is concerned. But this doesn't mean that adverse consequences shouldn't flow from what is known about his conduct at the present time. And it certainly doesn't mean that he should be allowed to go about his life unimpeded while there's an outstanding warrant for his arrest.

Then again, the District of Columbia Boxing and Wrestling Commission is not known for competence. Let's not forget, this is the commission whose PED-testing protocols failed to detect elevated levels of testosterone in Lamont Peterson's system at a time when Peterson, by his own later admission, had testosterone pellets surgically implanted in his hip.

I didn't go to Pacquiao-Bradley III, which was contested at the MGM Grand in Las Vegas on April 9, 2016. It was an intriguing match-up. But I'd been to eleven Manny Pacquiao fights, including five when I was privileged to be in Manny's dressing room before and after the bout. I'd had similar experiences with Tim Bradley. So when it came time to deal with a cataract in my left eye, I decided to schedule the procedure, get it over with, and watch the fight on television.

Pacquiao–Bradley III in Perspective

Trilogies in boxing usually occur because the first fight was great and bout number two was good enough to warrant a third. Neither Pacquiao-Bradley I or II was particularly scintillating. But economic rivalries and political considerations dictated that Pacquiao-Bradley III happen.

The fight was contested at the MGM Grand in Las Vegas.

"I never thought Pacquiao would fight me again," Bradley said at the January 21, 2016, kick-off press conference, announcing their April 9 confrontation. "Then [Top Rank president] Todd duBoef called, and I said, 'Wow! Okay!'"

Pacquiao is in the twilight of a ring career that has captured the imagination of fight fans around the world and elevated him to iconic status in his native Philippines.

Bradley hasn't enjoyed Pacquiao's fame. But he has crafted an admirable record that includes victories over Juan Manuel Marquez, Lamont Peterson, Ruslan Provodnikov, Devon Alexander, and Pacquiao (on a controversial split decision in 2012). Two years later, Pacquiao evened the score in a rematch.

"Everyone has their own opinion regarding the first fight," Bradley says. "I thought I won. The second fight, Pacquiao definitely won that fight, hands down."

"It was a good fight," Bradley says, continuing his thoughts on Pacquiao-Bradley II. "I did as well as I could, but I knew he beat me.

I was sad. I was pissed off. I don't like to lose. How I was able to deal with that loss was, I realized that defeats do happen. Just because you get defeated doesn't mean your legacy ends. When you get defeated, it's how you rebound, how you come back from a defeat, that makes you."

Bradley gives everything that boxing can ask of a fighter. He's always in shape. Once the bell rings, he pours what he has into the war. He's courteous and accessible to the media and fans. He's a good role model.

"Just because you can get away with something," Tim says, "that doesn't make it right."

Boxing politics are part of the sweet science. With Pacquiao-Bradley III, politics of a different kind intruded.

In February, Pacquiao put his foot in his mouth with a string of homophobic remarks. During a March 16 media conference call, Bradley was asked about the cunundrum that Manny found himself in and responded, "I don't want to get into any of that stuff. It's pretty much irrelevant to boxing and what we're here to talk about. You can ask Pacquiao about that. But if you ask me a question about gay people, I love all people for what they are. I respect people for what they are. I judge people by their heart. That's the most important thing. I have a gay uncle that passed away. He had the biggest heart out of all of my uncles, and I miss him to death. I still miss him today, right now."

Top Rank CEO Bob Arum, a self-described "proud liberal" (who supported John McCain over Barack Obama in 2008 and was promoting Pacquiao-Bradley III), took issue with Manny's remarks. But Arum then delved further into the political arena in an effort to engender pay-per-view buys for the fight by capitalizing on anti-Hispanic comments made by Donald Trump.

Branding Trump "an opportunist," Arum proclaimed that Pacquiao-Bradley III would have a "No Trump" undercard featuring Gilberto Ramirez, Jose Ramirez, and Oscar Valdez, and that buying the pay-per-view would be an ideal way for people to register their opposition to Trump's bigotry and prejudice.

"I'm standing up for my Hispanic neighbors and all the Hispanic kids who fight for me," Arum declared. "Somebody has to stand up to this crap."

That left unresolved the issue of whether abstention from buying the pay-per-view would be a good way to register opposition to Pacquiao's homophobic comments.

The promotion also sought to market Pacquiao-Bradley III as a confrontation between the fighters' respective trainers: Teddy Atlas and Freddie Roach.

Roach and Pacquiao have been together for thirty-two fights over the course of fifteen years. The Bradley-Atlas union is more recent. Bradley had been trained by Joel Diaz throughout his career. But after surviving a twelfth-round crisis against Jesse Vargas last year, Tim decided that a change was necessary.

"The respect was gone," Bradley said of his parting from Diaz. "I didn't listen to him anymore. I just did what I wanted to do."

Atlas wasn't sure he wanted to work with Bradley. He'd walked away from training fighters a long time ago. But he liked Tim and decided to give it a try. In their first collaborative effort, Bradley stopped an out-of-shape Brandon Rios in the ninth round last November.

"I understand the privilege of this opportunity," Atlas said at the kickoff press conference for Pacquiao-Bradley III. "But part of me is unhappy being back in this part of the boxing world because I know what some of the people in it are like. I get reminded of why I didn't like it before and still don't like it. What brought me back was a good human being. Tim Bradley is a good person. I like this guy. I feel good being with him. Working with Tim, I enjoy this kind of teaching again."

"Teddy is always on me," Bradley noted. "He's a guy that cares. He's a guy that loves. He's a guy that knows what he's doing. He's a guy that believes in what he's doing and he's a guy that believes in me. I trust everything that Teddy is telling me and teaching me. Teddy can instill everything that I need."

In keeping with these thoughts, one promotional storyline for Pacquiao-Bradley III was the idea that Bradley would be a different fighter this time around because he was being trained by Atlas and would have Teddy in his corner. Atlas fed into that thinking with the observation, "Tim didn't always connect his mental fortitude and his athleticism in the most effective way possible." But Atlas also observed, "Tim Bradley was successful for ten years before I came along. He's a real good athlete and he knew how to win."

Seeking to further develop the rival trainer theme, the promotion sought to turn it into a fistic version of the Republican party's unruly presidential debates.

Roach willingly obliged. Talking about Bradley's knockout of Brandon Rios, Freddie declared, "You have to take into consideration the kind of shape the opponent was in. He really looked bad, overweight. I mean, he looked really fat. I'm not going to give Teddy Atlas credit for that win because that guy wasn't there to fight."

Other Roach comments included:

★ "I know that ESPN announcer who is coaching Bradley is a good storyteller and likes acting. Let's see how well they do when we go off-script and hit them with a dose of reality TV."

★ "I've never faced Teddy before. I'm not his biggest fan. I don't have a lot of good things to say. He's had two champions, I think, in his career; Michael Moorer and the kid from Rhode Island, Pazienza, at the end of his career."

★ "I don't think Teddy is gonna help anything. He's a good storyteller between rounds. I don't know what the fuck that has to do with boxing. I mean, firemen and shit like that. It doesn't impress me, never has. I don't really think that's motivating your fighter. I'm not a cheerleader, I don't tell my fighters stories about firemen. I respect firemen, but what does that have to do with throwing a jab or blocking a punch? Nothing. I would rather give my fighter direction and tell him what he has to do to change to win the fight."

Atlas then responded:

★ "I don't want to be part of a circus with this Roach bullshit. But I'll react to it as best I can. Maybe he should have been a cheerleader in Manny's last fight [against Floyd Mayweather]. Maybe it would have helped a little bit. Maybe it's called being a motivator."

★ "I didn't ask for this to come about or to grow into the ways that it has. I made myself a promise, and that was to be as restrained as I could be and, when it was appropriate, to respond. But I didn't fire the first shot across the bow, and I waited a while before I responded. At the end of the day, if some of those responses help the promotion, that's a good thing. I started with Cus D'Amato always reminding me to help the promoters in any way you can. But I could tell you now that I would have preferred that it wasn't initiated."

★ "I don't care what he thinks. I would need a lot of help if I was influenced by what Roach thinks. He's going to steer me with the kind of man I am, the kind of trainer I am? Are you kidding me?"

Ironically, the similarities between Atlas and Roach are more striking than their differences. Teddy is fifty-nine years old; Freddie is fifty-six. Each man came out of a troubled home and sought refuge in boxing, although Atlas's ring career was cut short by a chronic back problem before it began. Each man was influenced by a master trainer. Atlas was molded by Cus D'Amato when he was young. Roach was trained by Eddie Futch. And each man takes his fiduciary duty to his fighter seriously, extraordinarily so.

The dictionary defines "extraordinary" as "beyond ordinary, very unusual, remarkable."

"You have eight weeks to get a guy perfectly ready for one night," Atlas says. "And if he loses, you blame yourself and ask yourself over and over again, 'What did I do wrong.'"

"I lay in bed last night, trying to fall asleep," Freddie acknowledged two days before a recent fight. "I was asking myself, 'Is he going to try to box us? Bang with us? Will he go to the ropes and try to sucker us in?' I ran through every scenario that might happen. And when I'd gone through them all, I fell asleep."

Pacquiao-Bradley III would be the first time that Roach and Atlas faced off against each other as trainers. However, a trainer can do just so much. Atlas did a very good job of preparing Michael Moorer to fight George Foreman. But when Big George hit Moorer on the chin, all that fine-tuning went out the window. Pacquiao doesn't hit as hard as Foreman. But neither did Kendall Holt, Ruslan Provodnikov, or Jesse Vargas, each of whom hurt Bradley badly and had him in trouble.

Pacquiao and Bradley both weighed in at 145.5 pounds, comfortably under the 147-pound contract limit. When fight night arrived, Manny was a slightly better than 2-to-1 betting favorite. The announced attendance was 14,665, meaning that more than one thousand tickets were unsold. The buzz that once surrounded Pacquiao has diminished.

The televised "no Trump" undercard had all the excitement of a Martin O'Malley presidential campaign rally.

Then Pacquiao and Bradley took center stage. Round one was tactically and evenly fought. Thereafter, Manny was the aggressor; cautiously at first, more so as the bout progressed. By round four, he was dictating the rhythm of the fight.

Bradley did relatively little offensively. One of the keys to his past success has been the constant grinding aggression that he brings to fights. He doesn't fight well circling or backing up. But Tim wasn't grinding on Saturday night. He looked awkward and mechanical, proving again the theory that a new trainer can make adjustments with a veteran fighter but not major changes in his fighting style.

As the bout progressed, Bradley rarely took away what Pacquiao wanted to do or made Pacquiao do what Manny didn't want to do. And Pacquiao was simply too fast for him.

When the fighters exchanged, more often than not, Pacquiao was the one who got the better of it. He scored a flash knockdown in round seven with a quick right hook that landed awkwardly and caught Bradley off-balance, causing Tim's glove to touch the canvas. There was a more convincing knockdown in round nine, when a straight left shook Bradley and a follow-up left deposited him on his back.

Last December, Bradley served as an expert analyst for the TruTV telecast of Nonito Donaire vs. Cesar Juarez. Commenting on Juarez's lack of aggression, Tim observed, "Trying or not trying, either way, he's going to get hit. So he might as well try."

On Saturday night, Bradley didn't try the right things often enough. According to CompuBox, he threw only twenty-five punches per round, landing an average of eight. That was perfect for Pacquiao, allowing him to dictate the pace of the fight. Equally telling, Bradley landed a total of twelve jabs. That's one jab per round. Fighters rarely win by landing one jab per round.

By way of comparison, in Pacquiao-Bradley I, Bradley threw seventy punches per round. In Pacquiao-Bradley II, he threw an average of fifty-two.

When Pacquiao-Bradley III was over, Manny had outlanded Tim by a 122-to-92 margin. All three judges scored the contest 116-110 in Pacquiao's favor.

Prior to the bout, Pacquiao was adamant in saying that Pacquiao–Bradley III would be his last fight. Arum was equally adamant in saying that he wasn't sure Manny would stick by that pledge.

For now, let's give the final word on the subject to veteran newspaperman Bill Dwyre, who recently wrote, "A boxer's retirement is like a politician's campaign promise."

Noted trainer Naazim Richardson knows a thing or two about boxing, having trained Bernard Hopkins during the latter years of The Executioner's sojourn through boxing. Looking ahead to Errol Spence vs. Chris Algieri, Richardson declared, "I've watched Spence for a long time. He likes to hurt people. If he can't hurt Algieri the way he wants to, it could turn into an interesting night."

But Spence could hurt Algieri the way he wanted to.

Errol Spence Jr Looks Like the Real Thing

Twenty-six-year-old Errol Spence Jr is the brightest prospect on Al Haymon's Premier Boxing Champions roster. On Saturday night, April 16, the 2012 US Olympian (he was defeated in the quarter-finals in London) obliterated Chris Algieri at Barclays Center in Brooklyn, raising his professional record to 20-and-0 with seventeen knockouts.

Haymon likes to keep his favored fighters away from punchers. In that regard, Algieri was a safe opponent. The thirty-two-year-old Huntington, Long Island, native entered the ring with a 21-and-2 record and has shown a willingness to go in tough. He moved into the spotlight with a gutty split-decision triumph over Ruslan Provodnikov in 2014. Next, Manny Pacquiao turned him into a yo-yo, knocking Algieri down six times en route to a unanimous-decision verdict. Then, going in tough for the third time in less than a year, Chris lost a unanimous decision to Amir Khan. He was brought back against trial-horse Erik Bone in December 2015 and prevailed in a less-than-stellar performance.

Equally important, Algieri had scored only eight knockouts in his ring career. And the only stoppage in his last nine fights was a seventh-round KO of Wilfredo Acuna (who has lost twelve of his last fourteen bouts and been knocked out eleven times).

In sum, Spence-Algieri was made for Spence. The thought process wasn't, "Who can we bring Algieri back against who will make Chris look good?" It was, "Paulie Malignaggi is out. Who's a name without a big punch that will make Errol look like the next big thing in boxing?"

The conventional wisdom was that Algieri represented a step up in class for Spence and a test that would indicate how far the prospect has progressed. Errol reinforced that view, saying, "I think I'm one of the top talents of all the young guys. But I've got to prove myself. Everybody wants to see what I've got. They've got a lot of questions that aren't answered, and they want to see me answer those questions. He's just a measuring stick to see how good I really am. Every time he stepped up, he lost. That's my stepping-stone. I'm ready for it. I'm looking for a coming-out party."

Two fights preceded Spence-Algieri on the NBC telecast. Based on their presentation, it looks as though some belt-tightening is underway at Premier Boxing Champions. The huge set that was symbolic of last year's telecasts was missing. More significantly, Kenny Rice and B. J. Flores called the action. That's a far cry from last year's NBC-PBC "dream team" headlined by Al Michaels, Marv Albert, and Sugar Ray Leonard.

Former cruiserweight beltholder Steve Cunningham faced off against Krzysztof Glowacki in the first featured fight of the evening. Glowacki (25-0, 16 KOs) was toiling in near anonymity last June when he climbed off the canvas to knock out Marco Huck in the eleventh round and claim the WBO cruiserweight crown. Cunningham (28-7, 13 KOs) is three months shy of his fortieth birthday and, over the past five years, has won only four of eleven fights.

After a slow first round, Cunningham came out aggressively in round two, got sloppy on the inside, and was decked by a straight left . . . Twice . . . That put Steve in a hole that he was unable to climb out of. He fought well in spurts and rocked Glowacki with straight right hands from time to time. But he couldn't sustain a fight-winning effiort for three minutes a round.

In round ten, Glowacki dropped Cunningham again, this time with a right forearm that referee Arthur Mercante Jr. mistakenly called a knock-down. In round twelve, Krzysztof did it once more, this time with a body shot while Cunningham was flurrying on the inside.

The CompuBox totals were roughly even, with Cunningham out-landing Glowacki by a 124-to-117 margin. The judges' scores of 115-109, 115-109, 116-108 were a bit wide of the bullseye but hit the target.

In the second featured fight of the night, Marcus Browne (17-0, 13 KOs) squared off against Radivoje Kalajdzic (21-0, 14 KOs) in a light-heavyweight bout. Browne, like Spence, was a 2012 US Olympian (although he didn't make it as far as Errol did, losing in the first round). He almost lost to Kalajdzic, and arguably should have.

Midway through round one, Kalajdzic visited the canvas on what was clearly a slip. And Browne clearly hit Kalajdzic with a jolting straight left when he was down. Instead of warning Browne for his transgression (and possibly deducting a point), referee Tony Chiarantano mistakenly called a knockdown. That loomed large on the scorecards later on.

Kalajdzic isn't a big puncher. But he's a tough guy who can take a punch. Browne landed hard again and again in the first three stanzas. Then, in round four, Marcus got rocked by a right and the momentum of the fight changed. In round six, another right deposited Browne on the canvas, and he was slow getting up. Kalajdzic ran the table from that point on.

In the end, Browne was saved by the bell. In an unusual way.

Browne-Kalajdzic had been scheduled for ten rounds. But because Glowacki-Cunningham went the full twelve-round distance, Browne-Kalajdzic was cut just prior to the bout to eight rounds to accommodate the time restraints imposed by the NBC telecast. Even then, it looked to this observer as though Kalajdzic had eked out a 76-75 triumph. The judges ruled otherwise, giving Browne the victory on a 76-74, 76-75, 74-76 split verdict.

Then it was time for the main event. Depending on where one looked, Spence was listed as a 12-to-1 to 20-to-1 favorite. With good reason.

Spence was in control from the opening bell, digging to Algieri's body and going upstairs with hard punishing blows. Errol was faster, better schooled, and hit harder than Chris.

In round four, a straight left put Algieri on the canvas. Twenty seconds into round five, another straight left dropped him for the second time. Chris rose on wobbly legs and looked to be in no condition to defend himself. Worse, more than two minutes remained in the round.

At that point, referee Benjy Esteves (whose refereeing credits include Magomed Abdusalamov vs. Mike Perez and Arturo Gatti vs. Joey Gamache) allowed the fight to continue. Fifteen seconds later, with Algieri pinned against the ropes, a brutal left hand put him on the canvas for the final time.

Spence outlanded Algieri 96-to-36 with a 73-to-33 edge in power punches. It wasn't that he beat Algieri so much as the way he beat him that was impressive. Errol did what Pacquiao, Provodnikov, and Khan were unable to do. He knocked Chris out.

"It was pretty one-sided," Spence said afterward. "I want a title fight next. Hopefully, it's Kell Brook, I'm his mandatory and I want him. Danny Garcia and all the rest of the welterweight champions; I want them all."

It's too early for a coronation. By way of comparison, Andre Berto blew out a lot of guys early and was extolled by his proponents as the future of boxing. When Berto was twenty-six (the same age Spence is now), Andre's record stood at 25-and-0 with 19 KOs. But he fizzled when things got tough.

We don't know how Spence will respond when he's in the ring with someone who forces him to walk through fire. But for that moment to come, the opponent has to be good enough to test Errol in ways that he hasn't been tested so far. Spence has speed, ring savvy, and power. The fact that he's a southpaw makes him even more difficult to deal with.

More than a year after PBC began—and after scores of time buys on multiple networks—no PBC fighter has made his way into the consciousness of mainstream sports fans. It's possible that Spence will. But to get there, he'll have to fight more challenging opponents.

And a closing note . . .

Refereeing a fight is one of the most difficult jobs in sports. It's also one of the most important.

Arthur Mercante and Tony Chiarantano can be forgiven for calling two knockdowns that weren't. Sometimes a referee simply isn't in position to clearly see a moment in time unfold.

The fact that Chiarantano didn't penalize Browne for hitting Kalajdzic when he was down, and Esteves allowed Spence-Algieri to continue for as long as he did is more troubling.

Las Vegas is the land of make-believe. So why not market Canelo Alvarez vs.
Amir Khan as a world middleweight championship fight?

Canelo–Khan and the Shadow of Gennady Golovkin

When boxing was boxing, as the saying goes, big events were built around long-anticipated fights that the public hungered for and thought would be great. Canelo Alvarez vs. Amir Khan (which took place on May 7, 2016, and was the first fight card at the new T-Mobile Arena in Las Vegas) was a bout that virtually no one lobbied for in advance. The selling point was Canelo. Boxing fans were told, "Watch him because he's a star."

Alvarez, the current pride of Mexico, is twenty-five years old. He began boxing professionally at age fifteen and has compiled a 47-1-1 (33 KOs) record. At present, he's the most marketable pay-per-view fighter in the United States, having engendered 900,000 pay-per-view buys when he beat Miguel Cotto last November.

There are two blemishes on Canelo's record: a draw in his fifth professional bout (when he was one month shy of his sixteenth birthday) and a loss by decision to Floyd Mayweather in 2013. Thereafter, Canelo showed that he could deal with a slick boxer by outpointing Erislandy Lara. And he outpunched slugger James Kirkland en route to a third-round knockout last year.

Outside the ring, Alvarez projects a solid image. He takes questions from the media in English but answers in Spanish.

"My job, and I'm very fortunate," he says, "is to box. I train hard and I give the best of me. I'm not trying to tap into my market. It's just something very fortunate that I've been able to have in my career. I don't like to talk trash just to sell fights. I train hard and do my talking in the ring. I want people to respect me and to follow my fights, not because of what I say but what I do."

In keeping with that philosophy, Alvarez steers away from controversial utterances. But he spoke movingly when asked three days before the fight about presidential candidate Donald Trump's comments regarding Mexico and the Mexican people.

"It hurts and offends," Canelo answered. "I want him to understand and for people to know that, when I'm out there running, I see a lot of countrymen working hard, working in the fields. Not everybody is coming here to rob and steal. A lot of immigrants, we come here to succeed."

Meanwhile, Khan was in Las Vegas as a sacrificial offering. Like Alvarez, he was a child prodigy, winning a silver medal at the 2004 Athens Olympics at age seventeen. Now twenty-nine, he entered the ring with a 31-3 (19 KOs) record and two "KOs by."

The "KOs by" were a problem. Amir is a natural 147-pound fighter with a notoriously brittle chin. Breidis Prescott (KO 1) and Danny Garcia (KO 4) reduced him to rubble with one punch.

Canelo weighs in at 155 pounds, enters the ring above 170, and was far and away the hardest puncher that Khan had faced.

"You never know," Amir told the media on Wednesday of fight week. "This could be a good weight for me. I'm respecting his power. I know he can hurt me, but that works in my favor. When I fought Danny Garcia and Breidis Prescott, I didn't think they would hurt me and I wasn't as careful as I should have been."

But Amir acknowledged, "I'm not supposed to win this fight. Normally I'm the favorite. This is the first time I've been the underdog. I know I'm not going to be stronger than Canelo. I'm going into this fight thinking that I might not have the power to hurt him. One little mistake in a fight like this could get me in trouble, so I'm making sure that I'm not making any mistakes. I believe that my skills can win this fight."

Most observers thought otherwise. By fight night, the odds in Las Vegas (which had opened at 3-to-1) were 5-to-1 in Canelo's favor. The assumption was that, at some point, Alvarez would catch up to Khan and knock him out. If Amir won, it would be the biggest upset by a British fighter since Lloyd Honeyghan stopped Donald Curry in Atlantic City thirty years ago. Or phrased differently, Canelo-Khan was expected to be "no Khan-test."

The fight-night attendance of 16,540 was well short of a sell-out. But this was Cinco de Mayo weekend. And the crowd, which was highly partisan in its support of Canelo, came to life for the main event.

Khan had seen how decisively Alvarez was outboxed by Mayweather three years ago and said to himself, "I can do that." But Amir doesn't have Mayweather's defense. Or chin. In the end, Canelo's fans got what they came for.

Khan started well, circling away from his foe, mounting a quick in-and-out attack highlighted by fast right hands. The pattern for round two was similar to round one. Canelo stalking; Amir getting off first; Alvarez failing to cut the ring off effectively; Alvarez missing with wild left hooks.

But Canelo did land a solid right to the body in the second stanza that was a harbinger of things to come.

In rounds three and four, Canelo's rights to the body began to add up with each one taking something out of Khan. By round five, Amir was throwing with less conviction than before and had started to slow down. Then, with a half minute left in round six—

BOOM!!!

Canelo feinted with his jab, which blinded Amir to the right hand that was coming behind it. The punch landed flush on Khan's jaw, and he corkscrewed to the canvas, unconscious before the back of his head hit ground zero with a sickening thud. Referee Kenny Bayless dispensed with the formality of counting to ten and ended matters by waving his arms over Khan's prostrate body.

Great punch. Suspect chin. It was a highlight-reel knockout.

Afterward, Amir predictably declared, "I stepped up too far. I tried to eat and put more weight on. But for some reason, I just couldn't."

Meanwhile, throughout fight week, Gennady Golovkin cast a shadow over the proceedings.

The last World Boxing Council "middleweight" champion to compete in a genuine middleweight championship bout was Sergio Martinez, who claimed the throne by decision over Kelly Pavlik in 2010. Miguel Cotto defeated Martinez in 2014 to seize the crown. But that bout was fought at a catchweight of 159 pounds at the insistance of Cotto (a smaller man who had the greater economic leverage). Cotto then lowered the catchweight to 157 pounds for a successful title defense against Daniel Geale and 155 pounds for a losing effort against Alvarez. One hundred fifty-five pounds suits Canelo just fine and was the contract weight for Canelo-Khan.

"I'm not a middleweight," Alvarez acknowledged before the bout. "I'm a super-welterweight. However, I wanted to fight this fight for some sort of title."

The problem is that the middleweight limit is 160.

Gennady Golovkin has been knocking out opponents at 160 pounds en route to claiming multiple championship belts and has been installed by the WBC as the mandatory challenger for Canelo's crown.

Virtually every time that Alvarez or Golden Boy CEO Oscar De La Hoya (Canelo's promoter) had a microphone thrust in his face during fight week, the subject of Golovkin arose. Neither man seemed anxious for a Canelo-Golovkin encounter and maintained that, if one were to occur, it would have to be at a contract weight of 155 pounds.

"One fifty-five is not a division," Abel Sanchez (Golovkin's trainer) countered. "We have seventeen divisions in boxing. Why would we need any more? Gennady is not going to bow down to a diva. It's not the Canelo title. It's the middleweight title, which is 160 pounds."

As fight week progressed, Alvarez looked and sounded like a man who was tired of hearing about Golovkin. After disposing of Khan, Alvarez invited Golovkin into the ring to—in his words—"prove I'm not afraid." But he might be. And he now finds himself between a rock and a hard place.

Everyone understands that, if Canelo instructed De La Hoya to "make the Golovkin fight happen," Golden Boy would see that it happened. After all, Oscar is the man who, on September 30, 2014, told a media gathering at HBO, "My focus is Canelo, one hundred percent. Whatever he asks, I have to do."

If Alvarez refuses to fight Golovkin at 160 pounds, he risks seeing his name change in the headlines from "Canelo" to "Pollo."

One might add that, throughout Canelo-Khan fight week, the assumption was that Canelo would beat Khan. The more intriguing issue was how many pay-per-view buys the bout would engender. And more specifically, does Canelo need a good dance partner to generate stratospheric pay-per-view numbers? The early returns on Canelo-Khan suggest that he does.

Trainer Dan Birmingham once opined, "Courage is the willingness to fight anyone." Right now, it appears as though Golovkin wants to fight Canelo far more than Canelo wants to fight Golovkin.

"My whole thing," Canelo said during an April 19 media conference call, "is I want to be a legend."

Beating Golovkin at 160 pounds would make him a legend. Still, a word of caution is in order.

Richard Russell was one of a dozen southern Democratic senators who controlled that legislative body in the mid-twentieth century. Russell never had occasion to comment on fighting Gennady Golovkin. But he often told the tale of a bull that charged head-first into a locomotive.

"That was the bravest bull I ever saw," Russell would tell listeners. "But I question its judgment."

Arnie Boehm (who trained Lennox Lewis as an amateur in Canada) once said, "The key to this man is that he doesn't like to be beaten at anything. If you beat him at anything, he'll go out and practice all night. Then, the next day, he'll come back and beat you."

Lennox Lewis Is Still a Class Act

On May 5, 2016, I had lunch with Lennox Lewis at the MGM Grand Hotel and Casino in Las Vegas.

Not long after retiring as an active fighter, Lewis told me, "When I was boxing, I could feel the big fight atmosphere. I was part of it. But I wasn't focused on it."

Now Lennox was in Las Vegas for the May 7 fight between Canelo Alvarez and Amir Khan. It wasn't a huge fight, but there was a bit of a buzz.

Lewis lives each day with the satisfying sense of accomplishment that comes from a job well done. He's fifty years old, thirteen years removed from his last professional fight, and aging like fine wine. The trademark dreadlocks are gone, but he still cuts an imposing figure. Heads turned when he entered the restaurant.

Lennox has become more social in retirement than he was before. He goes out more often and enjoys spending time with his four children (Landon, eleven; Ling, nine; Leah, six; and Livia, three).

"I don't miss being an active fighter," Lewis told me. "I went through it. I enjoyed it. It was a great experience. But it's over now. It was important for me to retire on my own terms, for my legacy and my health. I love it that I ended my boxing career as a champion."

Looking back on that career, Lennox pointed to five fights that were particularly important to him

⋆ June 3, 1991—KO 7 over Gary Mason: "Mason was undefeated [35-0, 32 KOs], and the fight was for the British and European heavyweight titles. It was my first big test, and I passed it with flying colors."

⋆ May 8, 1993—W 12 over Tony Tucker: "That was my first world championship and also the first time I fought a Don King fighter that King thought would beat me."

★ October 1, 1993—KO 7 over Frank Bruno: "I was born in England, moved to Canada to be with my mum, and won an Olympic gold medal for Canada. Then I went back to England to pursue my professional career. Frank was already there. He was the darling of the British media. And British boxing fans were divided. It was important to me to win them over, and that fight did it."

★ November 17, 2001—KO 4 over Hasim Rahman: "I disliked Rahman a lot at that time. I gave him the opportunity to fight me for the title. He beat me, and I accepted that. But when Rahman became heavyweight champion, he had a responsibility to act like a champion. And he acted like a thug. He was rude and arrogant. There was the whole gay thing [when Rahman suggested publicly that Lennox was gay]. He tried to avoid the rematch even though he had a legal obligation to fight me again. Getting my belt back was a must. Knocking him out was extremely satisfying. I had several one-punch knockouts like that in my career. Frans Botha was another. In a way, it's surprising. You've thrown that punch thousands of times before. And you don't know it's perfect this time until it lands and you see the result."

★ June 8, 2002—KO 8 over Mike Tyson: "Tyson wasn't Tyson anymore. But I had to beat him. Otherwise, people would have said forever, 'Lennox was good, but he never beat Mike Tyson.' So I needed that win, not for my own self-respect but so other people would respect me. I'm happy for Mike now. He seems to have remade himself. There was a time, even long after we fought, where I was always on guard when I was with him. I didn't know what crazy thing he might do. I feel safe now when I'm around Mike. But I still always cut the deck."

Inevitably, the conversation turned to Emanuel Steward, who began training Lennox in 1995 and was with him until the end of Lewis's ring career. When Lennox retired in 2004, he told the world, "Emanuel did as much for me as any trainer ever did for a boxer. There were times when Manny believed in me more than I believed in myself."

Looking back on his years with Steward, Lewis told me, "Every day with Manny, I was learning. As I got older, my body got older. That makes a big difference if you're a boxer. Toward the end of my career, there were things I could no longer do physically that I could do before. But at the same time, my mind was getting sharper and my boxing skills kept improving. My biomechanics got better. I was more relaxed in the ring. I could do things more efficiently and put less demands on my body to do what I had to do to win. Manny was a big part of that."

Steward died in 2012 as a consequence of colon cancer that had metastasized throughout his body. By the time it was diagnosed, he had six weeks to live. He chose not to share that knowledge with many of those who were closest to him.

"If I could have Manny back for a day," Lennox told me, "I'd say to him, 'I didn't know you were sick. I wish you'd let me know so I could have gone through it with you and done everything I could to comfort you.'"

Then I asked Lewis to critique today's leading heavyweights. His thoughts follow:

★ On Tyson Fury: "His style of boxing is right for him, especially since his power is limited. He has no strength. His power definitely needs to be worked on. But his boxing ability is better than most people realize."

★ On Wladimir Klitschko: "He accomplished a lot. It's never easy in boxing, but I have the feeling that it was particularly hard for him. To be a complete fighter, you have to be able to box on the inside and go to the body. Wladimir never did those things, so I don't think he mastered his craft in a way that enabled him to live up to his full potential. If he had, he might have been great."

★ On Anthony Joshua: "There's a lot of potential there. But he has been moved along pretty fast against relatively weak competition. Let's see what happens when he reaches a level where he can't knock everybody out. You never know how great a boxer is until you see how he performs when he's tired. Joshua could become the best in the world or he might fall short. We just don't know."

★ On Deontay Wilder: "He started boxing late, which is a drawback. And he depends almost entirely on his power, which isn't good because boxing is about so much more than power. Also, I question his chin. But he might be better than I think."

★ On Alexander Povetkin: "He's a physically strong, typical European heavyweight. No more, no less."

★ On Luis Ortiz: "This is The Bogeyman. Everyone is afraid of him. He has good power and good boxing ability. I think he's the best one out there for now."

★ On David Haye: "He's in the stew, but he's not choice meat."

Meanwhile, two days before my lunch with Lennox, Donald Trump had won the Indiana primary to become the Republican party's presumptive presidential nominee. What did Lennox think about the 2016 presidential campaign?

"I've never heard this type of rhetoric in politics," Lewis answered. "The candidates sound more like clowns in a circus than statesmen. But obviously, America loves it because people are voting for Trump and they're putting him on TV all the time."

And if Trump wins?

"I'm not worried," Lennox said with a smile. "I have a home in Florida. But I also have homes in Jamaica and Canada [where his eighty-six-year-old mother lives]."

In other words, Lennox can always move the family to Ontario to live with his mum.

Keith Thurman and Shawn Porter are friends. The last thing they wanted to do was hurt each other. But when they met in the ring, it was on each man's list.

A Look Back at Thurman–Porter

The June 25, 2016, fight card at Barclays Center in Brooklyn featured WBA welterweight champion Keith Thurman (Florida) versus challenger Shawn Porter (Ohio) in a battle of fighters from swing states that may well decide the 2016 presidential election. Politics aside, it was everything that a fight should be.

When Thurman dials back the hype, he comes across as thoughtful and intelligent. There's the glib Keith Thurman and the deeper, more introspective persona.

Trainer Dan Birmingham says, "I've known Keith since he was kid. He started coming to the gym when he was eleven years old. I've been working with him since he was fifteen and I still don't really know him. He's very opinionated. He has an opinion about everything. And he reminds me of a hippie from The Sixties. Outside the ring, Keith is all peace and love. He's a giver. He plays the flute, guitar, and a little piano. He would have done well at Woodstock. But when the bell rings, he'll rip your head off."

To that, Thurman adds, "I want to make it difficult for the writers to put me in a box and say, 'Keith Thurman is this' or 'Keith Thurman is that.'"

Three years ago, at age twenty-four, Thurman knocked out Diego Chavez and was acclaimed as one of boxing's rising stars. He entered the ring to face Porter with a 26-and-0 (22 KOs) ledger. But some of the air had gone out of his balloon since the Chavez fight, largely because Keith had gone in relatively soft since then.

Thurman is a smart fighter with good power. Sound bites roll off his tongue. "The number one rule in boxing," he says, "is protect yourself at all times. When I don't produce a knockout, it's not my bad. It's the other fighter's good." But lest one worry about a lack of action, Thurman also opines, "If two men are fighting, someone should end up getting hurt."

Thurman-Porter was the first fight on CBS in prime time since the initial meeting betweeen Muhammad Ali and Leon Spinks in 1978.

Porter, age twenty-eight, is trained by his father, Kenny Porter. Prior to facing Thurman, Shawn's record stood at 26-1-1 with 16 knock-outs. There were victories over Adrien Broner and a badly faded Paulie Malignaggi on his resume and also a loss by majority decision to Kell Brook.

Both Thurman and Porter were coming in after long periods of inac-tivity. Keith hadn't fought since July 11, 2015, when he stopped Luis Collazo in seven rounds. Shawn had last entered the ring on June 20, 2015, when he decisioned Broner.

The promotion was refreshingly free of the ugly posturing and name-calling that passes these days for "marketing" in boxing. Thurman and Porter have known each other since their time as decorated ama-teurs. They've sparred and socialized together, and evinced mutual respect throughout the build-up to the fight.

Thurman was the more voluble:

★ "I got lots of love and respect for Shawn. I'm happy for my success, and I'm happy for Shawn's success. But on June 25, my friend is about to become my enemy."

★ "When Shawn Porter was in my camp, we spent a lot of time together. He got to meet my mother. I know his father. It's a very fun process to have a rival be so personal, somebody that you really know, somebody that you've been cheering for. June 25 is the only day that I'm not allowed to cheer for Shawn Porter."

★ "There really is nothing awkward in it. If anything, there's a very very cool factor. To be really honest, there's an extremely just super-cool factor that I remember this dude when he was a teenager. He remembers me when I was a teenager."

★ "We know each other very well. [But] we've never seen each other under the bright lights. Fight night is a different kind of night. He's in the way of my dreams. I'm in the way of his dreams."

Porter responded in kind, saying, "You see the respect. But I want to prove to ourselves and to everyone out there in the world that I'm better than Keith. And I know he has that same mindset. I'm coming for his head. It doesn't matter that we're friends. And I know at the end of the day it doesn't matter to him. We both have families to take care of. We both have legacies to build, careers to continue, and goals to reach. To anybody that's wondering if we're too friendly with one another to take one another out, no, we're not."

Thurman was an early 3-to-2 betting favorite. But as fight night neared, the odds moved closer to 2-to-1. The general feeling was that the bout would reveal more about Thurman than it would about Porter (whose strengths and weaknesses as a fighter had been more clearly defined by earlier fights).

When the bell for round one rang, Thurman-Porter quickly evolved into a classic bull-versus-matador encounter.

Porter likes to apply constant pressure and outwork opponents with an aggressive mauling attack. As Paulie Malignaggi observed, "Shawn fights like a linebacker. Most guys punch their way in. He looks for physical contact first and then he throws punches."

Meanwhile, Thurman thinks of himself as a cerebral fighter. In words that could have been taken from *The Art of War*, by Sun Tzu, Keith says, "If people want to move forward [engage], I'll move backwards. If they want to move backwards, I move forward. I go with the flow. I do what I think is necessary to win. The key to victory is to not let your opponent have his way. I like to stay open-minded and see what presents itself in the fight. The game plan is victory."

But Porter made victory difficult. He came in low throughout the night, leading sometimes with his head and shoulders, scoring off of bull-rushes, hitting arms, hips, and anything else his fists could find. His best work came when he pinned Thurman against the ropes and unleashed a torrential two-fisted body attack.

Thurman's plan had been to jab and pick his shots against Porter's bullrushes.

"Keith will control the rushes with his jab," Dan Birmingham had said. "Or time him and take his head off with a right hand when Shawn rushes in."

But Thurman didn't jab as often or effectively as Birmingham had hoped for. Instead, he fought fire with fire; sometimes because he wanted to and other times because Porter gave him no choice.

There was spirited back-and-forth action throughout the battle. When Thurman was able to dictate the distance between Porter and himself, he landed the sharper, more effective punches. Shawn kept coming forward, throwing from all angles. But it wasn't always effective aggression.

Referee Steve Willis did a good job of letting the fighters fight. Porter was cut by the outside corner of his left eye in round four. Thurman suffered a gash beneath his left eyebrow in round nine (the first time in his career that Keith had been cut).

Thurman wobbled Porter on several occasions with sharp hard counterpunches but was noticeably hurt by a hook to the body in round eight.

Both men dug deep. It was a difficult fight to score. Thurman prevailed by a 115-113, 115-113, 115-113 margin. The judges agreed that Keith won rounds one, four, eight, and eleven, while giving a unanimous nod to Porter in the second and seventh stanzas. That left six rounds up for grabs, which they divided evenly between the fighters.

The CompuBox statistics reflected the even nature of the battle, with Thurman being credited for landing 235 of 539 punches and Porter 236 of 662.

"This is what we live for," Keith said afterward. "This is what it was advertised to be. He weathered the storm. I weathered his storm. It was a great fight."

As for why he got the decision, Thurman observed, "Shawn did what he's good at. He brings it. But he brings it in a fashion that's not fully effective. It's seven rounds for victory. I might have dropped out of high school, but I know how to count. And math was my favorite subject."

As for what comes next, the first point to make is that Thurman-Porter was an important fight for reasons that go beyond who won and lost. Both men are Premier Boxing Champions fighters. And PBC has been struggling.

The April 30, 2016, PBC card on Fox headlined by Andre Berto vs. Victor Ortiz attracted 1.6 million viewers, a 22 percent decline from the January 23, 2016, Danny Garcia vs. Robert Guerrero show on Fox that averaged 2.1 million viewers.

PBC's April 29, 2016, card on Spike featuring Andre and Anthony Dirrell in separate bouts averaged 513,000 viewers (26 percent less than the 693,000 viewers that Spike's earlier 2016 telecasts averaged).

Worse, PBC's June 18, 2016, card on NBC featuring Andrzej Fonfara vs. Joe Smith in prime time had an 0.8 overnight rating. That was down

20 percent and 39 percent from NBC's two most recent PBC telecasts prior to that (1.0 in April 2016 and 1.3 in December 2015). As reported by Dan Rafael of ESPN.com, "The 0.8 is the lowest for a prime-time PBC card on network television since PBC debuted in March 2015. According to Sports Media Watch, the 0.8 is one of the lowest metered market ratings ever for a sporting event on prime-time network television. Every NBC prime-time PBC telecast has had a worse rating than the one before it."

Indeed, the PBC brand has been so diminished that Thurman-Porter was branded as "Showtime Championship Boxing on CBS" rather than a PBC fight.

What happens next will be instructive.

Thurman-Porter was what Premier Boxing Champions should have given the public from the start. It was the kind of fight that boxing fans expected on a regular basis when PBC was born.

The 147-pound division is boxing's deepest. Even with Floyd Mayweather and Manny Pacquiao on leave, Thurman, Porter, Kell Brook, Danny Garcia, Errol Spence, and Tim Bradley are in the mix. Terence Crawford, Amir Khan, and Adrien Broner would be welcome additions to the fold.

Thurman has said that he wants to fight Garcia next. At the post-fight press conference after beating Porter, Keith proclaimed, "Danny Garcia, undefeated. If you loved this one, you gotta love that setup."

That was consistent with Thurman's earlier statement, "I have an 'O' and I'm not afraid to let it go. If you can beat me, beat me."

Meanwhile, David Avanesyan is the WBA's "interim welterweight champion" and the "mandatory challenger" for Thurman's belt by virtue of a desultory twelve-round decision over a long-past-his-prime Shane Mosley.

One year ago, the assumption was that PBC wouldn't need phony belts in 2016 to prop up its champions.

So what will Al Haymon (who controls PBC) do next? Keith Thurman has the potential to be a breakout star. Will PBC backslide and match him in an unappealing defense against Avanesyan? Or will it build on the excitement generated by Thurman-Porter and give sports fans another fight that we care about?

Thurman wants the big fight. Speaking of the legacy he hopes to build, he says, "Legacy is a process. You gotta ride the train. Mayweather didn't become Mayweather overnight. It's not one fight. It's the continuation of fighting at this level and coming out on top."

And he has cautioned the media, "Claiming [that someone is] the best is cool. There's nothing wrong with finding the best. But to get the best is going to take a little bit more time. It's not even going to happen this year. Mayweather was at the top for over a decade, and you want somebody to replace him. But you need to really see who's going to be the top dog for the next three to five years. Then you got a king. I look forward to the journey and the process."

Thurman is a very good fighter. He has not yet shown that he's the best. It would be a shame for Keith and for boxing if he were denied the opportunity to find out if he's great.

And one thing more . . .

I don't know how many times this has to be written before the powers that be get the point.

A fight that looks good on paper (which Thurman-Porter did) is more likely to be a good fight than one that shapes up as mediocre to begin with. Most of the fans who were enthralled by Thurman-Porter had no idea which belt was at stake, nor did they care. They didn't want to see world sanctioning body officials in the ring. They didn't want anything to "marinate." They wanted to see a good fight.

It's not rocket science. Televise good fights and people will watch them.

The heavyweight division is wide open. In 2016, Jarrell Miller was looking to fill the void.

Jarrell "Big Baby" Miller

The romance of boxing has always been inseparable from the allure of heavyweights who can punch.

Jarrell "Big Baby" Miller can punch. Ranked in the top ten by the IBF, WBA, and WBO, he has compiled a 17-0-1 (15 KOs) ring record and is on the verge of becoming a viable heavyweight contender. On August 19, 2016, he'll face journeyman Fred Kassi in a bout that will be televised on ShoBox.

Miller has lived most of his life in Brooklyn with stops in Belize (Central America) and Queens (one of New York's five boroughs) along the way. He graduated from Thomas Edison High School and attended Borough of Manhattan Community College for two semesters before deciding to concentrate on boxing. His most significant business interest apart from the sweet science is an ownership stake in the Purehart Training Center in Queens. He and his girlfriend have a five-year-old son named Achilles.

Dmitry Salita met Miller in 2004 when Salita was training with Harry Keitt. Jarrell was sixteen years old at the time. Dmitry is now Miller's promoter and recently entered into a co-promotional agreement with Greg Cohen.

Steve Nelson and Michael Mihalitsas have co-managed Miller since October 2015. Nelson has experience in the heavyweight ranks, having previously co-managed Hasim Rahman, Monte Barrett, and Lawrence Clay-Bey.

I wanted to write about Miller and reached out to set up an interview. Salita and Nelson each telephoned me on August 1 to say that Jarrell would be at the Mendez Gym in Manhattan at 10:30 the following morning and would be expecting me.

"Call Jarrell to confirm it," Dmitry suggested.

So I called Jarrell.

"Looking forward to it," he said.

At 10:30 on Tuesday morning, I was at the Mendez Gym. So was trainer Harry Keitt.

Jarrell wasn't.

"Jarrell and ten-thirty aren't good friends," Harry told me.

Keitt is one of hundreds of amateur and professional boxers who got their start in New York under the tutelage of trainer George Washington. Harry and I chatted for a while.

"Jarrell was sixteen years old when I started working with him," Keitt reminisced. "He was kickboxing at the time. I told him, 'Kickboxing and boxing don't go together. You got to do one or the other.' So for a while, he put his energy into kickboxing. He did one and then the other. Jarrell has his own mindset. He does his own thing and says what he wants to say."

At eleven o'clock, Harry called Jarrell. He was at home in Queens, giving serious thought to leaving for the gym, which meant he might arrive around noon. I had other things to do. It's one thing to wait an hour and a half for LeBron James. But Jarrell Miller isn't LeBron James.

I went home. Thereafter, we rescheduled for 3:00 p.m. on August 11. This time, Jarrell arrived as promised.

Miller is personable and outgoing. He likes to talk and is a good self-promoter. His confidence is genuine. He means it when he says, "I'm the best out there. It's just a matter of time for the whole world to see it."

How does Miller define himself?

"I'm Jarrell. I'm a big kid at heart. I love to fight. Family means the world to me."

"What makes you happy?"

"Food. Cheeseburgers."

"Why are you boxing?"

"I haven't seen big money yet. But it's a money thing. And an ego thing. That's what motivates me."

Miller has an opinion about everything. The historical figures that he admires run the gamut from Jack Johnson to Gandhi to Albert Einstein to Malcolm X with James Brown thrown in.

He's also passionate about politics.

"Look at the election campaign now," Jarrell told me. "It's making a mockery of the whole country. Ignorance and stupidity make me angry, and we're seeing a lot of ignorance and stupidity these days. Trump is racist. He's disrespectful of other people. Obama didn't solve all the country's problems. No one can. But he tried and he's done a lot. We need to keep going forward now, not go backward. Racial justice, religious tolerance, income inequality, global warming, education. People got to get on the same page."

That brings us to Miller as a fighter.

Jarrell was born on July 15, 1988 (eighteen days after Mike Tyson obliterated Michael Spinks). "Mike Tyson was what got me interested in boxing," he says. "When Tyson fought, everything else stopped. Everyone in the neighborhood was watching it on television. When he knocked guys down, everyone went crazy. I was like "WOW! I want to have that same impact on people."

Miller began combat sports training in Muay Thai at age fourteen. He took up boxing at sixteen. Then he focused on kickboxing, establishing a 23-and-2 record as a professional kickboxer. His first professional boxing match was a one-round knockout victory on July 18, 2009. Twenty-two months passed before he committed fully to the sweet science and entered the ring with only his hands as weapons for the second time.

Is there a danger that Jarrell will have a brain blip someday and kick an opponent?

"I don't think so," he answers. "I programmed myself a long time ago. No boxing shoes; kick. Boxing shoes; no kick."

Miller was brought in for one fight as a sparring partner for Vitali Klitschko toward the end of Vitali's career. He was in Wladimir Klitschko's camp as a sparring partner on multiple occasions.

"The first few times with Wladimir were tough," Jarrell recalls. "There's constant pressure because he's got a stiff jab and cuts off the ring well. When you're taking four steps, he's taking two. He's a hard hitter. He can crack. And when you get inside, he lays on you, wears you down, tires you out. Those were hard sessions for me. I wasn't as experienced then as I am now. I still have a lot to learn, but I had more to learn then. It took a while. But I finally learned how to land an overhand right on him. Then they stopped inviting me to camp."

The right hand is Jarrell's money punch. Talk with people in boxing about him and it always comes down to the same thing.

Matchmaker Ron Katz: "He's a big guy. He's improving. And he can punch."

Ring announcer David Diamante: "He's fun to watch. So far, he's passed every test they've put in front of him. And he can punch."

Promoter Lou DiBella: "Jarrell has a big personality. He's getting better as a fighter. And he hits like a motherfucker."

That said, there's a school of thought that Miller could, and should, shed some pounds. In his last fight (a May 27, 2016, knockout of Nick Guivas), he weighed in at 283.

"A lot of Jarrell's weight is in his thighs," Harry Keitt says. "His legs are like tree trunks and that's okay. But I'd like to see him at 250. He'd be more flexible and get a little less tired as a fight goes on. Jarrell has the ability. He has gifts. The heavyweight division is wide open now. If Jarrell stays in the gym and works like he should, he could be the guy. But he has to do what it takes."

"Jarrell dances to his own music," adds Dmitry Salita. "There are times when he's like a big kid. One of the questions he has to answer is, as he gets bigger in boxing, will he do what he has to do in training or hang out and be a celebrity?"

It's hard to not think of Chris Arreola, another heavyweight with a big personality and the punch to match, whose lack of discipline caused him to fall short of his potential.

What will happen when Miller faces a world-class heavyweight? That's the multi-million-dollar question. The fighter most often mentioned in conjunction with Jarrell is Deontay Wilder. At present, they're the two hardest-punching American heavyweights, and maybe the two best.

"If Jarrell keeps improving," Salita posits, "it won't be long before he's better than Wilder. So let me ask you something. Deontay Wilder is from Alabama. Jarrell Miller is from Brooklyn. Which one should be fighting at Barclays Center and be the face of Brooklyn boxing?"

"I'd love to fight Wilder," Jarrell says. "I know the things he does right, but I also see the things he does wrong. Certain situations put you in a spot where you put up or shut up. That's when you find out what's inside you. Sure, there are times when I think about the worst that can happen in a fight. All fighters do. Then I'm like, 'Fuck it. Do what you gotta do.'"

And he can punch.

*It speaks poorly for would-be elite fighters when they avoid the toughest chal-
lenges in their own weight division and call out opponents they have no intention of fighting.*

The Middleweight Division

A championship belt once meant that a fighter was the best in the
world in his weight class. Now, too often, it means that he's a good fighter
who has been cleverly managed, matched, and promoted. With that in
mind, let's review the recent nine-day, three-fight merry-go-round that
reaffirmed what we already knew about the middleweight division.

On September 9, 2016, WBA "world" champion Danny Jacobs scored
a seventh-round knockout over a badly faded Sergio Mora. Jacobs (now
32-1, 29 KOs) had fought one round in the previous thirteen months.
Mora, a 20-to-1 underdog who has won only six of twelve fights over
the past eight years, had fought none.

One day later, thirty-four-year-old Gennady Golovkin, who's widely
recognized as the best middleweight in the world, fought Kell Brook in
London.

Golovkin is the WBC, WBA, and IBF middleweight champion. But
the WBA belt comes with a catch. In its never-ending quest for sanctioning fees, the WBA designated Gennady as its "super champion" and
bestowed its "world" championship belt on Jacobs.

Brook, age thirty, entered the ring with a 36-0 (25 KOs) ledger
and the IBF welterweight championship belt. Despite weighing in a half
pound heavier than Golovkin, he was a 6-to-1 underdog, in part because
of their past weight-class differential.

Brook's backers noted that Bernard Hopkins went up two weight
divisions to wrest the 175-pound title from Antonio Tarver in 2006. Ray
Leonard made the jump from welterweight to middleweight to dethrone
Marvin Hagler in 1987. But Kell Brook isn't Sugar Ray Leonard. And
Gennady Golovkin is more formidable than Antonio Tarver.

Give Brook credit for making the fight interesting. After being hurt
by a hook to the body early in round one, he fought back hard, won the

last ninety seconds of the round, and had an edge in the second stanza. He outboxed Golovkin at times, landed some sharp power punches, and made Gennady look mortal.

But Golovkin's punches were harder than Brook's. He took everything that Kell had to offer. And Brook couldn't keep Golovkin at bay. By round five, Kell was getting hit more and landing less. And his right orbital bone was fractured.

A trainer knows when his fighter is getting beaten up and is about to get beaten up worse. One minute fifty-five seconds into round five, Dominic Ingle (Brook's trainer) stepped onto the ring apron and waved a white towel of surrender.

"Kell Brook is good fighter," Golovkin said afterward. "He has great distance. But he is not middleweight. He touch me. I don't feel. After second round, I understand, don't box him. Just street fight with him."

The victory raised Golovkin's record to 36-0 (33 KOs) with knockouts in his most recent twenty-three fights.

Then the scene shifted to Texas, where former WBC "world" middleweight champion Saul "Canelo" Alvarez challenged Liam Smith for the WBO 154-pound crown on September 17.

Alvarez (now 48-1-1, 34 KOs) claimed the "lineal" and WBC "world" middleweight championships when he decisioned Miguel Cotto last November in a bout with a 155-pound weight limit. After beating Cotto, Canelo should have said, "It was a great honor to fight Miguel Cotto. It's a great honor to have won the WBC's middleweight championship belt. But I'm not a middleweight, so I'm returning to the junior-middleweight division."

But that's not what Alvarez did. Canelo was matched next against a blown-up Amir Khan and scored a sixth-round knockout in another "middleweight championship" fight with a 155-pound limit. That same night, immediately after the fight, Canelo called out Golovkin from the safety of the ring. And Oscar De La Hoya (Alvarez's promoter) told the assembled media, "Canelo wants to be a legend. He wants to take risks. He dares to be great."

Talk is cheap.

Eleven days after beating Khan, rather than contracting to fight Golovkin, Alvarez relinquished his WBC middleweight title. That led to Canelo vs. Liam Smith.

Smith claimed the WBO 154-pound belt in December 2015 with a seventh-round stoppage of "Jimmy" Kilrain Kelly and defended it successfully earlier this year against Predrag Radosevic. He entered the ring to face Alvarez as a 10-to-1 underdog with a 23-0-1 (13 KOs) record. Prior to facing Alvarez at AT&T Stadium in Texas, he'd never fought outside the United Kingdom as a professional.

Smith fought as well as he could against Alvarez. But the outcome of the fight was never in doubt. Canelo was bigger, faster, stronger, better, and hit harder. Like Golovkin against Brook, Alvarez got hit with some sharp clean punches. But Smith simply didn't have the power to hurt him. Liam fought courageously through adversity only to find more adversity. Canelo softened him up with a brutal body attack, dropped him in rounds seven and eight, and ended matters with an excruciatingly painful hook to the liver at 2:28 of round nine.

Meanwhile, WBO middleweight titleholder Billy Joe Saunders (23-0, 12 KOs) has watched the past two weeks unfold with more than casual interest.

Saunders shows what a belt is worth. Golovkin, Jacobs, and Alvarez have all expressed interest in contesting his hold on the WBO crown.

Golovkin's promoters tendered a seven-figure offer and would be amenable to fighting Saunders in England. Golden Boy is expected to make a similar offer for an Alvarez-Saunders match-up in the United States. Team Saunders was also reportedly offered $500,000 plus UK television rights to fight Danny Jacobs in America. Or Billy Joe could opt to stay at home against a local challenger.

One day after Golovkin beat Brook, Billy Joe posted a video on Twitter in which he addressed Gennady as follows: "Let's get one thing right. I'm a fully fledged middleweight. I definitely want you on your next available date. The date you come back to me with will be a date that I will accept because I'll give the fans what they want to see."

That challenge was soon supplemented by "He [Golovkin] keeps banging on about wanting a chance at my belt. I'll give him a chance if he wants it. I'm ready to fight wherever he wants, I don't care if it's in England, America. I don't care if it's in a field. I'll fight him wherever he wants."

The proof of the pudding will be in the eating.

Alvarez would also like a crack at Saunders and his 160-pound belt.

As for Danny Jacobs, on September 9, Keith Idec posted a column in which he noted correctly that Jacobs is "accessible, likeable, charitable, intelligent, respectful, and a devoted father to his young son." Idec then wrote, "For some reason, though, Jacobs hasn't become quite as big an attraction in this star-starved sport as he and many within the boxing industry believe he should be. Jacobs can't comprehend why he isn't doing bigger business than a Friday night slot on basic cable."

Jacobs was then quoted as saying, "It's very frustrating because I have an amazing story, I'm very well spoken, I'm a philanthropist. I have all the ingredients of a superstar, yet all the backing is not following through."

Okay, Danny. Here's why. There's one "ingredient of a superstar" that you're missing. The reason athletes become superstars is that they prove themselves in competition again and again.

LeBron James didn't win his first NBA title in 2012 against the lowly Philadelphia 76ers. His team beat the Oklahoma City Thunder. You won your "championship" against Jarrod Fletcher. LeBron James didn't lead the Cleveland Cavaliers to victory in the NBA Finals this year against the New Orleans Pelicans. The Cavs beat the Golden State Warriors led by Stephen Curry, Klay Thompson, and Draymond Green. You beat Peter Quillin last December, sat out for nine months, and came back against Sergio Mora.

In early September, Jacobs declared, "We called out Triple G months ago. I truly want that fight." In the ring immediately after beating Mora, Jacobs repeated that sentiment, proclaiming, "I want to prove to the world that I'm the best middleweight. So if Triple G gets the victory [against Kell Brook], that's what I want."

Well, Golovkin got the victory over Brook. And the WBA can now order a purse bid that would be enforceable against either Jacobs or Golovkin. If one of the fighters refused, he could be stripped of his belt.

But that leads to numerous unanswered questions. First, Jacobs would in effect be the challenger. What would the purse split be? If Golovkin-Jacobs went to purse bid and a promoter affiliated with Al Haymon won the bid, how would HBO feel about Golovkin fighting on another network? How can a promoter monetize Golovkin-Jacobs to pay Danny what he wants? Gennady can sell out an arena in New York or

Los Angeles. But Golovkin-Jacobs isn't a big-money pay-per-view fight. Gennady has had one pay-per-view outing (against David Lemieux at Madison Square Garden in 2015). He sold out the main arena, but the pay-per-view numbers were disappointing.

Meanwhile, Golovkin applies pressure and cuts off the ring too well to simply run from him. He gets hit reasonably often but takes a good punch and is willing to take one to land one in return, which forces opponents to fight with him. And he can whack.

Thanks to Kell Brook, we know that Gennady can be outboxed. He doesn't have to be outpunched to be beaten; just punched hard enough.

With that in mind, Golovkin vs. Alvarez would be a marvelously entertaining fight. Gennady is an aggressive fighter. Canelo is an excellent counterpuncher. Golovkin beats his opponents down mercilessly. Alvarez has scored highlight-reel knockouts in three of his last four fights.

After beating Smith, Alvarez was asked yet again about fighting Golovkin and answered, "I fear no one."

But Canelo's handling of the Golovkin situation is fast becoming his own personal "no mas." Win or lose, he needs to fight Golovkin to be fully respected.

2016 saw a mix of fights, some good and some bad.

Fight Notes

PBC's first telecast on Fox's big broadcast network began in entertaining fashion on Saturday night (January 23, 2016) when Dominic Breazeale took on Amir Mansour in the opening bout.

The thirty-year-old Breazeale (now 17-0 with 15 KOs) represented the United States in the super-heavyweight division at the 2012 London Olympics.

Forty-three-year-old Amir Mansour (22-2-1, 16 KOs) spent eight and a half years in prison at the start of the new millennium after being convicted of cocaine trafficking and received an additional fourteen-month sentence in December 2011 for violating the terms of his probation.

Each man was looking for victory in the hope that it would give him a semblance of credibility in the heavyweight sweepstakes.

Breazeale (an amiable man who outweighed Mansour by thirty-five pounds) fights like someone who's learning to box by the numbers. He looked soft around the middle and in a few other places as well.

Mansour, who seems less amiable, sought to overwhelm Breazeale with swarming aggression. Dominic didn't have the technique to keep him off and was decked by a solid right hand in round three. That left Breazeale simply trying to survive.

Mansour, arguably, won every round of an entertaining fight. But by the fifth stanza, he had the look of a fighter who had punched himself out. He quit before the start of round six, saying that he couldn't close his mouth. Post-fight tests revealed that, fortunately, his jaw was not broken.

Mansour might be a bit softer than he looks. And Breazeale might be a bit tougher.

In the second televised fight of the night, Sammy Vasquez dominated Aron Martinez, who chose to stay on his stool at the close of round six. In the main event, Danny Garcia pounded out a workmanlike unanimous decision over Robert Guerrero.

A word on the announcing team for Fox's first PBC telecast is also in order.

The always reliable Brian Kenny opened the show from the host's seat and returned from time to time.

Charissa Thompson did spot reporting in a manner that suggests she's better suited for her role as a co-host of *Fox Sports Live*.

Gus Johnson, who handled blow-by-blow chores, advised viewers that Breazeale (a former quarterback at the University of Northern Colorado) once threw a football seventy-two yards.

Johnson tends to be a cheerleader and uses superlatives like "great" and "terrific" so frequently that they lose their meaning. He's prone to hyperbole: "Shawn Porter is coming off a HUGE upset of Adrien Broner ...We all LOVE Floyd Mayweather ... Danny Garcia throws that Puerto Rican left hook."

Keith Thurman was the telecast's boxing expert. When Thurman dials back the hype, he's thoughtful and intelligent. "Power is the easiest way to earn respect," he noted. Thurman was also candid and right-on when he said of Martinez in round five, "He's not looking to fight."

Mark Kriegel was in the analyst's chair (thought of by some as "the Larry Merchant seat"). His comments were on point all night. When Johnson suggested during Mansour-Breazeale that the heavyweight division might be wide open, Kriegel noted, "It is wide open. You've got a forty-three-year-old and an ex-football-player." Later, referencing the role that Angel Garcia and Ruben Guerrero play in training their sons, Kriegel observed, "If you think Little League fathers are bad, this is the ultimate expression of male vanity."

Time and again, when Johnson verged on going overboard, Kriegel brought him back to solid ground. Late in Garcia-Guerrero, with the dialogue focusing on which fighter wanted it more, Mark said simply, "I don't think it's a question of desire. I think it's a question of talent."

Kriegel has talent.

★ ★ ★

Seanie Monaghan sat on a chair in a dressing room on the second floor of The Theater at Madison Square Garden. It was Saturday, February 27,

2016. In a matter of hours, Terence Crawford would defend his WBO 140-pound crown against Hank Lundy. In a matter of minutes, Monaghan would walk down a flight of stairs and enter the ring to do battle against Janne Forsman of Finland in the second bout of the evening.

Seanie has been boxing professionally for six years. During that time, he has compiled a 26-and-0 record with seventeen knockouts. He was a "project" with no boxing experience beyond brawling in bars when he walked into a gym in Freeport, Long Island, where Joe Higgins was training amateurs eight years ago. In some ways, he's still a project.

Monaghan's advocates characterize him as a technically sound fighter who mounts an aggressive inexorable assault. His critics say that he's plodding and predictable. Everyone agrees that Seanie does the most with what he has.

In each of his fights so far, he has gotten the job done.

Making weight for the Forsman bout had been easier than usual because the contract weight was 180 pounds instead of the standard 175-pound light-heavyweight limit. Seanie had weighed in a day earlier at 179.8; Forsman at 177. The Finnish fighter had a respectable 21-and-3 record with thirteen knockouts, but it had been built against limited opposition.

Monaghan was sharing the dressing room on the second floor with three other undercard fighters. Each team had its own space. Seanie was surrounded by four men who have been with him from the start of his ring career: Higgins, Joe's son, manager P. J. Kavanagh, and cutman George Mitchell.

Monaghan is the only fighter that Kavanagh has managed. "Seanie is a guy you'd want next to you when you're in a foxhole and the bullets are flying," P. J. says.

Higgins was focused on the combat at hand. "Forsman looked soft in the body at the weigh-in," the trainer noted. "He has a respectable record. And you can't take any fighter lightly. But I think, when Seanie goes to the body, he'll take him out."

One of the other undercard fighters—Miguel Gloria (a lightweight with one win in two bouts who was slated for the fourth contest of the evening)—approached and asked if he could take a selfie with Monaghan. Seanie obliged.

As a matter of course, Monaghan is remarkably self-sufficient in the dressing room before a fight. Other than taping his hands, putting his gloves on, and warming him up, his team lets him be. Seanie likes it that way. He prefers to sit alone with his thoughts.

"Mostly, I'm focusing on my game plan and what I want to do in the fight," Monaghan explains. "If I had better mind control, that's all I'd think about. But sometimes I think about my kids and the lifestyle that my being successful in boxing can give them. I have to keep winning for that to happen."

Losing would be worse than getting banged up. Seanie is used to getting banged up. He's not used to losing.

"I'm old school," he says. "Getting hit doesn't bother me. Losing would."

Emanuel Taylor stopped Wilfredo Acuna in round six of the opening bout of the evening. It was Seanie's turn now.

Monaghan-Forsman was a typical Seanie Monaghan fight. Seanie moved steadily forward from the opening bell, digging a well-schooled hook to the body whenever the opportunity presented itself. He got hit too much. But over time, he broke Forsman down. Shortly before the end of round four, an accumulation of body blows put the Finnish fighter on the canvas. Midway through round five, referee Allan Huggins halted the beatdown.

In the dressing room afterward, there was a little redness and swelling around Seanie's left eye. But there were no cuts, which was a happy departure from the norm.

"Seanie keeps getting better," Higgins said. "Guys who gave him good sparring two years ago can't hang with him now. His reaction time is improving because he doesn't have to think as much before doing what he has to do. It's more second nature than it was before."

"Seanie has paid his dues," Kavanagh added. "It would be easy for him to get lazy in training, slough off a bit. But he doesn't do that. He's extremely disciplined and strong mentally. He works hard and never cuts corners."

If Monaghan keeps winning, it's likely that he'll have the opportunity to fight for a world title. When that happens, he'll go as far as his skills and his heart can carry him.

★ ★ ★

Gennady Golovkin and Roman Gonzalez continued their destructive ways on April 23, 2016, with dominant victories over Dominic Wade and McWilliams Arroyo. It was the third time in a row that the two champions (who are widely regarded as the top pound-for-pound fighters in the world) were paired on an HBO telecast.

Gonzalez (now 45-0, 38 KOs) is twenty-eight years old and plies his trade at the 112-pound flyweight limit. The thirty-year-old Arroyo (now 16-3, 14 KOs) was the best available opponent.

Arroyo said all the right things during the build-up to the fight. "I didn't just start yesterday," he told the media during an April 18 conference call. "I've been boxing all my life. I'm in boxing to fight the best. It has been my dream since I was a little kid to fight on HBO and to fight the best in the world."

But the problem with fighting the best is that you're fighting the best. And while Arroyo takes a good punch, he doesn't have one. By round three, the beatdown had begun and McWilliams's face was showing signs of bruising and lumping up. Then, to make matters worse for Arroyo, two minutes into the fourth stanza, the sole on his right shoe fell off.

Gonzalez dominated throughout, throwing punches like a non-stop assault weapon; 1,132 over the course of twelve rounds. He outlanded Arroyo by a 360-to-193 margin with a 311-to-148 advantage in power punches en route to a 120-108, 119-109, 119-109 triumph on the judges' scorecards. The only negative in "Chocolatito's" performance was that he couldn't knock Arroyo out.

Golovkin didn't have that problem.

Most devastating knockout artists have an aura of menace outside the ring as well as in it. Golovkin is cut from different cloth. In a social setting, Gennady might be mistaken for a computer geek. Inside the ropes, think merciless . . . inexorable . . . relentless . . . "Boxing is not a game," he says. "This is fighting."

Wade, age twenty-six, was the mandatory challenger for Golovkin's IBF middleweight belt by virtue of a split-decision triumph over forty-one-year-old Sam Soliman last June. Dominic entered the ring with eighteen victories and twelve knockouts in eighteen fights. But there were zero wins over world-class fighters on his resume.

At a February 18 kickoff press conference, Wade, like Arroyo, said all the right things regarding the mountain he had to climb: "All Golovkin has is his strength. It ain't no style I've never seen . . . Willie Monroe had the style to beat him, but he didn't have the power and he got tired . . . I'll prepare for whatever I have to. That's what training camp is for . . . I'll adjust the way I have to when we get in the ring . . . You do what you gotta do when you get hit. When I get hit, I'll do what I gotta do."

Nine days before the fight, Wade proclaimed, "I'm ready for April 23. It's going to be a beautiful night. Everybody is kind of underestimating what I can do and how I perform. That night I can show it."

Not.

When fight night arrived, the odds were roughly 40-to-1 in Golovkin's favor.

Gennady has turned into a ticket seller. The Forum in Inglewood was sold out with 16,353 fans in attendance.

Late last year, trainer Abel Sanchez said of his fighter, "They all think Gennady is overrated until they get in the ring with him."

Other testimonials have come from vanquished opponents.

Matthew Macklin, who Golovkin knocked out with a body shot at Madison Square Garden three years ago, recounted, "It's easy to be relaxed when someone can't hurt you. When they can, it's a different story. With Golovkin, you burn up a lot more nervous energy and you're panicked into making mistakes."

Daniel Geale, who met a similar fate at Gennady's hands the following year, observed, "Golovkin can do anything he wants in there."

Wade felt Golovkin's power in the first minute of the fight, spent the second half of round one trying to tie Gennady up, and was decked by an overhand right near the end of the opening stanza. One minute fifty seconds into round two, a left uppercut followed by a right to the shoulder put Dominic on the canvas for the second time. A third knockdown, courtesy of a straight right hand, ended matters with a ten count at the 2:37 mark of round two.

"His power is real," Wade said afterward. "It was more than I expected."

Golovkin has now knocked out twenty-two consecutive opponents. His record stands at 35-and-0 (32 KOs) with victories in seventeen consecutive middleweight championship fights. Sixteen if one discounts his June 14, 2010, knockout of Milton Nunez, when Gennady won an "interim" WBA belt. That puts him four successful consecutive title defenses behind Bernard Hopkins's record of twenty.

As for Wade, he had his 517 seconds of fame and is unlikely to be in the spotlight again.

★ ★ ★

Top Rank's fight card at Madison Square Garden on June 11, 2016, was all but lost in the worldwide tributes that followed the death of Muhammad Ali.

Ali fought in the big arena at the current Garden on five occasions. Against Oscar Bonavena, Joe Frazier (twice), Floyd Patterson, and Earnie Shavers. There were hopes that his spirit would find its way to The Theatre at MSG, where Saturday's fights were contested. But it never quite got there.

The first co-featured fight of the evening matched Felix Verdejo against Juan Jose Martinez.

Verdejo (21-0, 14 KOs) has been touted by Top Rank as the next Puerto Rican ring icon. He has good skills coupled with speed and charisma. But as of late, Felix has been going in soft and, even then, has failed to close the show.

Juan Jose Martinez (25-2, 17 KOs) was chosen as Verdejo's opponent with an eye toward making Felix look good. He's a plodding, straight-ahead fighter without much power. The only issue was whether—and if so, when—Verdejo would knock him out. That occurred at the 2:40 mark of round five.

After the bout, Verdejo said he wanted to fight the best. He hasn't so far. Given the level of opposition that Felix has faced to date, one wonders whether he'll peak as a world champion or a beltholder.

The second fight of the evening saw Vasyl Lomachenko move up in weight to challenge WBO super-featherweight titleholder Roman Martinez.

Lomachenko (who entered the ring with a 5-1, 3 KOs professional record) is one of the most decorated amateurs in ring history, having won gold medals at the 2008 and 2012 Olympics as a representative of

Ukraine. He turned pro on October 12, 2013, lost a split decision in a championship fight against Orlando Salido in his second pro bout, and impressively conquered Gary Russell Jr. in his next outing to claim the WBO featherweight crown. This is known as a fast track.

Martinez (29-2-3, 17 KOs) annexed the WBO super-featherweight title in 2015 via decision over Salido (who had moved up in weight) and retained the title on a draw against Salido in his most recent fight. A decision loss to Ricky Burns and knockout defeat at the hands of Mikey Garcia plus three draws spotted Roman's record.

It would be hard for any fighter to live up to the accolades that Lomachenko's most ardent proponents have heaped upon his shoulders. But he's a complete fighter and very good. Against Martinez, Vasyl didn't disappoint, ending matters with an impressive left-uppercut right-hook combination at 1:09 of round five.

Lomachenko means it when he says he'll fight anyone.

Both endings were expected. Lomachenko and Verdejo were 15-to-1 favorites. Neither opponent won a round. As a general rule, fights are more entertaining if the audience doesn't know in advance who will win.

That said, Lomachenko is particularly intriguing. Vasyl lost to Salido in part because of a significant weight differential between them and more so because the referee failed to clamp down on Orlando's over-the-line roughhouse tactics.

Indeed, Lomachenko recently noted, "The biggest concern coming from amateur to professional was to adapt to that dirty style of boxing. It's not that there are not dirty fighters in the amateurs. It is that, in the amateurs, the referee will put a stop to it right away."

Lomachenko has matured as a professional fighter. He would beat Salido convincingly today.

★ ★ ★

Coming on the heels of Keith Thurman vs. Shawn Porter, the July 30, 2016, match-up between Californian Leo Santa Cruz and Carl Frampton of Northern Ireland was the second good main event in a row at Barclays Center.

Santa Cruz, age twenty-seven, came into the fight with a 32-0-1 (18 KOs) record. He's an action fighter with a signature win over Abner Mares in which he claimed the WBA 126-pound title.

Frampton, also twenty-seven and entering the bout undefeated (22-0, 14 KOs), held the WBA and IBF 122-pound belts by virtue of a split-decision victory over Scott Quigg earlier this year. The assumption going in was that both men would throw a lot of punches, but Frampton wouldn't be able to hurt Santa Cruz as much as Santa Cruz would hurt him. Leo was an almost 3-to-1 betting favorite.

Santa Cruz-Frampton was contested in front of an enthusiastic, sometimes roaring, crowd of 9,062.

In the early going, Frampton was able to get inside, neutralize his opponent's longer reach, and score effectively with hooks both to the body and up top. Santa Cruz landed well with straight right hands and, in round six, seemed to take control of the fight. But Frampton hung tough.

The action was spirited. Both men were willing to engage and fired back when hit. According to CompuBox, Santa Cruz outlanded Frampton by a 255-to-242 margin. But Frampton prevailed on a 117-111, 116-112, 114-114 majority decision. 114-114 was the most accurate of the three judges' scorecards.

Santa Cruz vs. Frampton showcased boxing at its best. One of the undercard bouts—Paulie Malignaggi vs. Gabriel Bracero—showcased boxing as it shouldn't be.

There was a time when Malignaggi was a world-class craftsman. But he'll never be as good a fighter as he once was. Now thirty-five, he entered the ring on Saturday night with a 35-7 (7 KOs) ledger. He'd had six fights since 2012 and lost three of them (including two "KOs by").

Bracero, also thirty-five, was coming in off a first-round knockout victory over Danny O'Connor last October. Thereafter, Gabriel was in the news when he was arrested for assault, criminal possession of a weapon, obstructing government administration, and resisting arrest. Prior to that, he'd been arrested twelve times on charges ranging from attempted murder to armed robbery and spent almost six years in prison.

Bracero and Malignaggi had trained together as amateurs and young pros. "When I was away," Gabriel reminisced at the final pre-fight press conference, "I used to read boxing magazines. I read about Paulie on a regular basis."

Malignaggi was then a world champion and Bracero was in prison. But that was then, and now is now.

Paulie shouldn't be fighting anymore. The people who care about him the most (his brother Umberto, mentor Anthony Catanzaro, and longtime friend Pete Sferazza) have told him that time and time again.

But Malignaggi won't quit. "I feel like I can still box very well," he told David Greisman of Boxing Scene last December. "I have a very good sense of timing when I get the proper amount of sparring."

That quote came in conjunction with Paulie's explanation as to why he'd been knocked out by Danny Garcia at Barclays Center on August 1, 2015 (his most recent fight on American soil prior to facing Bracero). Paulie said he hadn't gotten in enough sparring for the Garcia fight—only twenty rounds—because he'd suffered a cut in May prior to a bout that had to be canceled due to the cut and he was wary about testing the eye.

"I've always been very heavily reliant on sparring," Paulie explained. "I'm a reflex type of fighter. I always rely on my eyes and my reflexes."

Four days before fighting Bracero, Malignaggi was more introspective when he spoke with writer Tom Gerbasi.

"Maybe it's just a dream," Paulie confessed. "We get into this sport as dreamers to better our lives. We're all dreamers; we all come from garbage. Anybody else who laces on the gloves for a living is the same way. So maybe I just don't want to stop dreaming. Whenever I'm in an arena that's roaring and yelling, I don't care if they're with me or against me. I'm the center of attention, coming from a place in my life where I was never the center of anything. I didn't have shit and people never expected me to become anything. So I can still take the stage and have all eyes on me, and maybe I just want to keep dreaming and feeling that a little bit longer."

Paulie has fought in main events at Madison Square Garden in New York and the MGM Grand in Las Vegas against the likes of Miguel Cotto and Ricky Hatton. At Barclays Center on July 30, he wasn't even deemed worthy of a slot on the three-fight Showtime Championship Boxing card. Instead, Malignaggi-Bracero was relegated to Showtime Extreme.

Against Bracero, Paulie wasn't sharp. He moved as well as his thirty-five-year-old legs allowed him to, circling out of harm's way for most of the bout. He feinted and postured. What he didn't do was fight well. There were moments when he established his jab and showed flashes of the fighter he once was. Bracero is a fading fighter too, and he was never as good as Malignaggi. But Paulie couldn't sustain excellence for three minutes a round. And he got hit with punches he wouldn't have been hit with a few years ago. He outlanded Bracero by a 164-to-134 margin and emerged with a 98-92, 98-92, 96-94 victory on the judges' scorecards. But the best that can be said of his performance is that he beat a good club fighter.

Paulie can blame all sorts of things for his showing. He can say that Bracero is a slick veteran who didn't want to engage. He can say he didn't get the right sparring for the fight. He might even say that his reflexes were dulled by the aroma of weed that wafted through the arena on fight night and led to Barclays Center security personnel being called into action.

But a better coda for the fight came when Malignaggi was leaving the arena and a fan asked, "Hey, Paulie; who do you want to fight next?"

"I just want to go home," Paulie said.

There are people who could stop Malignaggi from fighting again. Right now, Paulie is as good as any expert boxing commentator on television. The fear is that, if he continues to dance with self-destruction, his commentating skills will decline like his boxing skills have.

If Malignaggi's words don't come out quite the same in five years, the powers that be will simply replace him.

"We're sorry, Paulie. You're a great guy. We love you. But you know how things are. We have an obligation to our viewers."

It would be better if these people insisted that Malignaggi stop boxing now.

A fighter shouldn't wait until he's showing signs of brain damage to stop boxing. By then, it's too late.

★ ★ ★

HBO and Showtime rang down the curtain on their 2016 boxing telecasts with a flurry of activity on December 10 and December 17 that said good-bye to the past and offered a glimpse of the future.

Let's begin at the end. Bernard Hopkins fought Joe Smith on December 17 in a fight televised by HBO.

Hopkins (now 55-8-2, 32 KOs) will turn fifty-two years old next month. He hadn't fought since losing to Sergey Kovalev on November 11, 2014. He'd won four of eight fights over the past six and a half years, and his last knockout was a ninth-round stoppage of Oscar De La Hoya in 2004. That's the year Barack Obama was elected to the United States Senate. When Bernard turned pro, on October 11, 1988, Ronald Reagan was president of the United States and there were fewer than 80,000 Internet hosts. Today there are approximately one billion.

Smith was born on September 20, 1987, eleven months after Hopkins turned pro. Joe entered the ring with a 22-1 (16 KOs) record that had been cobbled together against mostly pedestrian opposition. The one bright spot on his ledger was a first-round upset victory over Andrzej Fonfara earlier this year.

Hopkins-Smith shaped up as a match between a very old, skilled veteran against a tough club fighter. Prior to the bout, Smith voluntarily entered a VADA testing program designed to detect the presence of performance-enhancing drugs. Hopkins declined to do so.

Last month, I spoke with Ron Katz (possibly the best matchmaker in the United States east of the Nevada-based Bruce Trampler) and asked Katz what he thought would happen in Hopkins-Smith.

"Joe will knock him out," Katz said.

Of course, Katz is the matchmaker for Star Boxing (Smith's promoter).

"Are you just saying that because Smith is your guy?" I pressed.

"You know me better than that," Katz countered. "There have been times when I told you our guy had next-to-no chance. Hopkins is an old man, and he's a lot older now than he was when he fought Kovalev. Unless Joe freezes, he'll walk through Bernard."

That thought was supported by the words of John David Jackson, who trained Sergey Kovalev for his whitewash victory over Hopkins. Last month, before being tabbed to train Hopkins for the Smith fight, Jackson said, "Bernard is an old fighter. Even though he says he's an Alien and The Executioner and all that, the bottom line is he's an old fighter. So you have to treat him like an old fighter. You have to do things that take him out of his comfort zone. You have to make him work. Sergey was able to use his jab to offset Bernard's trickery. Bernard is very well schooled and he's a student of the game. He was just older [against Kovalev] and unable to do what he once did."

Hopkins had pledged that, win or lose, Hopkins-Smith would be his last fight. The HBO telecast was packaged as The Final Fight of The Legendary Bernard Hopkins.

Smith ruined the script.

In round one, it was clear that Hopkins isn't close to being a great fighter anymore. Smith went after him from the opening bell and kept the pressure on throughout the fight.

Smith suffered a cut along his left eyebrow from a head butt in round two that HBO blow-by-blow commentator Jim Lampley observed "wasn't anything near accidental." But as the fight progressed, Joe began landing to the body and hit Hopkins with increasingly clean punches up top that wouldn't have landed on Bernard several years ago. Hopkins fought mostly to conserve energy and avoid punishment while attacking occasionally with right hands that carried less power than in years past. Also, Bernard began to tire.

Early in round eight, Smith cornered Hopkins and connected with a series of punches punctuated by a solid right hand and two hooks to the head that blasted Bernard through the ropes. Hopkins was unable to make it back into the ring within the twenty seconds allotted for such matters and was counted out at fifty-three seconds of the round. It was the first "KO by" loss of Bernard's sixty-five-bout career.

"He got frustrated," Hopkins said somewhat disingenuously after the fight. "And I might have gotten grazed with a left hook and next thing I know he was throwing me out of the ring."

At the time of the stoppage, Smith was ahead on two of the judges' scorecards by margins of 69-64 and 67-66. The third judge (Pat Russell) had an inexplicable 67-66 score in Bernard's favor.

According to CompuBox, Smith outlanded Hopkins in seven of the eight rounds en route to an 86-to-54 advantage in punches landed. "I came here to do my job," Joe said afterward. "I had to finish him. His career was going to end, but I needed mine to continue."

Mythmakers were quick to note that Hopkins, like Joe Louis, ended his career after being knocked through the ropes en route to an eighth-round knockout defeat. The difference is that Louis was knocked through the ropes by Rocky Marciano. Hopkins was knocked through the ropes by Joe Smith. Also, after Louis lost, The Brown Bomber acknowledged, "What's the use of crying. The better man won. That's all."

There was also action this month on the heavyweight front.

Showtime began its December 10 festivities with a live telecast of the IBF heavyweight title fight in Manchester, England, between Anthony Joshua (now 18-0, 18 KOs) and Eric Molina (who was knocked out for the fourth time).

Molina fought like the 30-to-1 underdog he was and was stopped in three rounds. Next up for Joshua is Wladimir Klitschko in a bout scheduled for April 29, 2017, at Wembley Stadium in London. Joshua-Klitschko will be interesting.

Also on December 10, HBO showed a tape delay of the WBO "world heavyweight championship" fight between New Zealand's Joseph Parker (now 23-0, 18 KOs) and California's Andy Ruiz (29-1, 19 KOs).

Parker-Ruiz would have been acceptable as the main event at a good club show. To call it a world championship fight was absurd.

Ruiz deserves respect as a professional fighter who had won all of his previous bouts, albeit against limited opponents. That said, he looked like the Pillsbury Doughboy when he toppled the scales at 255 3/4 pounds and fought in a manner that evoked images of an overweight competitor in a tough-man contest. Parker won a narrow majority decision. It doesn't say much for Joseph that Ruiz had him in retreat for much of the night.

Alexander Povetkin was supposed to face Bermane Stiverne in a WBC "heavyweight championship elimination bout" in Russia on December 17. But the fight was called off twenty hours before the bell for round one was scheduled to ring because a blood sample taken from Povetkin by VADA on December 6 tested positive for ostarine (a banned drug that produces effects similar to anabolic steroids). After the positive result (the second for Povetkin this year) was reported, the WBC announced that it was withdrawing its sanction of the fight and Stiverne withdrew from the contest. Povetkin then knocked out late-substitute Johann Duhaupas in the sixth round.

Congratulations to the WBC and VADA for their commitment to clean sport. Shame on Povetkin.

A new biography of Ingemar Johansson provided an entertaining look at the former champion.

Ingemar Johansson

Ingemar Johansson created an enormous amount of excitement in the world of boxing for a short period of time.

After an ignominious appearance (he was disqualified for refusing to engage) in the final round of the heavyweight competition at the 1952 Helsinki Olympics, Johansson returned to his native Sweden, turned pro, and defeated a series of undistinguished European opponents.

He was technically lacking as a fighter and fought cautiously, waiting for the opportunity to land his only destructive weapon: a big right hand later known as "The Hammer of Thor."

Victories over Henry Cooper and Joe Erkine raised Johansson's standing a bit. Then, on September 14, 1958, he knocked out previously undefeated American heavyweight contender Eddie Machen in the first round. Given the fact that Machen would go the distance with Sonny Liston, Floyd Patterson, Cleveland Williams, Zora Folley, Jerry Quarry, Doug Jones, and Ernie Terrell during the course of his own twelve-year career, that was no mean accomplishment. And it earned Johansson a June 26, 1959, title shot against reigning heavyweight champion Floyd Patterson.

Johansson was a heavy underdog against Patterson, a "Swedish meatball" who, it was thought, would be pulverized by the champion. The odds grew even longer when the challenger defied tradition by cohabitating with his girlfriend, eating cheesecake, and going dancing at night during training camp. It had worked for him in the past, so why change now?

When the hour of reckoning came, Johansson knocked Patterson down seven times en route to a third-round stoppage. Suddenly, the heavyweight champion of the world was a good-looking, charismatic Swede, who enjoyed listening to Frank Sinatra, was media friendly, and charmed virtually everyone within his orbit.

Ingemar Johansson by Ken Brooks (McFarland & Company) is the first major biography to be written about Johansson.

Early on, Brooks states, "I will make no claim that Johansson belongs on the same tier with Joe Louis, Muhammad Ali, Joe Frazier, Jack Dempsey, or any of the other giants of the game. His infighting was non-existent, his jab without sting, his chin suspect, his title reign too short. In retrospect, one could be excused for dismissing Ingemar as a lucky one-shot champ, one of those ignominious few who won the heavyweight title only to lose it in their first defense."

That's a good start because it signals that the author will avoid the pitfall of praising his subject beyond what is deserved.

Brooks then goes on to note that Johansson "hated school, disdained reading, despised teachers, and disliked books." He starting boxing at age thirteen and quit school two years later.

By the time Johansson was seventeen, he'd fathered two children by two different women. Both babies were put up for adoption. At age eighteen, he married Barbara Abramson. The couple quickly had two children and separated soon after. In 1951, at age nineteen, Johansson fathered a fifth child by yet another woman.

Adding to his resume, in 1954, Johansson spent sixty days in prison for insubordination during an eleven-month stint in the Swedish navy occasioned by Sweden's mandatory military service law.

In 1954, Johansson, then twenty-two years old and separated from his wife, met seventeen-year-old Birgit Lundgren, who became his longtime companion. They married in 1963, had two children together, and separated in 1969.

Johansson was a popular champion. As Brooks notes, sports coverage in the 1950s "bordered on hero worship. Columnists and beat writers tapped out glowing hagiographies on ballplayers and prizefighters. Sportswriters who interviewed Johansson mostly stuck to the script, depicting Ingemar as debonaire, witty, educated, sophisticated."

When Johansson dethroned Patterson in 1959, all was forgiven in his native Sweden (although Ingemar ruffled feathers later that year by becoming a Swiss citizen in an attempt to avoid high Swedish taxes).

A 1959 poll of three hundred sportswriters awarded Johansson the Hickout Belt emblematic of the year's outstanding professional athlete.

The Associated Press named him "male athlete of the year." He was honored by *Sports Illustrated* as its "sportsman of the year." And the Boxing Writers Association of America designated him "fighter of the year."

Johansson also appeared on myriad American television shows and engaged in flings with a bevy of head-turning women, including Elizabeth Taylor and *Playboy* centerfold Stella Stevens.

The party came to an end in 1960. One year less a week after dethroning Patterson, Johansson was knocked unconscious in the fifth round of their June 19 rematch. Nine months later, they squared off for the third time with each man visiting the canvas before Patterson emerged victorious on a sixth-round stoppage that many observers considered premature.

Johansson retired from boxing in 1963 with a 26-and-2 record. Still commercially viable, he steadfastly resisted comeback offers. Promised one million dollars to fight Sonny Liston, he responded, "I like money, but not that much." As a footnote to his career, it should be noted that Johansson never faced an opponent with a losing record.

With the arrival of Cassius Clay, who would become Muhammad Ali (the ultimate charisma machine), people forgot how charismatic Johansson had been.

In 1974, Johansson moved to Florida, where he purchased and operated a motel in Pompano Beach. "I got tired of running around, tired of parties," he said. "You can't be a swinger all your life. I've had my glory. Now it's over. I loved the old life. I love this one too. I don't sit and dream of the old days. I never thought of boxing as my life, just some fun I had when I was younger."

Johansson enjoyed his early years in retirement. He was polite to autograph seekers. "It takes longer to say 'no' than it does to sign my name," he noted. In 1979, he met a Swedish journalist named Edna Alsterlund. They began living together in 1981 and later married.

1981 also saw Johansson succeed on a quixotic quest. His weight had ballooned to almost three hundred pounds. And on a whim, he decided to enter the Stockholm Marathon. He shed fifty pounds and completed the run in four hours and forty minutes. Later that year, he entered the New York City Marathon and, fifteen pounds lighter, shaved ten minutes off his time.

Asked about the difference between long-distance running and boxing, Johansson replied, "In a marathon, you might get sore feet, a sore body. But in a day or two, you are all right. After a fight, it might be forever."

Forever came too soon.

In the mid-1980s, Johansson returned to live in Sweden. Ten years later, he began having noticeable memory-loss problems. Eventually, his mind decayed into a hellish dementia. In 2001, Edna told an interviewer, "It is best not to remember Ingemar as he was, but to learn to love him as he is."

Meanwhile, Floyd Patterson was suffering from a similar fate. Patterson died in 2006 at age seventy-one. Johansson followed him to the grave at age seventy-six three years later.

Brooks writes objectively rather than over-praising his subject. His book humanizes Johansson and is engagingly written. The stunning first-round knockout of Eddie Machen and three Patterson-Johansson fights are nicely told. There's also an interesting look at some of the shady financial maneuvers engaged in by Cus D'Amato, who served as Patterson's longtime trainer and manager.

But there's a problem. What appears to be a generally well-researched book is marred by factual errors. Some of these errors are just sloppy. At one point, Brooks writes that Johansson and Lundgren married in 1962. At another juncture, he says they wed in 1963.

Other errors are the result of more serious lapses. For example, Brooks writes, "Patterson-Johansson I marked the first heavyweight title fight in history to be simulcast live to theaters via closed circuit."

That's simply wrong. Several previous heavyweight championship fights were telecast live in theaters via closed circuit. Indeed, when Rocky Marciano defended his title against Archie Moore, 400,000 paying customers watched via closed circuit in 133 venues across the country.

Brooks also occasionally lapses into misleading hyperbole (e.g., writing that Sonny Liston quit in his first fight against Cassius Clay because his shoulder was "torn from its socket from swinging at air"). Liston did claim an upper-arm muscle injury after the fight, although that claim was suspect. His shoulder was certainly not "torn from its socket."

In another misstatement, Brooks writes that "Patterson served competently for years on the New York State Athletic Commission" until dementia robbed him of his cognitive abilities. In truth, Patterson's appointment as chairman of the NYSAC was a cynical ploy by corrupt power brokers from the start. He never functioned as a competent chairman.

These inaccuracies undermine an otherwise entertaining and informative book. Instead of saying, "This is interesting; I didn't know that," readers have to wonder what other errors might lurk beneath the surface.

That said, *Ingemar Johansson* is a good book. In the introduction, Brooks writes, "The time has come to more fully appreciate boxing's most overlooked and under-appreciated champion. Hopefully, this book is a start."

It is.

Roberto Duran's autobiography added little to what boxing fans already knew about "Manos de Piedra" in the ring. But there was an interesting look at Duran outside of boxing.

I Am Duran

Roberto Duran had an epic career and is widely regarded as one of the greatest fighters who ever lived. His first pro fight was contested on February 23, 1968, when he was sixteen years old; his last, on July 14, 2001, when he was fifty. He fought during the terms of eight presidents of the United States.

At one point, Duran's ring record stood at 72 wins against a single loss. He won championships in four weight divisions and was part of a fistic round-robin with Ray Leonard, Marvin Hagler, and Thomas Hearns that electrified boxing fans in the 1980s. His final ledger consists of 103 victories in 119 fights with 70 knockouts. One can fantasize that, but for a near-fatal car accident suffered on October 4, 2001, he might still be fighting.

Duran is now a warm, almost cuddly presence on the boxing scene. He's often in the media center before big fights, having been brought in by the promotion to tap into the Hispanic market. As recounted in *I Am Duran*, told by Duran to George Diaz (Blue Rider Press), it wasn't always that way.

Duran's mother was Panamanian. His father, Margarito Duran, was an American soldier of Mexican and Cherokee descent who impregnated Clara Samaniego while serving with the US military in the Canal Zone.

"He made me and then left when I was one and a half," Duran recounts. "I wouldn't see him for another twenty years. He was nothing to me. All he did was make me, see me, and then leave me."

Roberto's mother already had a son and daughter from two previous relationships when Roberto was born.

"Life wasn't easy, but she didn't make it any easier for herself or us," Duran recalls. "I'm a child of the streets. My neighbors were thieves, whores, and murderers. I never made it past third grade. I know what poverty is because my childhood sucked. But I survived. Boxing champions never come from rich neighborhoods. They come from the barrios, the gutter. It's God's law."

Duran fought with a combination of skill and savagery that was rare in any era. On March 2, 1975, he successfully defended his lightweight title with a fourteenth-round knockout of Ray Lampkin, who was hospitalized after the bout. "Today, I sent him to the hospital," Duran told the media. "Next time, I'll put him in the morgue." After brutalizing Davey Moore in 1983 to claim the WBA 154-pound crown, Duran surveyed Moore's battered swollen face and told him, "The next time, I'll kill you. You'll feel better."

"I was a fighter," Duran says. "I was paid to fight. That's who I was and what I did. In a lot of ways, I was Mike Tyson before Mike Tyson came along. Fighters would take one look at me and crap in their pants."

Duran's greatest triumph was a June 20, 1980, decision over then-unbeaten Sugar Ray Leonard to claim the 147-pound crown. Looking back on his state of mind prior to that bout, Roberto says, "Some fast little black kid from the United States wasn't going to beat me."

In the weeks and months after Leonard-Duran I, Duran, in his words, "went out drinking, dining, and partying. Night after night, we partied until everything was just one big haze. I got to the point where I weighed nearly two hundred pounds. What was I supposed to do after beating Leonard? Stay at home, go to church every day, not screw around and not drink? That's not who I am."

Then circumstances—including the incentive of an $8 million payday—forced Duran into a rematch against Leonard on short notice. He had less than two months to get into fighting shape and lose fifty pounds.

"I wasn't feeling well," Duran says of the days leading up to the November 25, 1980, rematch. "I spent almost every day in the sauna. I went two days without eating. When I stepped on the scale [to weigh in on the day of the fight], I was weak. I could feel nothing in my legs. I was nowhere near the fighter I'd been just months earlier."

After the weigh-in, Duran ate ravenously, including two steaks washed down by orange juice, coffee, and cold water. Soon after, his stomach began to hurt. That night, with both fighters in the ring, Ray Charles sang "America the Beautiful" before the bout.

"Leonard thought he'd psyched me out," Duran says. "But I wasn't intimidated by him or the blind guy singing the American's song. I just didn't feel good. My stomach trouble had been getting worse. In the eighth, we had an exchange against the ropes. But by then, I had had enough. My arms were weak. My body was weak. I couldn't move, couldn't breathe properly. I backed off and waved with my right hand. Leonard hit me a few times, but I kept motioning to the referee that I didn't want to fight. I never said 'no mas.' I just turned my back and motioned to the referee that I didn't want to continue. When the referee asked me what I was doing, all I said was 'no sigo [I do not follow].' I couldn't go on. I couldn't keep fighting. I felt like crap. But I never said 'no mas.'"

"I'm a proud man," Duran continues, "but also an impulsive one. Sometimes I make a bad decision and, in due course, think 'Oh, shit.' This was the biggest 'Oh, shit' moment of my life. But it was too late. I let my emotions get the better of me. I didn't know the world would react the way it did, and I didn't know I would get treated like shit for so long. I didn't know it would haunt me for the rest of my life. 'No mas.' It started then and it went on for years. Even now, thirty-six years later, people still bring up that 'no mas' shit. Fuck 'no mas.' I'm sick of hearing it."

I Am Duran has few if any new insights into boxing or Duran's magnificent ring career. But there are quite a few personal nuggets.

On Duran's first date with his future wife, Felicidad, he took her to a movie about killer rats.

Duran is also candid in the book about the lifestyle issues that have been tabloid fodder over the decades. There are accounts of debauchery, including a drunken threesome that Roberto engaged in with two women during the interval between the Hagler-Duran and Hearns-Duran fights.

"I'm a family man who loves his wife," Duran says. "But I've also slept around and fathered other children. I make no apologies for that. As world champion, as one of the most famous and honored men in Panama, I've been around temptation every day, and I'm not going to say sorry for the things I've done. I have three other children with three other women. These things happen. I'm just a man. Some people may look down on the way my life has turned out. But everyone in Panama knows my family situation, and I don't care what people think."

The other side of that coin was revealed when Duran's daughters started dating.

"I didn't mind them having boyfriends," Roberto acknowledges. "But if those boys stepped out of line with my girls, I threatened to kill their entire families. I think they understood what I was saying. We didn't have a lot of problems after talks like that."

After Duran (who is 5 feet 7 inches tall) retired from boxing, his weight ballooned to 260 pounds. Doctors told him that his obesity was life threatening. That led to a decision on his part to undergo gastric bypass surgery.

Meanwhile, throughout Duran's career, whatever money wasn't siphoned off before it reached his hands was quickly spent.

"People think I'm a millionaire," Duran says. "I used to be. I made about $60 million from my fights. But nowadays, the house is all that's left to show for it. The cash I do have goes to paying the bills for food, water, and electricity with a little bit put aside in case of emergency. The days of buying fancy cars are long gone. It's been years since I had a payout from a fight. And Panama being the place it is, I've had money problems."

Still, *I Am Duran* ends on an upbeat note.

"Look at the legacy," Duran urges in closing. "There were the Four Kings: Duran, Leonard, Hagler, and Hearns. We gave boxing fans everything and more when we fought each other. We were all stars and we all wanted to beat the shit out of each other. We shook hands and then we fought. We hated each other's guts. And now we smile, pose for pictures, and have a drink together every so often. That's boxing."

I sat with Gerry Cooney again—and this time, with Larry Holmes too—for a look back at a historic night.

Larry Holmes vs. Gerry Cooney: Through Their Eyes

On June 11, 1982, Larry Holmes and Gerry Cooney entered the ring at Caesars Palace in Las Vegas for one of the most highly anticipated fights of all time. In some respects, Holmes-Cooney marked the long-overdue end of an era. It was the last major championship bout to be marketed—and not subtly—as black versus white.

Cooney was "the great white hope." He didn't want it that way. Ironically, years later, he would learn that one of his maternal great-grandmothers was black. And Holmes was angry, believing that his journey through boxing had been on a road paved with jagged glass while Cooney traveled on a red carpet.

Millions of words have been written about Larry Holmes vs. Gerry Cooney. But the two men who did battle that night have a unique perspective. I talked with them recently. The memories that they shared with me follow.

In the Dressing Room before the Fight

Holmes: I did what I always did to get ready . . . Wait for the time to go by . . . Stretch . . . Shadow-box . . . Stay limber . . . Work up a sweat . . . Windmill both arms . . . Then someone came in and said, "Larry, it's time to go." I asked, "Is Cooney out yet?" The guy said no. And I told him, "I ain't going first. I'm the heavyweight champion of the world." He said, "That's the way they want to do it." And I said, "It's not the way I'm doing it. I'm the champ. Hell, no." So Cooney went first. And right before I left for the ring, I said a prayer, "Lord, don't let me hurt him, and don't let him hurt me." I wanted to knock him out. But I never wanted to hurt anyone in boxing so that they weren't okay after the fight was done.

Cooney: I was angry about the black-white thing, the way it had been built up and the way Holmes had talked about me. There was nothing I could do except keep my mouth shut and not make it worse. But I was so mad that it was the first time in my career I didn't have butterflies in the dressing room before a fight. I just wanted to go out and hit him.

The Ring Walk

Holmes: Walking to the ring, I saw a lot of white people and a lot of people wearing green. There was people shouting, "Nigger; he's gonna kick your ass." They hated me when I fought Ali. And they hated me when I fought Cooney, but this was a different kind of hate. I kept saying to myself, "Don't lose your concentration. Stay focused on the fight."

Cooney: I heard the crowd and knew it was behind me. I couldn't see the top of the stands. They seemed to go on forever. People were reaching out to touch me, grabbing at me. I tried to stay focused and went through my game plan. Use the jab, get inside, everything I had to do to win the fight.

The Ring Introductions

Holmes: They introduced me first. That was wrong. I was the champ. I didn't know they were going to do that. All I could do was say to myself, "Okay, it's done. There's nothing you can do to change it now. But when you leave the ring, you're still gonna be the champ."

Cooney: I knew they were going to introduce Larry first. That was Rappaport and Jones [Cooney's co-managers, Dennis Rappaport and Mike Jones] and Don King [Holmes's promoter]. I couldn't have cared less.

Referee Mills Lane's Instructions

Holmes: I remember Gerry looking down during the instructions. And when we touched gloves, I told him, "Let's have a good fight." A lot of people were paying a lot of money to see Larry Holmes and Gerry Cooney fight. I wanted them to get their money's worth.

Cooney: I wasn't looking down. When I fought someone, the last impression I wanted them to have of me before the fight started was of me looking at their body, at their ribs because that's where the punches would be coming. Then Mills Lane said, "Let's get it on," and Larry said, "Let's have a good fight." I still wanted to hurt him. But right then, all the racism went out the window. This was a fight, two guys trying to beat each other. That's all it ever should have been, not a big racial thing.

The Fight

Holmes: In the second round, I threw a one-two that landed on the button and knocked him down. But I still had to be careful because Gerry was a big puncher and he had a lot left. There was a punch he hit me with—a left hook to the body [in round four]—that hurt me bad. The bell went "ding" and ended the round a second after that, which was good because I wasn't feeling so good right then. And the other time he hurt me was with a low blow [in round nine]. The referee gave me time to recover and deducted two points. Gerry was strong. He hit hard. But I wore him down. I was beating on him pretty good when Victor Valle [Cooney's trainer] stopped it [in the thirteenth round]. The way I felt at the time, I wished it had ended with Gerry on his back and the referee counting to ten. But I'd won so I was happy.

Cooney: So much of what I'd heard before the fight was, I couldn't go the distance. And I fell into that trap. I worried too much about going the distance instead of fighting my fight. In the second round, I got dropped. I remember asking myself, "What are you doing down here?" I know I hurt him a couple of times, but he covered up how hurt he was. Mills Lane took a couple of points away from me. That was deflating. I should have told myself, "Okay; I'm going to knock him out." Instead, I got discouraged. By the thirteenth round, I was tired and I was almost like, "Go ahead; hit me. You can't hurt me." Victor Valle wasn't going to let that happen and stopped the fight. Larry had all the tools. He was patient. He was a very smart fighter. His experience won it for him. The truth is, I wasn't ready for him that night. I needed a few more fights.

The Next Day

Holmes: The next day, Gerry and I did an interview with Howard Cosell. Before it started, I told him, "You're a good fighter. You fought a good fight. Don't let people get you down." You know how people are. The critics, the boxing writers who don't know shit about boxing. A lot of them turned on Gerry after he lost. "Gerry Cooney is a bum. Gerry Cooney can't fight." Trust me. Gerry Cooney could fight. I know. I was in the ring with him. If Gerry Cooney was young and fighting today, he'd be the best in the world. He was one of the best back then. It's just that he fought a guy who had more than he did that night.

Cooney: I really thought I was going to win the fight. When I lost, I didn't know how to process the emotion. It seemed worse than it was. I felt like a failure. I kept thinking about all the people I'd let down. My father beat me every day when I was a kid and told me I was nothing. I try not to think about that today. I've dealt with it and come to terms with my past. But the day after the fight, I was thinking maybe my father was right. It didn't help that the doctor who stitched me up after the fight had booze on his breath.

Later

Holmes: There was a distance between me and Gerry after we fought. But I called him from time to time. I do that with some of the guys I fought, just to talk. Win or lose, we shared something important. Then, after a while, Gerry and I started showing up for each other at events and got to know each other as people. I learned about some of the problems he had in his personal life. And I respected the fact that he dealt with his problems in a good way. He doesn't let the bullshit life throws at you get to him anymore. And the way I feel now, I like Gerry. He's fun to be with; he's articulate; he's a good guy. I'm a nice guy too, so it makes sense that we should like each other.

Cooney: Larry Holmes was one of the greatest heavyweights of all time. He was a real champion. As time went by, I came to understood that it was a good fight, that I belonged in the ring with Larry that night. Then he reached out to me and things got good between us. You know, more people in the world were paying attention to Larry and me than anything else that happened that night. That's pretty cool, knowing I was part of that. Looking back, I appreciate now that it was part of my life journey. I wish I'd performed better. But I'm fortunate to have been part of boxing history and to have had that moment.

Curiosities

"As a play-by-play announcer," Steve Albert has said, "I won't get on a player for missing a shot. I will get on a player for not hustling."

Steve Albert: From Boxing to Hoops

Steve Albert is best known to boxing fans for having been the voice of Showtime Championship Boxing for two decades. But his interests extend far beyond the sweet science. He's a sports junkie.

If there's a ball, puck, or net, Steve will be there. I can attest to that through firsthand knowledge. I was an undergraduate at Columbia, which has lost more football games than any college program in history except VMI. Once a year, as an exercise in masochism, I go to a Columbia football game. Several years ago, I asked Steve if he wanted to join me.

"Oh, boy! Wow! Columbia football! That would be fantastic!"

Okay. So I'm exaggerating a bit. But Steve did come to the game. And he brought brother Al with him, which shows that insanity runs in the family.

"Marv would have come too," Steve said apologetically. "But he's calling a basketball game tonight."

In July 2012, Steve signed a five-year contract to serve as the play-by-play TV announcer for the NBA Phoenix Suns. His basketball roots run deep. In high school, he was a ball boy for the New York Knicks. Over the years, he has been the lead television play-by-play announcer for the Nets, Warriors, and Hornets (who, at the time, played in New Orleans).

"It was easier to call NBA games thirty years ago than it is now," Steve told me recently. "The game was slower back then. As good as television is, it doesn't really show viewers how fast these guys are. The way they move, the bullet passes. It's also a much more physical game now. These guys are so big and powerful. It's uncanny how they move with so much finesse."

Have any fights broken out in games that Steve has called for the Suns?

"Not yet," he answered. "But I think I can handle it if one does."

He paused for effect.

"No ears have been bitten either."

Phoenix missed the playoffs this season for the sixth year in a row, finishing eighteen games out of a playoff spot with 23 wins and 59 losses. Meanwhile, the Golden State Warriors won an NBA-record seventy-three games during the regular season and cruised through the first two rounds of the playoffs.

Then Golden State hit a speed bump. The Oklahoma City Thunder, led by Kevin Durant and Russell Westbrook, took a three-games-to-one series lead over the Warriors in the Western Division finals. Golden State fought back, winning games five and six. That set the stage for a dramatic game seven.

I suggested to Steve that we watch the game together. At nine o'clock eastern time, we were in my apartment awaiting the action.

"Years ago, I was close to some of the players," Steve reminisced. "Chris Mullin when I was with the Warriors; Buck Williams when I was with the Nets. I fraternize with the players less now than I did when I was young. Part of that is an age thing. And part of it is that they're all connected to their devices. On the plane, on the bus, they're always on the phone or listening to music or something else with a plug in their ear. They're cordial, but there's not a lot of conversation."

"The traveling is hard," Steve said, continuing his thoughts. "It's a real grind. And that's for me. You can imagine what it's like for the players. The injuries and the fatigue factor when you get to the playoffs are brutal."

Years ago, Al Bernstein (then Steve's TV partner at Showtime) told me, "I've worked with a lot of very good commentators, but none of them prepared for a telecast as exhaustively as Steve. He researches; he studies; he has more notes at ringside than you can begin to imagine. He's the best-prepared commentator I've ever seen."

That work ethic continues to this day.

"Basketball is particularly demanding," Steve told me as the Warriors-Thunder pre-game commentary segued to a commercial. "You're talking about eighty-two games. So as soon as one game ends, I'm preparing for the next. I'm always watching NBA League Pass to scout out the next opponent. I probably watch more games than some coaches. I take notes. I organize them. I'm not just watching the players. I'm listening to the announcers for whatever insights they might have. I feel better going into a game when I'm prepared."

How far does that never-ending preparation extend?

Sitting on the sofa in my apartment, Steve had a yellow legal pad in front of him.

"I never know when I might see or hear something that helps my announcing in the future," he told me. "It could be an idea on how to improve my presentation; a piece of information I might use sometime; anything."

The final pre-game commercials ended.

"It's funny," Steve said. "After all these years of knowing each other, we've never seen a fight together. And we wind up watching a basketball game together on television."

The action began with brother Marv calling the play-by-play.

"What does it feel like, sitting here listening to Marv?" I asked.

"When I was a kid, it was a thrill. 'Hey, that's my brother!' I'm used to it now, but I always root for Marv while the game is going on. I feel good when he does a good job."

The Thunder jumped to an 8-4 lead.

"OKC has come out more methodically than they did in game six," Steve observed. "Let's see if they can keep it up. Once Curry hits a shot, the game will officially be on."

Curry hit a three-pointer.

"There it is."

And another.

"Curry is amazing. When he's on, he puts up shots and doesn't even look to see if they're going in."

Durant hit a three-point basket to put the Thunder ahead 14-10.

"The best shooters release the ball so fast. They don't even look at the rim."

The Thunder led 24-19 after one quarter and extended their lead to 29-19 as the second stanza began to unfold. Marv Albert informed viewers that Klay Thompson had missed his first six shots from the floor and the Warriors as a team were 9 for 29.

"Sometimes, I'll watch a game like this and do play-by-play in my head," Steve said. "Marv and I think alike. I would have put that in there then too."

Oklahoma City 35, Golden State 22.

"The Warriors are making too many lazy passes," Steve noted. "But this is a game of runs. They can tie it up in the blink of an eye with the three-ball."

OKC maintained its lead at 45-33.

"Golden State is better than this," Steve said.

Klay Thompson came alive, hitting a trio of three-point baskets.

"What a beautiful stroke. This could be a classic."

The Thunder took a 48-42 lead into the dressing room at halftime.

"I still think Golden State wins it," Steve said. "They're more experienced and mentally tougher than OKC. I have the feeling that, right now, there are players in the OKC dressing room who are waiting for the other shoe to drop. From a straight talent point of view, the Thunder might have the better players. But basketball is a game where the better team can beat the better players. Golden State will go on another run and OKC will get demoralized."

Oklahoma City scored the first basket of the second half to go up 50-42.

Steve backtracked a bit. "This is not the well-oiled Golden State machine we're used to seeing. The Warriors have to get their act together."

Then it happened. Stephen Curry started raining threes.

"It's like boxing," Steve posited. "The Warriors are into OKC's head now and are taking them out of their comfort zone."

The Warriors surged ahead 59-56.

"Right now," Steve noted, "Stephen Curry looks like he's having a lot more fun than Russell Westbrook."

"Shaun Livingston of the Warriors took a pass off a defensive rebound and slammed down an uncontested dunk on a transition play."

"[Oklahoma City coach] Billy Donovan's got to be pissed," Steve said.

A second later, Reggie Miller (Marv's broadcast partner) declared, "If you're Billy Donovan, you can't be happy with your transition defense."

Golden State lead 71-60 after three quarters, having outscored Oklahoma City 29-to-12 in the third stanza.

"One of the great things about being Marv right now," Steve noted, "is you know that everyone is watching and listening to you call this game. Not only is Lebron James watching; I'll bet Barack Obama is watching this game."

The Thunder went on a seven-point run, narrowing Golden State's lead to 73-69.

"It still feels as though Golden State is in the driver's seat," Steve said. "But maybe not. This is a great game."

The Warriors hung tough, expanding their lead to 88-77.

"I love the way Golden State plays. Look at the way they're setting things up. Three passes for the best shot on each possession. When OKC has the ball, Westbrook or Durant tries to do it by himself."

Ultimately, Golden State emerged triumphant 96-88 behind 36 points from Stephen Curry and 21 from Klay Thompson.

"What an amazing comeback," Steve said, putting his pen away and readying to go home. "Down three games to one against an OKC team that was playing at its peak and beating the crap out of them. It will be a great story if the Warriors make it all the way, but they have one more mountain to climb. Golden State against Cleveland will be great."

It's one thing to wear a swimsuit in a beauty pageant or walk down the runway in a fashion show. Climbing into a boxing ring to sashay around in front of a horde of testosterone-charged fans is an entirely different matter.

Round-Card Girls

Emanuel Steward was on edge. The legendary trainer was working Wladimir Klitschko's corner against Nigerian heavyweight Samuel Peter in a bout in Atlantic City. Klitschko was ahead on points but tiring.

"What round is coming up?" Steward asked as he readied to give instructions to his fighter during the one-minute break.

No one answered, so Steward did what a lot of people in the arena were doing. He turned away from his fighter and looked at the round-card girl.

Round-card girls came out of the Nevada desert in the late 1950s, when Las Vegas casinos began hosting fights. They're now a fixture at boxing matches throughout the world. The women serve two purposes. First, they advise fans which round it is. That's fairly straightforward since a number is printed on each card that they carry around the ring. And equally important, round-card girls entertain the audience, particularly during slow-moving preliminary fights when fans tend to get restless. This function, of course, is directed primarily at male members of the crowd.

Round-card girls come in all shapes and sizes, some more desirable than others. As a general rule, their looks and styling reflect the character of the promotion. Casinos supply their own round-card girls. The bigger the fight, the more glamorously dressed and elegant looking the women are.

Lesser promoters offer an array of talent that ranges from local college students to strippers who ply their trade at nearby adult clubs. Some of the girls are clean-scrubbed with little makeup. Others look like hookers who were recruited off the streets an hour earlier. They're heavily tattooed and parade around the ring in raunchy leopard-print thongs while balancing on black-vinyl dominatrix-mode shoes with six-inch stiletto heels.

"I prefer the way round-card girls looked twenty years ago," cele-brated sports artist LeRoy Neiman opined several years before his death. "They were provocative but not vulgar and definitely more elegant than they are today."

"But looks can be deceiving," Neiman (who was Playboy's "artist in residence" for decades) continued. "I remember drawing one of those elegant round-card girls. Her manner and costume warranted a lot of respect. Then I went home and, later that night, I was watching a show called *Midnight Blue* on a local softcore porn channel. There she was, the same girl."

The script that round-card girls follow is familiar. With ten seconds left in a round, the timekeeper raps his microphone four times to warn the referee that the round is about to end. This is the round-card girl's wake-up call. When the bell rings, she walks up the ring stairs. An aide parts the strands, and she steps into the ring. Then the rope-splitter hands her a card.

The most popular round-card girls parade seductively around the ring, stopping where they get the most favorable reaction from the crowd. That might be from ringside or up in the balcony. Either way, a good round-card girl knows where her core constituency is and what it wants.

The response of the crowd depends on the looks of the girl and, more importantly, on how she plays to them. An average-looking woman with a big personality gets more cheers than a beautiful woman with little presence. Also, the crowd is more likely to voice its approval at club fights than at a glitzy Las Vegas championship match. Round-card girls fit well with a blue-collar environment and beer.

At times, there are complications. For starters, ring canvases have a soft spongy feel. They're very different from a regular floor. Thus, a bikini-clad woman who recently worked a night of black-tie boxing in New York observed, "Walking on the canvas in high heels feels funny. It feels like walking in high heels on a bed. Sometimes when I do my sexy dip and stick my bottom out, my ankles give way like I'm drunk."

Other times, the obstacles are more formidable.

Four round-card girls once arrived at a fight card in New York pro-moted by Cedric Kushner only to learn that Kushner had remembered to hire them but forgotten to arrange for round cards. Undaunted, they circled the ring between rounds, holding imaginary cards in the air and signaling which round was coming next by raising the appropriate number of fingers.

Round-card girls are usually paid $100 to $200 per show. For some, it's simply a night's work. Others dream of being discovered for bigger and better things. It's hard to think of a round-card girl who parlayed the job into a greater future. Leslie Glass served as a round-card girl and later became a porn star after shooting several photo layouts for *Penthouse*. But she died at age thirty-six.

Round-card girls are instructed to avoid playing favorites where fighters are concerned. In fact, they're not supposed to acknowledge the combatants at all. They flirt only with the crowd.

Do fighters notice the round-card girls?

"I had a fighter named Willie Pastrano," Muhammad Ali's longtime trainer, Angelo Dundee, once recalled. "Good fighter, slick boxer. Willie liked women and he was a girl-watcher. Sometimes between rounds, I had to tell him, 'Stop looking at the chick and listen to me.'"

But Pastrano was the exception, not the rule. Indeed, Dr. Margaret Goodman (who served for years as chief ringside physician for the Nevada State Athletic Commission) has observed, "If I see a fighter looking at the round-card girl instead of his trainer between rounds, that's a danger sign. It tells me that the fighter is losing concentration."

Then Goodman, who wore designer pants suits in the ring and has the requisite beauty to entice a male audience, added, "I think being a round-card girl is the coolest thing. There are very few jobs where you don't have to take your clothes off and are still automatically the object of sexual adoration. No one paws at the round-card girls like they might at the dancers in an adult club. And people don't focus on their imperfections because the girls are only on for a minute at a time and most of the crowd is too far away to see them well anyway."

Not everyone likes round-card girls. "I think they're totally unnecessary," Don Turner (who trained Evander Holyfield and Larry Holmes) opined. "They don't have inning-card girls in baseball. Why pay money to some half-dressed woman to walk around a boxing ring? If you have extra money, give it to the fighters. But you know they won't."

Be that as it may, round-card girls have spawned some of boxing's finest legends.

Don Elbaum has promoted club fights in the United States since 1958.

"I used to promote in Steubenville, Ohio," Elbaum recalled. "It was a wild town with some of the best-run whorehouses in the country. The guys who ran them would give me hookers to use as round-card girls for free. From my point of view, it was great. I didn't have to pay the girls, and I sold extra tickets because the people who ran the whorehouses bought seats for their customers in order to display their wares."

Another time, a round-card girl saved one of Elbaum's fighters from defeat.

"I had a light-heavyweight named Tom Girardi," the promoter recounted. "He was a prospect. Another fighter pulled out, and Tom took the fight on short notice against some guy whose record was 2-and-6. I figured it was safe, but Tom got tired. It was a six-rounder. After round three, he came back to the corner and said he didn't think he could go six."

"Anyway," Elabaum continued, "the referee had been staring at the round-card girl all night. She was a doll. After round four, I handed the girl a card that said '6' instead of '5.' Then I started shouting, 'Last round, Tommy; you can do it.' Well, of course, the referee is staring at the girl. He thinks it's round six, makes the fighters touch gloves, and says the fight is over after what's really only round five. I cut the gloves off real quick, and Tom, who was completely out of gas, won a split decision."

Those who consider Elbaum a sexist will be pleased to know that he got his comeuppance at a fight card in Brooklyn. Matchmaker Johnny Bos told that tale.

"Don and I were sitting together," Bos recounted. "The round-card girl was particularly flirtatious. She winked; she wiggled. Halfway through the show, Don turned to me and said, 'That's a hell of a broad; I wonder who's taking her home tonight.' Then, during the last fight, the girl reached up and pulled off her wig. It was a guy."

The lessons to be learned from that are: (1) beauty is in the eye of the beholder; and (2) in boxing, there's always an element of surprise.

Surprise and violence. But the round-card girl never looks at the carnage around her. She carries on, seemingly oblivious to the feverish activity of trainers and cutmen tending to fighters between rounds. Despite being in the midst of mayhem, she performs her duty with a smile and come-hither stare, memorializing her presence in the print of stiletto heels in blood on the ring canvas.

Consider this a bonus piece for fans of the sport once known as America's national pastime.

Brian Kenny: "Ahead of the Curve"

Boxing fans know Brian Kenny from his work on *ESPN2 Friday Night Fights*, *Showtime Championship Boxing*, and PBC on FOX. But his #1 area of sports expertise is baseball.

Kenny is currently an MLB Network host and anchors its most important studio programming, including *MLB Now* and *MLB Tonight*. He's also an ardent proponent of sabermetrics: the use of cutting-edge statistical analysis as a key component of decision making in virtually every aspect of the game.

Ahead of the Curve: Inside the Baseball Revolution (Simon & Schuster) is Kenny's presentation in support of sabermetrics. "Somewhere along the line," he writes, "we stopped thinking. In the most basic ways, a purposeful ignorance set in. We have received considerable baseball wisdom from the early days of childhood from our adult role models, our peers, the media, and the baseball industry itself. What is so fascinating is that all this nonsense survived. For nearly a century, no one even bothered to think about it deeply enough to give themselves an incredible competitive advantage. At a certain point—about the time we discovered penicillin—it was time to evolve past these 19th-century relics. Instead, our thinking calcified and then endured decades beyond its point of usefulness."

With that as his starting point, Kenny challenges longheld assumptions regarding baseball strategy.

He begins with the sacrifice bunt, studying how a simple scenario has played out over an eighteen-year study period.

Man on first base, nobody out. Your team needs a run. Sacrifice bunt, right?

That's what most managers do. But look at the numbers.

With a man on first base and nobody out, a team can be expected to score .94 runs in that inning. With a man on second base and one out, a team can be expected to score .72 runs.

"So let's be clear," Kenny writes. "Even with a successful bunt, you score fewer runs."

But by bunting successfully, the manager has taken himself out of the line of fire and absolved himself of blame.

"He put the next two batters in the spotlight," Kenny continues. "There's a man on second waiting to be driven in. When he doesn't score, it's those two hitters that didn't get it done. Failure is there visually in the hitter slinking off the field, having left a man on base. The manager walks off scot-free, even though he is the one who traded three chances for two."

Then there's the matter of third-base coaches, who are reluctant to send a runner home on a fly ball to the outfield that's caught for the second out of an inning. The current success rate for attempts to score from third base in sacrifice fly situations is 90 percent. In other words, the coach only instructs the runner to go for it when the odds are overwhelmingly in his favor.

But if the fly ball is the second out of the inning, the runner's chance of being driven in by the next or a succeeding batter is roughly 30 percent. Thus, Kenny writes, "Third base coaches send runners only when it's obvious they will score. Getting a runner thrown out at the plate looks bad for both the third base coach and runner. But taking more risks will lead to more runs even with more runners being thrown out."

The manner in which today's managers deploy their pitching staff also mystifies Kenny. He starts by asking, "Why do all major league teams pitch the way they do?" And he arrives at the answer, "Because that's the way we always have done it."

But times change. In 1904, pitchers finished 88 percent of the games they started. In 2014, that number was down to 2 percent. "The only reason we still have starters," Kenny writes, "is because, once upon a time, one pitcher was all you used for the whole day."

Kenny advocates starting games, not just with long-inning pitchers but with short-inning hurlers as well. And he heaps scorn on the way managers use their closers.

"Today's relief aces," he writes, "are treated like rare exotic flowers to be taken out only in certain conditions. They work the ninth inning only, preferably with nobody on base, and they top out at seventy innings for the season. Take a step back. You've established one pitcher as the best on your staff, batter for batter. You then artificially restrict his innings [and] keep him from the most important parts of the game."

But isn't the ninth inning the most important part of the game?

"Any manager who is saving his closer/relief ace/fireman/stud for the ninth inning," Kenny notes, "is thinking the following: 'I'm saving him to seal this win when the game is most on the line.' And this is simply not the case. The game is frequently on the line in the ninth. But the act of saving your best pitcher for a situation that may not come (a one-run lead in the ninth) is not worth the exchange. A 4-1 lead with the bases loaded in the fifth? Run the numbers! You think there will be a bigger threat? The ninth-inning closer model has bolstered the myth that the game is on the line only in that final inning. It certainly is more obviously on the line at that point. But the fact is, most games are decided before then."

The nerve center for decision making during a baseball game is the manager who, Kenny declares, typically stands on the top step of the dugout "like Washington crossing the Delaware." He then notes that 83 percent of the MLB managers who started the 2015 season had played previously in the major leagues. By contrast, only 19 percent of NFL head coaches and 50 percent of NBA head coaches had similar playing experience. That leads Kenny to ask the rhetorical question: "Do you think Major League Baseball requires some different level of understanding of its sport that the NBA and NFL don't?"

Then comes more sacrilege. Kenny states, "If you told me I would be an NFL head coach tomorrow—taking over on a Monday in the middle of the season—it would be a disaster. Same thing if you gave me an NBA team. Now tell me I'm managing the Cincinnati Reds tomorrow. You know what? I'd be fine. Understand the distinction. I'm not saying I could coach. I couldn't teach a cutter or even a good curve ball. I couldn't teach a hitter proper mechanics. But coaching isn't managing. The Reds would go along for days before you even knew I was there. It's not that hard."

He's probably right. A case study proves his point.

Game 5 of the 2015 World Series. The Kansas City Royals are leading the New York Mets three games to one. Mets ace Matt Harvey has thrown eight scoreless innings, giving his team a 2–0 lead. Mets manager Terry Collins tells Harvey he's done for the night. Harvey pleads to take the mound for the ninth inning. The crowd is chanting his name. Collins relents and sends Harvey to the mound to finish the game.

"So what's wrong with a manager letting his stud pitcher take the mound for three more outs?" Kenny asks.

Then he answers.

"Here's what's wrong: a mountain of evidence that pointed to Harvey fatiguing late in games. Harvey has a fairly clear fatigue point: 100 pitches. To that point in his career, in pitches 1–100, major league hitters hit an anemic .206 against Harvey. After Harvey reached 100 pitches, they hit a robust .373 with a Hall-of-Fame level .440 on-base percentage. Harvey, after eight innings against Kansas City, was at 102 pitches."

In the ninth inning, Harvey—predictably, to the sabermetrician's way of thinking—blew up. The Mets lost the game and, with it, the World Series.

"The mainstream media almost universally defended Collins for going with his heart," Kenny writes. "Nowhere that I can recall did anyone wonder where brains fit into this equation."

That leads to Kenny's next target: the media.

"It is a sportswriter's job," he states, "to help bring the game to a mass audience, to help the interested reader or listener understand the latest strategic innovations, explain the nuances, and keep them abreast of the ongoing revolution. During the sabermetric revolution, the sportswriting fraternity failed miserably."

And there are choice words for the self-important writers who are responsible for inducting players into baseball's Hall of Fame: "How hard is it to figure out that Bob Feller and Mickey Mantle are Hall of Famers? Most of the players voted into the hall by the writers would also have been voted in by a panel of fourth-grade baseball fans. The hard part for the baseball writers is at the border. This is where they continue to fail."

Kenny extols Babe Ruth as the greatest hitter of all-time. And he sets forth an intriguing theory (first advanced by Bill James) as to what enabled The Bambino to turn baseball upside down: "It happened only because he was a pitcher. No one much cared if he swung from the heels. His hitting was superfluous. The baseball culture therefore didn't pressure him into conforming. Ruth had the good fortune to break the single-season home run record while still a pitcher. By the time he was ready to convert to an outfielder, it was too late to stop him. He had already shown that swinging for the fences was a worthwhile risk."

Basic record-keeping also comes under Kenny's withering eye. He denounces what he calls "the tyranny of the batting average," noting, "In batting average, a single is as good as a home run and walks don't exist. Yet the very first stat cited in most baseball conversations for 120 years was the batting average."

He savages what he believes is an idiotic overemphasis on a pitcher's won-lost record, beginning with the question, "Do you care that Mariano Rivera, from 2001 to 2012, had an average [annual won-lost] record of 4-3?"

Then Kenny adds, "I'm sorry if I'm the one to break this to you, but the same goes for all pitchers." And he backs up his opinion with data showing that, between 1920 and 2014 (a ninety-four-year database), pitchers who threw eight innings in a game and gave up two earned runs were credited with a "win" only 33.6 percent of the time.

Further analyzing his data, Kenny calls Ted Williams the second best hitter of all-time, behind only Babe Ruth. Examining The Splendid Splinter's 1941 season (.406 batting average, .553 on-base percentage, and .735 slugging percentage), he writes, "Williams's numbers can barely be fathomed. Our minds aren't trained to see .553 as an on-base percentage. It's too high. No one does that past high school."

Kenny also notes that, while Joe DiMaggio set a major league record that still stands by hitting safely in fifty-six consecutive games, Williams owns three of the four longest streaks for getting on base in consecutive games, including a streak of eighty-four consecutive games in 1949. "In baseball," Kenny writes, "0-for-0 with three walks is likely better than 1-for-5 with a single."

Sabermetrics can be a daunting subject for those who grew up in a simpler time when batting average, RBIs, HRs, wins, losses, and ERA reigned. Old eyes tend to glaze over when faced with OPS, OPS+, WAR, DRS, and FIP. But Kenny ties snippets of data together in enlightening and entertaining ways and brings statistics to life with a non-stop parade of informative and entertaining anecdotes.

There's a tip of the hat to Bill James, the patron saint of sabermetrics, whom Kenny calls one of "the seven most influential figures in the history of baseball" along with the likes of Babe Ruth, Jackie Robinson, and Marvin Miller. Speaking first and foremost about James, Kenny writes, "The best thing about the sabermetric revolution is that the pioneers of the movement weren't looking to run teams. They were fans of the game who loved baseball and proved that we can see much more when we take a wider view."

Kenny also hails Billy Beane (who pioneered sabermetrics with the Oakland Athletics) and Theo Epstein (who refined the art, first with the Boston Red Sox and now with the Chicago Cubs). The Houston Astros are lauded as today's team leader in sabermetrics.

And yes, in recent years, teams have been learning. By way of example, the defensive shift (realigning the traditional placement of fielders) began in 1946 with an experiment by Cleveland Indians manager Lou Boudreau when Ted Williams was at bat. It wasn't until the second decade of the twenty-first century that the shift became more than an oddity. In 2011, MLB teams employed a defensive shift on 2,358 occasions. In 2014, the number rose to more than 13,000.

"If you give it about thirty seconds of thought," Kenny observes, "you realize why, for about 130 years, professional baseball players stood where they did on the field. That's where they always stood. With this inability to evolve, it makes you wonder: how do we even survive as a species?"

"Athletes train hard for hours every day," Kenny writes in closing. "Managers plot and plan, losing sleep. Organizations pour money into resources. Given how hard every player, coach, manager, and executive works, wouldn't you think they would leap at the chance to gain a tactical edge using information? Each loss is crippling. Things do not have to even out. You need to fight and scrap and give yourself the best chance to win in every half-inning of every game. Burn this into your mind. You cannot give away a game."

Some thoughts on the light side of boxing.

Fistic Nuggets

Richie Giachetti, who was best known in boxing circles for training and managing Larry Holmes, died on February 3, 2016, following a heart attack at age seventy-five.

Giachetti had more than a few rough edges. He once killed a man in a bar fight and was sometimes referred to as "Richie the Torch." Whether that designation was related to his ability to light a fire under his fighters or past employment as an arsonist was a matter of debate. Jack Newfield, in his 1995 biography of Don King, portrayed Giachetti in a particularly unflattering light.

I had a pleasant relationship with Giachetti. At least, I thought I did. So I was taken back when I went over to say hello at a Boxing Writers Association of America dinner about twenty years ago and Richie greeted me with, "I ought to punch you in the fucking face."

"What are you talking about?"

"You know what I'm talking about. Fuck you, you piece of shit."

"I have no idea what you're talking about."

"Fuck you, Newfield."

"I'm not Jack Newfield. I'm Thomas Hauser."

"Oh, Jesus! I'm sorry. No, you're okay. Forget what I just said."

We chatted amiably for several minutes, at the end of which Giachetti told me, "You know, I'm a lot calmer now than I used to be. In the old days, I would have just punched you."

★ ★ ★

This has been a disheartening election year. It has also been a fascinating one. The lords of the Republican party created a ravenous electorate and fed it red meat. Now the beast is threatening to devour them.

The focal point of this exercise in democracy looks like an overweight orangutan wearing an $8,000 Brioni suit the size of a circus tent.

He refers to his wife as a former supermodel, which (like most things Trump) is an exaggeration.

The term "supermodel" implies a worldwide reputation and extraordinary success in commercial modeling. A recent Internet search turned up no significant content featuring the current Mrs. Trump prior to her union with Donald. It was only after she became Trump's girlfriend and later his wife that she moved significantly beyond test photos and vanity shoots.

Of course, if Melania were really a supermodel, she would have married Tom Brady or Billy Joel, not Donald Trump.

The man who criticized Carly Fiorina's face has a face that looks like it's spray-painted orange each morning while he's wearing goggles. The mess on top of his head resembles a hair weave doused with industrial-strength glue.

His stomach is HUGE. His face is AMAZING. The hair is OOPS!

He has debased the political dialogue. I now respond in kind.

A half-century ago, Muhammad Ali nicknamed his opponents. Sonny Liston became "the big ugly bear." Other ring foes were denominated "the rabbit" (Floyd Patterson), "the washerwoman" (George Chuvalo), "the octopus" (Ernie Terrell), and "the gorilla" (Joe Frazier).

But Ali did it with a twinkle in his eye. And he wasn't campaigning for the presidency of the United States.

Trump wants to be president, so it has far greater meaning when Rafael Edward Cruz becomes "Lyin' Ted" and Marco Antonio Rubio is labeled "Little Marco."

The other candidates are either unwilling or afraid to play the name game with Trump.

I'm not, and I will.

What shall we call Donald Trump?

On the theory that turnabout is fair play, we could call him Lyin' Donald or Little Donald. But that wouldn't be very creative.

Then there are the obvious choices: Obnoxious Donald, Raunchy Donald, Sleazy Donald, Slimy Donald, Loathsome Donald, and Nauseating Donald.

We could reference Trump's physique in the form of Plump Trump, Obese Donald, or Fat Boy. But that would be cruel and miss the point.

We're electing a president, not crowning a new Mr. Universe. So it might be preferable to focus on ability and character.

Doing so alliteratively would give us Detestable Donald, Deviant Donald, Disgusting Donald, Despicable Donald, and Dopey Donald.

In keeping with the sometimes childish nature of Trump's conduct, we could respond in kind with Icky Donald and Creepy Trump.

But the best name is . . .

It's hard to improve on Ivana Trump's characterization of her former husband as "The Donald." But let's try.

In recognition of Donald Trump's high standing in the Hispanic American community, let's call him "El Donaldo."

The *Urban Dictionary* defines "Donaldo" as follows: "A crack-dealing guy . . . A mean disgusting really ugly kid who has no life. He likes to make fun of girls and bully them. He is a bossy friend who wants his friends to hate random people. He is an ass wipe and a big loser."

★ ★ ★

Dino Duva and Don King once co-promoted Nigerian heavyweight Samuel Peter. Recently, Duva reminisced about what happened after Peter beat Jameel McCline and Oleg Maskaev in consecutive fights to claim the WBC "interim" and "world" heavyweight crowns.

"It was early 2008," Duva recalled. "Don and I went to Nigeria and met with a former president of Nigeria and some businessmen. They were serious about wanting to promote Samuel's next fight in Nigeria. We were close to a deal. Then Don asked for fifty thousand barrels of oil as part of the package. I said, 'Don, don't kill the deal.' And Don told me, 'Don't worry; I know what I'm doing. When the deal is done, I'll give you ten thousand barrels of oil.'"

"And it killed the deal," Duva remembered. "But the most interesting thing about it was, Don and I were fifty-fifty partners on Samuel Peter. And there he was, telling me that we were going to split the oil eighty-twenty."

★ ★ ★

Boxing and hype go hand in hand. So it's no surprise that, after Deontay Wilder broke his right hand in a July 16, 2016, victory over Chris Arreola, the hype machine went into overdrive.

"Deontay hits too hard to be a human being," Wilder's manager Jay Deas proclaimed. "He hits too hard for his bone structure."

Is that right?

Consider the case of Paulie Malignaggi.

"Broken hands?" Malignaggi says when the subject is raised. "I lost count because I went into some fights when the hand was broken but I wanted to rack up wins and I needed money. I also suffered a hairline fracture at the base of my thumb during the Pablo Cesar Cano fight that I didn't have surgery for. In total, I had four surgeries to my right hand."

Was that damage caused because Paulie "hits too hard to be a human being?"

Over the course of fifteen years, Malignaggi has registered seven knockouts in forty-three fights. More to the point, after three relatively easy victories at the start of his career, Paulie has scored four knockouts in his last forty fights.

★ ★ ★

Notes on a Telephone Conversation with Don Elbaum

Don Elbaum: You're not going to believe this.

TH: Since I'm talking with you, that's probably true.

Elbum: No, you gotta listen to me on this one. It's a great story, and you're the first guy I'm calling. You're the only one who can write this the way it should be written.

TH: In other words, Dan Rafael, Ron Borges, Mike Rosenthal, and Norm Frauenheim all turned you down.

Elbaum: Don't be a wise guy. This is a great great story and I'm offering it to you first. I got a heavyweight. He used to be a banker. His name is

Jeremiah Williams. I'm promoting a card in Flint, Michigan, on August 20 to help with the water situation there, and Jeremiah will be on the card. He's a great guy, thirty-seven years old, used to play football at Wake Forest. His record is 2-and-7, which isn't so good. But here's the thing. Jeremiah looks exactly like O. J. Simpson. He could be O. J. Simpson's identical twin. If you could get O. J. Simpson out of prison, put him in a time machine, and make him thirty-seven years old again, he'd look exactly like Jeremiah.

TH: Don, I'm looking at Boxrec.com as we speak. Jeremiah isn't thirty-seven. He's forty-four. And his record is 2-and-9.

Elbaum: But he's won two of his last three fights.

TH: Against guys with a composite ring record of zero wins and eleven losses.

Elbaum: You know something? That's a problem you have. You always let details get in the way of a good story.

TH: Like the time you told me you had a seven-foot fighter from Bosnia who turned out to be 6'6".

Elbaum: There was an explanation for that. He was short for his height. Besides, I made up for it when I brought Nikolay Valuev to Atlantic City.

TH: For all I know, Jeremiah Williams looks like Stephen Curry.

Elbaum: If he did, I'd say so. That would be an even better story. Look, let me put Jeremiah on the phone. He's a great guy.

So Don put Jeremiah on the phone. He seems like a really good guy, articulate, friendly. He had a promising freshman year in 1991 as a running back at Wake Forest. Four touchdowns and 523 yards on 139 carries. Then his production trailed off. He graduated in 1995. I asked Jeremiah to e-mail me a photo. He did, at which point I called Elbaum back.

TH: Don, there is a resemblance. But Jeremiah doesn't look like O. J. Simpson's identical twin brother.

Elbaum: You know something? I've been thinking about it, and you're right. But people stop Jeremiah on the street all the time, thinking he's Dwayne Johnson.

★ ★ ★

When Sergey Kovalev fought Andre Ward in Las Vegas on November 19, 2016, the promotion brought in Julio Cesar Chavez Sr. to help engender pay-per-view buys in the Hispanic market.

An appearance fee is in order when a retired boxing legend travels to promote a fight. But other requests can be problematic. Over the years, fighters have demanded everything from a refrigerator full of Dom Perignon to a bedroom full of women.

And Chavez?

Not to worry.

The only extra that Julio Sr. asked for was that his room be fully stocked with Doritos and Cheetos.

★ ★ ★

Vasyl Lomachenko, age twenty-eight, is one of the most decorated amateurs in ring history, having won gold medals at the 2008 and 2012 Olympics as a representative of Ukraine. He turned pro on October 12, 2013, and conquered Gary Russell Jr. in his third professional fight to claim the WBO featherweight crown.

My most vivid memory of Lomachenko dates to an interview session he had with HBO's commentating team on October 10, 2013 (two days before his pro debut).

Max Kellerman asked a fairly convoluted question about Vasyl's fighting style that was translated into Russian.

"Ya ne paneemayu [I don't understand]," Lomachenko responded.

Kellerman tried again with a similar result and finally settled on, "What is the key to what you do in the ring?"

"I don't want to get hit in the head," Lomachenko answered.

★ ★ ★

Mike Tyson retired from the ring eleven years ago but still has a hold on the American psyche. That was clear when he became an issue in the 2016 presidential campaign.

Speaking in Indianapolis, Indiana, in late April, Donald Trump proclaimed, "Mike Tyson endorsed me. I love it. He sent out a tweet. Mike, Iron Mike. You know, all the tough guys endorse me. When I get endorsed by the tough ones, I like it. Because you know what? We need toughness now."

Tyson, of course, was convicted of rape in Indianapolis in 1992. With that in mind—and seeking to score political points—Trump rival Ted Cruz responded, "Mike Tyson spent three years in prison in Indiana for rape. And yet in Donald Trump's world, this convicted rapist is a tough guy. I've got news for Donald Trump. Rapists are not tough guys. Anyone who believes a convicted rapist is a tough guy, you can understand the whole race right there."

Greg Garrison (who successfully prosecuted Tyson and now hosts a radio show in Indianapolis) also got into the act, admonishing, "Mr. Trump, tough is one thing. A rapist is quite something else. A seventeen-year-old girl, her clothes ripped off her; I've been thinking about this all night. Kept me up. You know how I feel about this election stuff. I don't want to throw rocks at anybody. But this is where I want you to listen to me with both of your ears open. Did nobody in that whole entourage of yours know that that snake raped a lovely kid in this town? I think I'd beef up my intelligence operation a little bit."

Such is the state of politics in America today.

★ ★ ★

For fight fans who collect this sort of thing, here are two more quotes from promoters:

Don Elbaum: "I got a new fighter. He's a liar, a con man, a thief, and, boy, can he punch. I love him."

Bob Arum (responding to claims that he was trying to steal Hector Camacho Jr. from a rival promoter): "If I was going to steal somebody, I'd steal somebody good."

★ ★ ★

Over the years, I've written extensively about moments shared with Muhammad Ali. This is about one that didn't happen.

In 1996, Ali and I co-authored a short book about bigotry and prejudice. Then, to spread the message, we visited a half dozen schools across the country, talking with students about the need for tolerance and understanding. In February 1997, our journey brought us to Boston.

Muhammad loves bread pudding. It was #1 on his list of culinary pleasures. And Julia Child—perhaps the most famous chef ever—lived in Cambridge, which is part of the Boston metropolitan area.

Child was a personality in her own right: eighty-four years old at the time with numerous books and television shows to her credit. More than anyone else, she had popularized French cuisine in America.

I'd always wanted to meet Julia Child. And as it turned out, Child thought it would be fun to meet Ali. Thus, an idea was born. The most celebrated chef in America would invite Muhammad Ali to her home for homemade bread pudding. And I'd write about it.

Alas, as Robert Burns once wrote, "The best-laid schemes o' mice an' men gang aft agley."

Child was called to San Francisco at the last minute. The bread pudding festival never happened. And I never got to write "The Greatest Meets the Greatest."

★ ★ ★

How many people remember that Joe Frazier sang the national anthem before the September 15, 1978, rematch in New Orleans between Muhammad Ali and Leon Spinks?

★ ★ ★

"The Sweet Science is joined onto the past like a man's arm to his shoulder."

Those words, written by A. J. Liebling in an introduction to his famed collection of essays entitled *The Sweet Science,* are part of boxing lore.

To further the point, Liebling proclaimed, "It is through Jack O'Brien that I trace my rapport with the historic past through the laying-on of hands. He hit me, for pedagogical example, and he had been hit by the great Bob Fitzsimmons from whom he won the light-heavyweight title in 1906. Jack had a scar to show for it. Fitzsimmons had been hit by Corbett, Corbett by John L. Sullivan, he by Paddy Ryan with the bare knuckles, and Ryan by Joe Goss, his predecessor who as a young man had felt the fist of the great Jem Mace. It is a great thrill to feel that all that separates you from the early Victorians is a series of punches on the nose."

In a small way, I'm part of the chain.

In 1988, I was chosen by Muhammad and Lonnie Ali to be Muhammad's official biographer. One of the benefits inherent in the undertaking was that I spent a lot of time at Ali's home in Berrien Springs, Michigan. With Liebling's thoughts in mind, I decided one afternoon that it would be fun to insert myself into the historical sequence.

Muhammad and I were watching tapes of old fights in Ali's living room.

"Could you touch me with a jab?" I asked.

I explained the request, and Muhammad weighed his options. The ensuing conversation went roughly as follows.

"I might hurt you bad."

"I said 'touch,' not 'punch.'"

"I'm a bad man."

"No, you're not."

"I might think I'm hittin' Joe Frazier and put you in the hospital."

"Don't."

"Are you sure?"

"Am I sure I don't want you to put me in the hospital? Yes."

"There's times I don't know my own strength."

"Be gentle."

Ali stood up, gestured for me to do the same, and positioned me in front of the sofa. He was closing in on age fifty at the time.

"Put your hands up," he instructed.

I did as ordered.

Muhammad gave me a long look, extended his upper teeth over his lower lip in that famous I'm-gonna-get-you pose, assumed a fighting stance, and did a modified Ali shuffle.

"Here comes the jab," he warned.

Then he hit me on the cheek with a right hand that felt like a caress.

"Want more?"

"Bring it to me."

The jab that followed had the weight of a feather.

I've experienced some pretty cool things in my life. One of them is that I was "punched" by Muhammad Ali.

Issues and Answers

Sunlight is the best disinfectant.

The New York State Inspector General's Investigation

PART ONE

On November 2, 2013, Russian heavyweight Magomed Abdusalamov fought Mike Perez at Madison Square Garden. Hours later, Abdusalamov was in a coma following the removal of a portion of his skull and other surgical procedures to treat bleeding and swelling in his brain.

Abdusalamov will never have a normal life. He's partially paralyzed on his right side, cannot walk, and has limited control over the rest of his body. He recognizes family members and close friends, but is unable to carry on a coherent conversation. He struggles to make sounds that resemble words and can communicate thoughts like hello, good-bye, yes, and no. He points to his mouth when he's hungry. He understands simple instructions and can identify shapes and colors by pointing on command. It's impossible to quantify his cognitive abilities and know how much he understands.

The Magomed tragedy set a chain of events into motion. In January 2014, his family filed a notice of claim with the New York State Court of Claims against the New York State Athletic Commission and the State of New York. On March 26, 2014, they filed suit in New York State Supreme Court against five commission doctors (Barry Jordan, Anthony Curreri, Osric King, Gerard Varlotta, and Avery Browne), Matt Farrago (the NYSAC inspector assigned to Abdusalamov's dressing room), Benjy Esteves (who refereed the fight), K2 Promotions (which promoted the bout), and Madison Square Garden.

Some of plaintiff's claims seem unfounded on their face. For example, Dr. Browne was the ringside physician assigned to Perez's corner and had nothing to do with Abdusalamov's medical care. Nor were K2 Promotions and Madison Square Garden responsible for the conduct of the fight or Abdusalamov's post-fight medical treatment. On February 26, 2015, Madison Square Garden was dismissed from the lawsuit. The dismissal of claims against Browne and K2 is expected to follow in the near future.

That said, many of plaintiffs' claims raise serious issues and Abdusalamov has suffered grievous wounds.

The Abdusalamov tragedy led to an external investigation of the New York State Athletic Commission. On November 11, 2013, Secretary of State Cesar Perales (who has oversight responsibilities with regard to the NYSAC) sent a letter to Catherine Leahy Scott (the inspector general of the State of New York), asking that her office "determine whether the policies and procedures in place to protect the fighters were properly administered in connection with the fight" and "take all other actions that you deem necessary and appropriate."

The inspector general's office is a government monitoring agency. Its investigations are often criminal in nature. But the office is also charged with uncovering abuse in state government and identifying which systems and protocols aren't working properly.

This wasn't the first time that the inspector general's office investigated the New York State Athletic Commission. Most notably, in March 2000, a New York County assistant district attorney assigned to the Rackets Bureau advised the inspector general's office of alleged improprieties by NYSAC officials. This came at a time when the NYSAC had become a microcosm of incompetence and corruption and a dumping ground for Republican party political patronage employees.

The inspector general's investigation of that unfortunate era unearthed numerous no-show jobs. An NYSAC satellite office in Poughkeepsie that was rented from a politically connected landlord was used so infrequently that mail sent there went unopened for months. Eventually, all NYSAC mail sent to the Poughkeepsie office was returned to the parties who had sent it. One commission employee with a no-show job and state cell phone accumulated more than $400 in monthly phone charges on a regular basis. On one occasion, his monthly bill exceeded $1,500. A review by the inspector general's office showed that most of his calls were personal, not NYSAC related.

By contrast, the inspector general's inquiry into the Abdusalamov tragedy began, not as an investigation of corruption, but as a review of the NYSAC's medical practices and an inquiry into whether Magomed received adequate medical care. However, it soon expanded into a broader study of the overall operation of the commission during the tenure of chairperson Melvina Lathan.

The available information suggests that the inspector general's staff members conducted their investigation diligently and conscientiously. Their written report was largely complete in December 2014. Third parties (including this writer) were advised that the report would be released by January 2015 in accord with the following protocol.

The report would be sent initially to the secretary of state, who would forward it to the New York State Athletic Commission for comment. The secretary of state and NYSAC would have ten days to review the findings and recommendations contained in the report and send their comments to the inspector general's office. Then, subject to possible revision, the report would be posted on the inspector general's website with the commission's comments.

But that's not what happened. The report was never released. John Milgrim (a special deputy who handles media inquiries for the inspector general's office) says that's because "the investigation is ongoing."

Other sources (including several in state government) say they believe that a "political hold" has been put on the report to (1) save the governor's office from embarrassment, and (2) make it more difficult for the Abdusalamov family to pursue its lawsuit against the State of New York, the New York State Athletic Commission, and some of the other defendants.

Milgrim rejects that notion, saying, "There has been no contact whatsoever between this office and anyone in the governor's office regarding this investigation."

During the course of its investigation, the inspector general's office interviewed dozens of individuals. In the interest of full disclosure, I should note that I was interviewed by investigators on January 2, 2014. In addition to myself, those present at the interview were Philip Foglia (deputy inspector general and chief of investigations), Kenneth Michaels (investigative counsel), Robert Werner (chief investigator), and Alla Korsunskiy (a forensic accountant). I also spoke with representatives of the inspector general's office on several later occasions.

Pursuant to New York's Freedom of Information Law, I now have transcripts of thirty-four interviews conducted by the inspector general's office, thirteen additional interviews in audio format, and hundreds of documents that have been gathered by the inspector general's staff during the course of its investigation.

The article that follows is based in part on these transcripts, recordings, and documents. The material in them goes far beyond Magomed Abdusalamov. It also deals with allegations of wrongdoing and incompetence by certain New York State Athletic Commission officials.

Some of the transcripts that were produced by the inspector general's office contain redactions (i.e., some material was blacked out). These redactions were made by a combination of people in the inspector general's office based on claims of attorney-client privilege, the attorney work-product doctrine, and the Health Insurance Portability and Accountability Act.

In writing this article, I've edited the interview testimony down to manageable size in an effort to report effectively, fairly, and accurately on the issues at hand.

The tragedy that befell Magomed Abdusalamov didn't happen in a vacuum.

The New York State Athletic Commission has better-qualified ring doctors and better medical protocols than most jurisdictions. But in recent years, medical oversight has sometimes been lax.

Melvina Lathan was appointed to the New York State Athletic Commission as one of three commissioners by Governor Eliot Spitzer in 2007. At the start of her term, the commission chairman was Ron Scott Stevens. On March 17, 2008, Spitzer resigned in the wake of a prostitution scandal and was replaced by Lieutenant Governor David Paterson. Four months later, Paterson removed Stevens from his post and replaced him with Lathan.

State athletic commissions don't "run" boxing. They regulate events. At the championship level where big money is generated, the sport is controlled by a handful of promoters, television executives, and world sanctioning body officials. In these situations, a state athletic commission is charged with doing three things: (1) enforce the laws that are in place regarding financial matters (most notably, the Muhammad Ali Boxing

Reform Act); (2) administer a fair fight; and (3) protect the health and safety of fighters in a reasonable manner.

The health and safety of fighters as it relates to the conduct of state athletic commission officials is dependent upon the enforcement of proper pre-fight medical standards and the performance of commission officials (most notably, the referee and ring doctors) on fight night. There are three primary areas of involvement: (1) who is allowed to fight; (2) whether or not a fight should be stopped; and (3) post-fight medical care.

These are important responsibilities. Lives are at stake.

During Lathan's tenure as NYSAC chairperson, the already danger-ous job of fighting was sometimes more dangerous than necessary. The most flagrant example of this involved the June 5, 2010, championship fight at Yankee Stadium between Miguel Cotto and Yuri Foreman.

Forty-five seconds into round seven of that fight, as Foreman was moving laterally to his right along the ring perimeter, his right knee gave way and he fell hard to the canvas. He rose in obvious pain, hobbling when he tried to walk.

"Walk it off, champ," the referee (Arthur Mercante) told him. "Suck it up, kid. I'll give you five minutes."

Foreman wanted to continue fighting. Less than a minute after he went down, the action resumed. At that point, Yuri was a seriously com-promised fighter. Forty-five seconds later, again with no punch being thrown, Foreman's knee buckled and he fell once more to the canvas.

During the one-minute break after round seven, trainer Joe Grier readied Foreman for the next stanza, hoping that his fighter could regain his mobility. But it was quickly clear that not only couldn't Foreman move to avoid punches, he couldn't get power on his own blows. At the 1:30 mark, while trying to move laterally, he staggered and almost fell again. At that point, following proper procedure, Grier asked Ernie Morales (the NYSAC inspector assigned to Foreman's corner) to tell the referee that he wanted to stop the fight. Morales stood on the ring apron and got Mercante's attention. But the referee ignored the request.

"Yuri was starting to get banged up," Grier recounted later. "He couldn't properly defend himself because he only had one leg. The referee wasn't listening to the inspector. I had to get it stopped. I asked if I could throw the towel in, and the inspector said 'go ahead.'"

With 1:15 left in round eight, Grier threw a white towel into the ring. Both corners came through the ropes to embrace their respective fighters. At that point, the referee shouted, "Everybody out of the ring. I don't want the towel. The corner is not throwing in the towel."

Grier didn't force the issue because he feared that, if he did, the commission would withhold Foreman's purse. The action resumed. Foreman was no longer able to properly defend himself. The fight was clearly unwinnable. Yuri's knee gave way and he staggered several more times before the end of the round. Thirty seconds into round nine, Cotto landed a hook to the body. Foreman's knee gave out again and he fell to the canvas. Finally, Mercante stopped the fight.

Six days later, Foreman underwent reconstructive surgery for a torn ACL and torn meniscus muscle in his right knee. He was never the same fighter again.

It has been an unwritten rule in boxing, honored for over a century, that, when a fighter's corner wants to stop a fight, the fight is stopped. A comprehensive look at the NYSAC's handling of Foreman-Cotto is detailed in my earlier book, *Winks and Daggers*.

Some other thoughts follow:

★ Al Bernstein: "I've been a commentator for literally thousands of fights, and I've never seen anything like that before. It's a time-honored tradition in boxing and a common sense rule: if the corner wants to stop a fight, the referee should stop the fight. This was horrible. Just horrible."

★ Naazim Richardson: "If I want it stopped, if I think my guy's health is in danger and the referee won't stop it, that's crazy. This isn't something we should even be having a debate about. You cannot overrule the trainer if he wants to stop the fight. It's dangerous. It's wrong. Something like that has no place in boxing."

★ Dan Birmingham: "It was blatantly wrong. Anyone who doesn't understand that doesn't understand boxing. I mean, really. Come on. What was the referee looking at? This isn't a game. Just because he wants to thrill the crowd, he lets the fight continue? That's scary. Thinking like that is dangerous. I don't care if you're talking about a four-round club fight or a world championship fight. That kind of thinking has no place in boxing. If the corner stops a fight too soon, so be it. At least then, no one dies. And make no mistake about it. Lives are at stake."

Larry Hazzard is uniquely qualified to comment on situations of this nature, having been inducted into the International Boxing Hall of Fame for his work as a referee and commissioner of the New Jersey State Athletic Control Board. Hazzard had this to say about Cotto-Foreman.

"Normally, I don't comment on situations involving a referee and a commission. And I don't like to criticize. But I'd be doing a disservice to the boxing community if I didn't speak out."

"You have to look at the total situation," Hazzard explained. "The most important mission of the referee is to protect the health and safety of the fighter. Fighters are in danger every time they step into the ring. It's the referee's job to protect them when the danger becomes too great. The referee's mission is not to tell the fighter, 'Suck it up. Walk it off.' Walk it off? What does that mean? The referee should have called in the doctor when the fighter's knee gave out. Instead, the referee, on his own, made a medical decision that the fighter should continue. One thing we should all agree on is that the referee is not empowered to make medical decisions. That's why we have a doctor in each corner. You call time and consult with the doctor. How can anyone argue with that? Suck it up and walk it off. What kind of refereeing is that?"

It's easy to criticize Arthur Mercante for his actions in Cotto-Foreman. But the overall handling of the situation represented a system-wide failure.

Hazzard highlighted this point when he said, "The fighter was hurt and shouldn't have been allowed to continue. If the referee couldn't see it, that's why you have other safeguards in place. Where was the ring doctor in all of this? Where was the rest of the commission? I know the corner inspector did his job, but where was everybody else? And how can you overrule the trainer when he wants to stop the fight? Nobody knows a fighter better than his trainer. When the inspector came up on the ring apron and told the referee that the trainer wanted the fight to be over, that should have been it. When Mercante threw the inspector out of the ring, what he was doing, really, was throwing the commission, which is represented by the inspector, out of the ring. He was throwing all the rules and a hundred years of boxing out of the ring. Right then, someone should have taken the fight out of his hands, because clearly, at that point, he wasn't acting properly."

"I hate to be this critical," Hazzard said in closing. "It's not my goal to criticize or upstage anyone. But I feel like I have to speak out. The actions that were taken on the night of the fight were totally incorrect. The way this fight was handled was horrible. In the whole history of boxing, to my knowledge, nothing like this has ever happened before. And it should never happen again."

Dr. Barry Jordan (the current chief medical officer for the New York State Athletic Commission) was asked about Cotto-Foreman by the inspector general's office. Excerpts from the transcript of that session read as follows.

Q: There's been some conversation about the Cotto-Foreman fight at Yankee Stadium. Are you familiar with that fight?

Dr. Jordan: Yes.

Q: Were you in attendance?

Dr. Jordan: No. I was watching it on television.

Q: Having watched it on television, did you have any concerns about that fight where Foreman slipped and fell down and his knee gave out and he clearly had less mobility?

Dr. Jordan: Yes, I did. I feel uncomfortable saying what my concerns were only because I don't want to criticize co-workers. But if I was working that night, I would have stopped the fight.

Cotto-Foreman was example of how, at times, the New York State Athletic Commission played Russian roulette with fighter safety during Melvina Lathan's tenure as chairperson. Lathan was at ringside during the fight and ruled that it should continue after Foreman's corner asked that it be stopped and a towel was thrown into the ring. Later, she told Michael Woods of TheSweetScience.com, "I think Arthur did a remarkable job. He did what he was supposed to do. He knows the rules. He responded appropriately. All in all, it was a magical evening of boxing."

Lathan also raised eyebrows with her handling of the December 3, 2011, fight between Miguel Cotto and Antonio Margarito at Madison Square Garden.

Dr. Jordan, Dr. Anthony Curreri (the New York State Athletic Commission's ocular specialist), and the commission's medical advisory board (including retinal specialist Dr. Vincent Giovinazzo) were unanimous in the belief that Margarito should not be licensed to box in

New York. In making that determination, they considered five problems Margarito faced after his 2010 fight against Manny Pacquiao: (1) a retinal detachment; (2) a large retinal tear necessitating the use of silicone oil as part of the repair process; (3) a fractured orbital bone; (4) a vitreous rupture; and (5) the removal of a cataract followed by the implant of an artificial lens. Taken together, these factors led to further concern regarding the total construction of Margarito's right eye.

However, Lathan attended a kickoff press conference for the fight and allowed pre-fight planning to proceed until after Madison Square Garden was sold out for the bout. Then she moved to deny Margarito a license to box on medical grounds, ran into a firestorm of protest, and chaired a NYSAC meeting in closed session at which Margarito was licensed, supposedly on the basis of a medical report submitted by an ocular specialist named Thomas Goldstein.

However, it's clear from a reading of the transcripts produced by the inspector general's office (including an April 28, 2014, interview with Lathan) that Dr. Goldstein's written report stated that Margarito was unfit to box. In that regard, the following exchange with Lathan is instructive.

Q: Was there any discussion about his [Dr. Goldstein's] written report?

Lathan: I don't think we [the three commissioners who cleared Margarito to fight] ever really read it. I mean, first of all, it's medical in nature. I read it. I don't understand what I read.

Q: Well, you understand the last part.

Lathan: Yeah. You know, forgive me, I think that night [when the commission met] I had—I was—had a temperature of 103 or 104. I had the chills. I couldn't talk. So I don't know. I don't say that's an excuse, but I can't recall what—when or how, what made us change anything. I remember listening to this person [Dr. Goldstein] and the way he spoke, what he said, was letting us know, in essence, that it was okay. And we had decided that we were going to go with whatever direction this person took us. That's what I'm recalling."

Barry Jordan was also asked about Margarito by the inspector general's office, and the following exchange occurred.

Q: What do you remember about that situation?

Dr. Jordan: I remember quite vividly. I denied him a license.

Q: Why did you deny him the license?

Dr. Jordan: He didn't fulfill our requirements.

Q: For medical reasons?

Dr. Jordan: Right.

Q: It was all about his eye?

Dr. Jordan: His eye, right. And I want to emphasize that my primary responsibility is to the health and safety of the boxer.

Q: So what happened?

Dr. Jordan: The commission had a hearing and they overruled me.

Q: Are those hearings routine? Have they happened before in your experience?

Dr. Jordan: This is the first [and last] time I've ever been overruled. And actually, to be quite honest, the physicians that were involved, Dr. Curreri and Dr. Giovinazzo, they were both rather upset, as was I.

Cotto-Margarito was stopped after nine rounds because Margarito's right eye was swollen shut and Dr. Curreri (the ring doctor assigned to his corner) ruled that the bout should not continue.

A motorist can run a red light ten times without adverse consequences. Then, one day, there's a truck. The New York State Athletic Commission was running red lights with regard to fighter safety. That brings us to Magomed Abdusalamov.

PART TWO

Tragedies happen in boxing. Some of the world's best, most conscientious referees, trainers, and ring doctors have been at ringside when fighters died. But some tragedies can be avoided.

There are three lines of defense to protect a fighter when he crosses over the line that separates bravery and courage from unacceptable risk: (1) the referee; (2) the fighter's chief second (usually his trainer); and (3) the ring doctor.

I've written at length about Magomed Abdusalamov. The most comprehensive of these articles examines, among other things, the actions of referee Benjy Esteves and trainer John David Jackson during Magomed Abdusalamov vs. Mike Perez and can be found my earlier book, *Thomas Hauser on Boxing*.

The inspector general's office focused its questioning with regard to Abdusalamov-Perez in significant measure on the conduct of the ring doctors.

Dr. Osric King was the ring physician assigned to Abdusalamov's corner. Benjy Esteves told the inspector general's staff, "Dr. King, at least seven times, I saw him come up to the ring."

Dr. Avery Browne (who was assigned to Perez's corner) concurred, telling investigators, "It's obvious the physican in Mago's corner was very attentive, was on the apron almost every round in clear view, assessing his responses and how did he generally look."

That testimony from Esteves and King is simply wrong. A study of video recordings confirms that there were two occasions when Dr. King stood on the ring apron near Abdusalamov's corner and looked on between rounds. But he was standing outside the ropes to Abdusalamov's left, and the fighter's head was turned to the right so he could hear one of his cornermen (Boris Grinberg Jr.) convert Jackson's instructions to Russian. Thus, Dr. King could see little more than the back of the fighter's head. There is no indication that he tried to communicate verbally with the fighter.

John David Jackson maintains that he acted properly during the fight and has aimed his fire at NYSAC medical personnel who were in Abdusalamov's dressing room after the bout. Jackson told the inspector general's office that Abdusalamov was groaning in the dressing room and said his head hurt and that Jackson told the doctors several times that Magomed should be taken to the hospital by ambulance.

Jackson's testimony is similar to that of Abdusalamov's brother, Abdusalam Abdusalamov, who testified through a translator, "In the dressing room, he [Magomed] sat down right away. The way that I remember, the doctor came to him. And he started to stitching his eye and they were saying something in English. Magomed said to do an MRI of his head. He said that he has big headache. The doctor was right in front of him and he was putting stitches on his eye, and he [Magomed] was holding his head and saying MRI. And he was asking for painkillers. And Boris Junior was translating that to the doctor. He was feeling worse and worse. I sat him down very quickly and said that we have to call for the ambulance. He was not able to dress himself, so I dressed him myself. After that, we practically drug him out to the street. And on the street, he vomited on the street a couple of times."

These statements by Magomed Abdusalamov's trainer and brother appear to be at odds with the facts. Indeed, Abdusalamov's own cutman, Melvin "Chico" Rivas, rebutted them when interviewed by the inspector general's office.

Q: To your recollection, was Mago's brother or Mago's father agitated in any way?

Rivas: No, sir.

Q: Did they appear concerned about Mago's health?

Rivas: No, sir.

Q: Did John David Jackson in any way express concern about Mago's medical condition, his well-being?

Rivas: Not that I recall.

Q: Did anybody from Mago's team say you should go to the hospital?

Rivas: No.

Rivas's testimony conforms to that of Dr. Gerard Varlotta, one of two NYSAC doctors who examined Abdusalamov in the dressing room after the fight.

Q: Did he indicate to you that he had a headache?

Dr. Varlotta: Absolutely not.

Q: Did he say that his head hurt?

Dr. Varlotta: Did not.

After Abdusalamov was examined in his dressing room by Dr. Varlotta and Dr. Curreri (who stitched up a cut on the fighter's left eyelid), Dr. Jordan (who was sitting at ringside) was handed the relevant medical reports and a suspension notice. Abdusalamov was suspended for sixty days because of the laceration and indefinitely because of two possible fractures. In relevant part, one of the reports stated, "Possible nasal/zygoma [cheekbone] fracture." Next to a line that read "final disposition," Dr. Curreri wrote, "To hospital."

There's an issue as to whether the examining doctors instructed Abdusalamov to go to the hospital immediately. The weight of the evidence suggests that they did not.

Boris Grinberg Jr. testified before the inspector general's office as follows.

Q: Just to be clear, did any of the doctors in the locker room say that Mago should go right away to the hospital?

Grinberg: No. They said that, in a day or two—you might have a broken nose—so go and check out the situation.

Q: In other words, go in a day or two and deal with the nose?

Grinberg: Yes.

Q: Was there any mention, to your recollection, of a doctor saying something about he could even do it when he was back in Florida?

Grinberg: Yes. He said when you go back, make sure you go to the hospital to check out your nose and take out the stitches. But he was talking about the nose. He said you can fly back to Florida.

If Grinburg's testimony stood alone, one might question it because of his ties to Abdusalamov. But it's confirmed by Dr. Varlotta.

Varlotta: When I finished with what I needed to do, Dr. Curreri then examined his nose and hand and confirmed that, if they needed to go to the hospital at some point, they could do it. But it wasn't urgent to do now.

Q: Dr. Curreri said that?

Dr Varlotta: Dr. Curreri said that. Both of us said that.

Q: So neither one of you thought it was an emergent situation?

Dr. Varlotta: No. Absolutely not.

Dr. Jordan's testimony before the inspector general's office was in accord.

Dr. Jordan: I want to just emphasize, these are routine injuries. They gave me an injury report for him. There's nothing here to suggest there was any neurological problem. This is facial injuries, laceration. Facial injuries are the most common injuries we have in boxing. There was nothing in these reports to suggest any neurological problem. So therefore, it was nothing out of the ordinary in my mind. He didn't present any symptoms, and it's very unlikely three experienced doctors [King, Varlotta, and Curreri], all three are going to miss a neurological presentation. They're some of the best doctors in the country in terms of ringside physicians. I can see if it was one doctor missing a neurological presentation. People do make mistakes. But all three missing a neurological presentation, no. All three of them said he didn't have any neurological symptoms. And I have faith in those doctors because they've been doing it for a very long time. They're qualified.

And there was more.

Q: When you read this and saw his [Dr. Curreri's] disposition of the case, which says "to hospital," what does that mean to you?

Dr. Jordan: That he was going to have his nose checked out. Either it was going to be that night or perhaps when he got back to Florida.

Q: Did you have any discussion with Dr. Curreri as to why he wrote "to hospital?"

Dr. Jordan: Because he was going to have it evaluated, because eventually he's going to get X-rays. Often, people don't do anything about nose fractures until after the swelling has gone down. Some boxers might not even get it repaired until after they finish their boxing career because they may just break it again. A nose injury is not an emergency.

Q: What about the zygoma?

Dr. Jordan: What about it?

Q: Is that an emergency?

Dr. Jordan: No. It's not an emergency. Now, those type of fractures, if it's up near the orbit, could be a problem in the sense that, if it's affecting the eye muscles—and you can tell that clinically because they'll have double vision—their eye movements won't be intact. But this was lower down.

Q: Should he have gone to the hospital immediately?

Dr. Jordan: No. Because there was no indication that he had any neurological problems. He did not become symptomatic neurologically inside the arena. That's the important thing. Now you're going to say, "Well, weren't there symptoms?" He didn't have any confusion, dizziness, headaches, double vision. He didn't have any neurological symptoms while he was in the arena.

It's likely that Abdusalamov's neurological symptoms at the time of his post-fight examination by commission doctors did not warrant sending him immediately to the hospital. His other injuries probably did. That said, going immediately to the hospital appears to have not become an issue until Matt Farrago (the NYSAC inspector assigned to Abdusalamov's dressing room) took a post-fight urine sample and saw blood in the fighter's urine.

At that point, Abdusalamov decided to go to the hospital. But Grinberg acknowledged that it was to check out the blood in his urine and possible fractures (including X-rays for a possible broken hand).

Grinburg then asked Farrago how they should get to the hospital. He later told this writer, "I asked Matt, 'Where do we go, what hospital, how do you get there?' He [Farrago] thought and said, 'I don't really know. Let me go find out.' So he left to find out and, when he came back, he said, 'There's nobody there [in the on-site NYSAC office, which was supposed to be staffed at all times on fight night]. I can't find anybody, I don't know.' So we're thinking, where should we go, and he said, 'Just take a taxi, and just tell them to go to the nearest hospital.'"

As Abdusalamov left Madison Square Garden in search of a taxi, his condition worsened. Grinburg told the inspector general's office, "I couldn't find anything, everything was full. I found one guy with a Lincoln Town Car. He pulled up, and he was actually Russian speaking. I told him, 'We have a boxer who has to go to the hospital. He's right there. Let me go get him.'" And as I went to get Mago, he left, he took off. I was freaking out because I couldn't get a taxi and I found out that he [Abdusalamov] threw up. I even asked a police officer to help me, and he didn't do much. But there was a restaurant across the intersection, so I crossed the street and I saw a couple wave down a taxi, and I told them the situation, that we have an emergency situation, we need this taxi. So they let me take the taxi."

Melvina Lathan has been an unreliable source of information with regard to the events of that night.

Executive Deputy Secretary of State Anthony Giardina told the inspector general's office, "This did come from Melvina—I don't think I read this—that he [Abdusalamov] left the ring, he was examined, he took a shower, and he came out into the stands to watch the last fight."

At that point, Phil Foglia (deputy inspector general and chief of investigations), who had studied Madison Square Garden surveillance tapes, responded, "She told us the same thing. She's wrong, by the way, about where he was after the fight."

Foglia had a similar exchange with Barry Jordan.

Dr. Jordan: The other thing, as far as what I was told, he [Abdusalamov] actually stayed and watched the final bout.

Foglia: Let me just dispel you. He didn't stay. That's just wrong. Whoever told you that is wrong. So let's get past that.

As for Lathan's own testimony as to why Abdusalamov went to the hospital by taxi instead of in an ambulance, the following questioning took place.

Q: Just generally speaking in terms of commission policy, if a fighter indicates he wants to go to the hospital irrespective of what the doctor has said, does the athletic commission arrange for him to be transported?

Lathan: Yes.

Q: And they would do that by ambulance, I assume?

Lathan: Yes.

Q: So if the boxer is indicating I want to go to the hospital, the athletic commission will arrange for that to happen?

Lathan: Yes.

Q: Is it the policy of the athletic commission that, if a boxer is to be transported to a hospital, that somebody from the commission should accompany him?

Lathan: Yes.

Q: So that's a policy?

Lathan: Absolutely.

Q: Not to be confrontational about this, but you said you didn't have any problems with what the inspectors did that night; is that correct?

Lathan: Yes.

Q: You subsequently learned that Matt Farrago told Mago and his team to take a cab to the hospital?

Lathan: Oh, I read about that in the newspaper.

Q: So what did you think about that?

Lathan: I think that was horrendous.

Testimony with greater credibility than Lathan's with regard to NYSAC policy at that time came from Dr. Jordan.

Q: Dr. Curreri indicated to us that he thought that Magomed should go to the hospital, and that's why he wrote "to hospital." Does that change your opinion any?

Dr. Jordan: As to what?

Q: Whether or not he should go to the hospital?

Dr. Jordan: He didn't say he should go to the hospital in an ambulance.

Q: Are you saying that, if he thought he should go to the hospital immediately, that he should have written "to hospital by ambulance?"

Dr. Jordan: Yes. And if he thought he should have gone to the hospital by ambulance, he would have been put in the ambulance.

Q: So in Magomed's situation, he might have a broken nose, he might have a broken zygoma, he's gotten nine stitches, he might have a broken hand, and his camp says, 'We want to go to the hospital.' What happens next according to athletic commission policy?

Dr. Jordan: You instruct them to go to the hospital. You can tell them which hospital they should go to.

Q: And that would be the extent of the athletic commission's participation post-bout?

Dr. Jordan: Yes.

Dr. Varlotta's testimony before the inspector general's office was similar to Dr. Jordan's.

Q: Had someone indicated that they wanted to go to the hospital just for his hand injury to be X-rayed, what would be the normal protocol for the athletic commission? Would he be sent by ambulance?

Dr. Varlotta: For a hand injury, no, he would not be sent by ambulance. He would be instructed to go to a hospital.

Q: On his own?

Dr. Varlotta: On his own.

Q: Would he be told what hospital to go to?

Dr. Varlotta: Yes. We would tell him what are the closest hospitals to go to.

Q: So the fighter for a non-emergent situation would be responsible for his own transport?

Dr. Varlotta: Correct.

Q: Is that the official policy of the athletic commission as far as you know?

Dr. Varlotta: I don't know the official policy, but that's what I've heard instructed.

Ralph Petrillo (the New York State Athletic Commission director of boxing at that time) was in accord.

Q: In a baseball game, if a pitcher breaks his hand or has some kind of hand problem or a batter gets hit by a ball, they're taken out of the game and, if they need to go to the hospital, they get taken in an ambulance. Why is it that, in this circumstance, you're saying, if the boxer just has a broken hand, he has to go by himself. Is that just the way it works?

Petrillo: Just the way it works.

Anthony Giardina conceded that things shouldn't work that way. Portions of Giardina's testimony relating to what Lathan said to him about Abdusalamov were redacted from his interview transcript before it was produced. But the following exchange was released:

Giardina: I called the commission, or wrote to the commission, and asked for the reports after the fight.

Q: Now, in looking at that form, it's a little more than what Melvina said to you about just a broken nose, isn't it? He received nine stitches, he had a possible broken nose, a possible fracture of the zygoma. And the disposition was to the hospital. We know that he was transported ultimately by a taxicab.

Giardina: On his own.

Q: Yeah. What do you think of that?

Giardina: I think this person should have been transported by ambulance to the hospital. We have ambulances there for a reason. Especially given the fact that, in this particular case, the commission knew, everyone there knew, that he had sustained a beating.

Paul Edelstein (the lead attorney for Abdusalamov's family) characterizes the litigation as follows: "This case is about a lack of proper procedures and a catastrophic failure of communication. The extra time it took to get Magomed to the hospital where he could be properly evaluated and treated destroyed his life."

In addition to the obvious medical issues involved, Edelstein is keying on the conduct of Matt Farrago.

Farrago, now fifty-four years old, boxed professionally and had twenty-eight fights over the course of eight years. He told the inspector general's office that, while fully functional, he suffers from chronic traumatic encephalopathy (CTE) and his memory today is not as good as it was two years ago.

"My recall is questionable," Farrago said. "I do the best I can."

Prior to the November 2, 2013, fight card, Farrago arranged with Gennady Golovkin's trainer to be given Golovkin's handwraps after Golovkin fought in the main event (which was contested immediately after Abdusalamov-Perez). Farrago wanted the handwraps so he could auction them off in support of Ring 10 (a charitable organization he's actively involved with that benefits retired fighters).

It's against NYSAC rules for an inspector to solicit and/or accept anything of value from a fighter's camp. Deputy Commissioner Keith Sullivan was in Golovkin's dressing room after the main event when Farrago picked up the handwraps and asked Golovkin to sign them. Sullivan reported Farrago's conduct to the appropriate authorities, and Farrago was placed on suspension by the commission. The wraps were later sold at auction for $350.

Edelstein (and possibly other parties in the litigation) will maintain that Farrago was distracted from his duties and didn't seek medical help for Abdusalamov as aggressively as he should have because his mind was on Golovkin's handwraps. However, Abdusalamov had left Madison Square Garden by the time the Golovkin fight ended and Farrago went to Gennady's dressing room to secure the handwraps.

Taking the handwraps was wrong. And it's clear that the delay in getting Abdusalamov to the hospital was crucial. But it's a stretch to say that Farrago's conduct interfered with proper medical care for the fighter.

PART THREE

In 2012, the secretary of state's office (which is responsible for overseeing the New York State Athletic Commission) began an audit of the commission's practices. Executive Deputy Secretary of State Anthony Giardina later told the inspector general's office that the audit report "noted several deficiencies in the commission's operations."

That's an understatement.

It's hard for good people to perform well when they're in a poorly managed system.

Glenn Alleyne is the NYSAC's community coordinator. He was interviewed by the inspector general's office on December 6, 2013, and the following exchange occurred.

Q: In your view, do Ralph Petrillo [the NYSAC director of boxing at that time] and the chair [Melvina Lathan] do the work that they're supposed to do?

Alleyne: No.

Q: Let's start with the chair. How often, on average, to your knowledge, does she actually come in?

Alleyne: I think she does four days a week.

Q: To your knowledge, is her job a five-day-a-week job?

Alleyne: Her responsibilities are—what she is asked to do is five-day-a-week work. Before I took over the licensing function, I did a great deal of the reporting and stuff that she was supposed to be doing. So yes, it's a five-day-a-week job in its constitution as a full-time job.

Q: What about Ralph Petrillo? Does he come in five days a week?

Alleyne: Rarely.

Q: Approximately how often does he come in?

Alleyne: Up till two or three months ago, three days a week. Three to four.

Q: Given that the chair and Mr. Petrillo don't come in all the time, do you see problems stemming from that? The work not getting done, first of all.

Alleyne: The problems from that are more the unavailability to handle what they need to handle. They don't actually do any hands-on moving-parts work. But there is work that can't—the chair takes the mail. She gets the mail. And when she's not there, she locks her door so we can't get the mail. There are things that Ralph Petrillo needs to approve to start the whole process of us doing what we need to do. When he's not there, he's not available, that's not possible. And for those, those being Eric [Bentley] and I, who have to try to stay in front of what we get, that becomes a problem. Right now, the commission is Eric Bentley because he makes sure the work gets done. The work that I do is money, it's ledgering, it's reconciling. And the shows would go on if what I did didn't happen or occurred incorrectly. Everybody would go to jail afterward, but it wouldn't affect the shows happening. But the shows would not happen without what he [Bentley] does. All of the mechanics, the actual mechanics of doing the work product of the commission, is now riding on one person.

Eric Bentley is highly respected within the boxing community. At the time in question, he was charged with coordinating medical data for the commission.

"I stopped going to the shows," Bentley told the inspector general's office on December 3, 2013. "If I'm asked to go because they need extra hands there, I'll go. But I stopped going to the shows."

Q: Any particular reason?

Bentley: Several particular reasons. First and foremost, I don't like the way things are handled at the shows. I kind of feel like [Deputy Commissioner] Robert Orlando is stuck doing all the work, while everyone else is just there for a dog and pony show and they just want to sit there at the ring and not take ownership of anything. And I feel like it's not very fair. It wouldn't surprise me that, if at an event, things were to get a little mishandled. So I thought it would be best, unless I'm asked to go, to just not go to the shows anymore until there is some sort of change implemented or some sort of more effective manner of running the shows. Felix Figueroa [then chief inspector] usually handles the back, and he's very good from what I've seen. Keith Sullivan is pretty good. I know he doesn't get to go to the shows as often, but he seems to be pretty thorough. But I know who handles the day-to-day at the office and who does what work. And I know the people that go to the events don't really do much work around the office. So I just figured it was a matter of time for something to blow up in our face.

Q: What about Ms. Lathan? Does she do any of the day-to-day work?

Bentley: She says she does.

Q: What does she say she does?

Bentley: She says [she's] always got reports that she's doing and she's always got meetings, and I've never seen these reports and I haven't seen too many meetings.

Then Bentley added, "There is probably going to be some sort of fall guy. I just want to make sure that the right outcome occurs. I feel like the entire Commission needs a reorg. I think responsibilities need to be altered. Certain people should have less responsibilities. Certain people should have more responsibilities. I want to make sure that the right people are held accountable for all the stuff that's gone wrong, not just this event [Abdusalamov vs. Perez], but the last two or three years."

Over time, the inspector general's office became painfully aware that proper procedures and protocols either were not in place at the New York State Athletic Commission or were not being followed. As Glenn Alleyne testified, "The commission is not a procedurally-correct driven entity. We have specific rules and regulations. Those are not always how we operate."

For example, portions of NYSAC fight night medical forms regarding urine samples were often filled out in advance of fights. In that regard, the following exchange between Melvina Lathan and the inspector general's staff took place.

Q: Commissioner, let me tell you, we've talked to your medical coordinator, and what he tells us is that he fills out step 2 in advance. So in other words, the forms are given to the inspector with step 2 already filled in.

Lathan: Really? He can't do step 2 [an affirmation that the temperature of the urine taken from the fighter was within an appropriate range].

Q: It's a problem. We have testimony that step 2 is completed by your medical coordinator.

Lathan: Is that right?

Q: Yes.

Lathan: Oh, that shouldn't be. That can't be.

Q: Yes, it creates a problem for the chain of custody and also for the validity of the test; am I right?

Lathan: I didn't know that.

Q: You've never looked at the forms before you've handed them out?

Lathan: Well, no, I've not really looked at them.

There was also evidence that urine samples, once taken from fighters, were mishandled.

Matt Farrago testified before the inspector general's office that, when he brought Magomed Abdusalamov's post-fight urine sample to the commission office, the office was unlocked and unattended, and he put the sample in an unlocked bag that contained other urine samples taken that night.

Abdusalamov's sample, like the other samples, was in a sealed envelope. "It could be tampered with," Farrago told investigators. "But you'd know it was tampered with."

And of course, samples could have been removed from the bag.

Q: There was nobody watching this bag. Is that correct?

Farrago: That's correct.

Similar testimony was elicited by the inspector general's office from Melvina Lathan.

Q: I'm concerned. I want the chain of custody of the urine samples.

Lathan: Yes.

Q: So once the urine samples are collected, they're going to be brought to that room, correct?

Lathan: That's correct.

Q: In terms of the chain of custody, somebody should have to be there to make sure there is no tampering with the samples. Am I right?

Lathan: Well, it's locked. It's in a locked container. So nobody else has access to it except the person with the key.

Q: You're talking about the valise or bag that it was—

Lathan: Yes.

Q: Is that ever left unattended?

Lathan: Ideally it would not be, but I'm sure that it has been. I can't say that it's been watched every moment. That wouldn't be realistic.

Q: But if somebody was not in the room, if the room was left unattended, would the door be locked?

Lathan: The door would be closed.

Q: But is it your policy that that room always has somebody in it?

Lathan: Yes.

Q: Do you know if that happened on the night of Mago's fight, that it was constantly manned?

Lathan: You know, I would be about 99.8 percent sure that somebody was there at all times. This particular night, we had twenty-four extra officials because we had a separate set for each title fight. We had like thirty-two, thirty-three officials in one night in one place. I'm not absolutely sure, but I can be almost sure that somebody was always in that room.

Q: But in terms of the actual protocols for the evening, nobody is assigned to be in that room to make sure that somebody from the commission is there at all times?

A. No.

That's poor management. What's just as bad is that, on the night Abdusalamov suffered his injuries, the commission neglected to take a mandatory post-fight urine sample from his opponent, Mike Perez.

Eric Bentley brought that matter to the attention of the inspector general's office.

Bentley: When I came in on Tuesday [three days after the fight], I went to my office and realized the show folder wasn't there. When I went to get the show folder from Ralph's office [Ralph Petrillo], I noticed there was a urine form [that hadn't been filled out] on his desk, and I assumed it was Magomed's. I just assumed he went right to the hospital and couldn't give a post-fight urine. [Then] I spoke to Robert Orlando, and he's like, "Yes, [Ernesto] Rodriguez told me he fucked up"—he didn't use the word "fuck"—"he forgot to take the urine." It's just dumb, it's ignorant. If you have a job to do, you do it one hundred percent. That's a reflection of leadership and the way they were trained, and that is probably the biggest issue that I hope you guys figure out when this is all said and done.

Ernesto Rodriguez was then interviewed by the inspector general's office:

Q: Who did the post-fight urinalysis?

Rodriguez: I have no idea.

Q: Is that usual that someone else would do it?

Rodriguez: Unfortunately, no. I was supposed to do it.

Q: What happened?

Rodriguez: I don't know. I didn't know it because all fights are not required to have post-fight urinalysis. Championship fights are, and I didn't do it. I actually went to watch the fight [Gennady Golovkin vs. Curtis Stevens in the main event] and forgot completely about it.

Q: Did you get any feedback?

Rodriguez: Tuesday when I talked to Ralph [Petrillo]. It was Tuesday or Monday. I'm not sure. Ralph called me.

Q: And what did Ralph say to you?

Rodriguez: Not too many kind words. He said, "What happened that you didn't do the post-fight?" And I said, "Ralph, I messed up. I thought—I didn't know—I forgot it was a championship bout. I wanted to get out of there." And then I think he said, "You know, this can be a problem."

Q: Why didn't you take it? Is it your testimony today that you completely forgot about taking the urinalysis?

Rodriguez: Yes, sir.

Q: But on the night of the event, nobody mentions to you, where's the urine sample? The first you hear is a couple days later?

Rodriguez: Yeah.

Ralph Petrillo might have been direct with Rodriguez regarding the inspector's failure to take a post-fight urine sample from Perez. But he was less direct with the inspector general's office. Thus the following exchange, which occurred on May 1, 2014.

Q: You were specifically asked about urine [during your November 14, 2013, interview] and how the urine is handled and urine tests and so forth and how it's done. Is there a reason why you didn't mention on November 14th that there was a missing urine test from that very bout?

Petrillo: No, no reason. No reason why I didn't mention it.

Q: But you were in front of the IG's office talking about that particular incident and what the procedures are for urine testing, and you did not bother to mention to the IG that, by the way, there was a missing urine sample.

Petrillo: Which one was missing?

Q: The last [sample] after Magomed and Perez.

Petrillo: Sometimes we don't do that.

Q: It was a title fight.

Petrillo: It doesn't matter. The post-fight urine is just street drugs. If I have an inspector there for that, now it's two o'clock in the morning and this guy can't go, maybe he's dehydrated, whatever the reason is. Listen, if the inspector wants to stay there, they stay there. If they don't, I don't blame them for not staying there. They make $52 a night, I wouldn't stay there.

Q: I just thought it odd because you're coming to the IG's office. We're asking about procedures. We're very interested in the Magomed-Perez fight. And this is not mentioned at all by you when you're here on November 14th.

Petrillo: Yeah.

The New York State Athletic Commission's problems also extended to its medical advisory board. Barry Jordan (the NYSAC's chief medical officer) told the inspector general's office, "I've had no influence in terms of who's on the board. Reason why, in the past, I would try and make suggestions because we've always been trying to make the sport as safe as possible, and I think it's important that the medical advisory board members know something about sports medicine and hopefully know something about boxing. But sometimes, since it's a political appointment, you may have a physician who doesn't know anything about boxing at all."

Then Dr. Jordan was asked, "Do you know if they receive any training while they're on the board?"

"No," he answered. "They don't."

"The weakest part of what we currently do is post-event," Glenn Alleyne told investigators. "Post-event would have to be all about going over what went wrong at the event, going over what could be done better next time. We don't do any of that."

In that regard, Dr. Jordan was asked, "Has the medical advisory board convened since the Mago fight?"

"No," he answered.

That question was put to Dr. Jordan on April 2, 2014, five months after the Abdusalamov-Perez fight.

The more the inspector general's office probed, the more problems it found.

Melvina Lathan acknowledged to investigators on April 28, 2014, that she had received a pair of earrings from someone who did business with the commission, but couldn't remember the donor's name.

Q: Do you have any idea of the value of the gift you received?

Lathan: No, I don't.

Q: When was that?

Lathan: About three years ago.

Q: How was it delivered to you?

Lathan: It was wrapped, gift-wrapped.

Q: Somebody physically gave it to you?

Lathan: Yes.

Q: Who was that? You don't know? You're shaking your head. Meaning no?

Lathan: Meaning I don't know.

On May 2, 2014, Kenneth Michaels (investigative counsel for the inspector general's office) had a follow-up telephone conversation with Lathan. His written notes of that conversation read in part as follows: "I referred to jewelry that she had previously testified, on April 28, that she had received as a gift, and asked her to bring the jewelry to the Inspector General's Office so we could evaluate it. She said she could not as she had given it away (to whom she did not say). She said that she had not received the jewelry from a promoter, as had been previously discussed; it was from a guy who was part of a 'crew' working with and trying to learn to be a promoter; he was 'hanging around' with the promoter. The promoter, she noted, had only brought a cake."

In that same conversation, Michaels's memorandum noted, "Lathan complained that she had felt railroaded at her recent interview." The memorandum goes on to state, "Lathan asked if I thought there had been any criminal activity. I pointed out that we were in the middle of an investigation, and this was like asking who had won a ten-round boxing match in the fifth round. She responded with words to the effect of, 'But you know who's winning.'"

Then, in a June 4, 2014, session with investigators, Lathan retracted her admission.

Lathan: I just want you to know that the last testimony about promoters and gifts, not.

Q: Not what?

Lathan: Not. I got no gifts from a promoter. Absolutely not.

Q: Didn't you tell us at one point that you got some earrings?

Lathan: Yeah, yeah, yeah. I thought that's what had happened, but it's not true. Not true at all. Absolutely not.

One of many problems with that testimony was that, six weeks earlier, the inspector general's office had interviewed Madeline Brady (the former director of licensing for the New York State Athletic Commission). Brady acknowledged having received a necklace from a promoter, which she brought to the interview and turned over to the inspector general's office. She then told investigators, "At the same time, Melvina and Ralph [Petrillo] got something. At the time, I didn't know [what] because they didn't open it in front of me. A subsequent conversation that I was part of, they were comparing notes. Ralph had gotten earrings for his wife. And Melvina, if I remember correctly, she got a watch."

Brady was also asked about free tickets that Lathan and Petrillo might have received from promoters, and the following exchange occurred.

Brady: For the big fights, there would be a credential list that was sent to Madison Square Garden or to Barclays Center. That used to be my job. That got taken away. It was as if she [Melvina] didn't want me to know who was going and who wasn't.

Q: Was there a reason for that?

Brady: I would say, "Why does this person have to go?"

Q: In other words, you questioned Melvina?

Brady: Yeah, and then you stop questioning when she tells you to mind your own business.

Q: Is that what she did?

Brady: Yes.

Q: In those words?

Brady: Yes.

Q: Was there ever a situation where friends or relatives were credentialed? Friends or relatives of commissioners or office staff to go to particular bouts?

Brady: Credentialed?

Q: Or permitted to come under the auspices of the athletic commission?

Brady: I know that, after a weigh-in when I determined the color of the wristbands and I was leaving for the night, I always gave Melvina and Ralph five to ten wristbands each. What they did with them, I don't know. If they gave them out, those people weren't necessarily sitting ringside but it got them entry.

Q: Entry to the arena?

Brady: Now at Madison Square Garden, that couldn't be done because Madison Square Garden and Barclays Center issued their own entries and we would have to get a list. For those events, I have seen family members in high-priced-ticket seats. I can't say with certainty that they weren't paid for. My gut tells me they weren't. You know, Ralph or Melvina's family are sitting in the $400 seats and there are four of them.

The inspector general's office also found itself in the middle of a sniping war between Lathan and John Signorile (who was appointed to the NYSAC as a commissioner by New York governor Andrew Cuomo).

Lathan complained in her testimony that Signorile told her he was going to take her job. Tom Santino, whom Signorile replaced as a commissioner, complained that Signorile lobbied to have him removed from the commission so he could replace him.

Signorile, for his part, told investigators, "When I go to the events, I'm treated very poorly and put to the side. And when I asked the chairwoman one day, I went to her office and I asked her, 'What do you need me to do at the events?' she replied, 'Just be a figurehead and sit there.' I said, 'Okay.' I said, 'I would like to sit up front at the table. The previous commissioners sat up front at the table.' She replied, 'We don't think that's a good idea.' I said, 'Who are we?' She said, 'We.' So I just nodded my head and went on my way. I'm not treated very well. I'm not welcome because I'm a threat. She assumes I'm looking for her job. She has discredited me to all the officials that I grew up with from the amateurs, telling them, 'He's after my job. He's after my job.'"

Later in the questioning, Signorile was asked why he hadn't attended the fight card at Madison Square Garden on the night that Adbusalamov was injured.

"It's a little bit of a hostile environment for me," Signorile answered. "I go in there, and all of my friends are afraid to associate with me, the officials that are my friends through the amateurs and the professionals because, if you associate with me, guess what, you're probably not going to get the coming title fight or you'll get a poor assignment. You'll get that Star Catering Hall with all four-rounders and a couple pro debuts."

Signorile also volunteered the information that "The chairwoman has a parking permit that says New York State Athletic Commission doctor on call—she's not a doctor—so she can park [where she wants]. A placard in the window."

Glenn Alleyne summed things up nicely when he told the inspector general's office, "We don't have what you would consider a classic managerial presence."

New York secretary of state Cesar Perales stated the obvious when he acknowledged to investigators, "The commission is not as well run as it should be."

Thus the question: How should the problems be fixed?

PART FOUR

On March 26, 2014, with the inspector general's investigation underway, Governor Andrew Cuomo announced the appointment of David Berlin to fill the previously vacant post of executive director of the New York State Athletic Commission.

Berlin assumed his position on May 1, 2014. Two weeks later, on May 15, Ralph Petrillo was dismissed as director of boxing. Eric Bentley was given Petrillo's duties on an interim basis.

Melvina Lathan had no input into the decision to terminate Petrillo. In discussing the matter with the inspector general's office, she stated, "What was said, if I'm recalling correctly, is that it came from the IG." Lathan was also concerned that her own job might be in jeopardy.

The chairmanship of the New York State Athletic Commission is a full-time position that pays approximately $100,000 annually. The other two commissioners serve on a per diem basis.

Before Berlin took office, primary authority for the daily operation of the NYSAC resided with the chairperson. But Lathan and Berlin were advised by the secretary of state's office that, after a June 7, 2014, fight card at Madison Square Garden, Berlin would be responsible for overseeing the daily operation of the commission.

The old guard resisted.

Felix Figueroa (the commission's chief inspector) had died suddenly on February 14, 2014. Thereafter, Lathan had named Mike Paz as acting chief inspector.

Two commission inspectors told Department of State officials that, over the 2014 Memorial Day weekend (the evening of May 23 through May 26), Paz made telephone calls to them and other inspectors asking for their help in undermining Berlin and shoring up Lathan's position.

The plan, as reported to the inspector general's office, was for inspectors to work the June 7 fight card at Madison Square Garden (which featured Sergio Martinez vs. Miguel Cotto). Then, after the transfer of power to Berlin (who was to be given additional authority on June 9), the inspectors would refuse to work or engage in a slowdown at a June 14 fight card at Barclays Center. At that point, it was allegedly planned, Lathan would show her mettle and restore order.

Lathan, when questioned by the inspector general's office, denied knowing of the plan until after it was reported to the secretary of state's office on May 27 and a state employee told her about it.

Lathan: I don't know anything about that. I mean, I heard it, yes. But did I know anything about that? Nah. Not at all.

Q: Who did you hear it from?

Lathan: Umm. Another employee from upstate, John Dantonio, said to me that there was some talk and if I had heard anything like that. I had not heard anything like that.

Q: Have you had any discussions with Mr. Paz about that?

Lathan: No.

Q: Our understanding is that Mr. Paz called a number of inspectors and suggested there be some kind of job action.

Lathan: I, you know, I wouldn't think that anyone, if he had in fact made that call; I don't see him making that call. But then, you know, human nature is human nature. Umm, I don't see anybody, our inspectors are paid below minimum wage, but I think they have integrity. I don't know. I wasn't involved in that. I don't know if he did in fact call anybody or that was what happened.

Q: Since Mr. Petrillo's departure, have you had any discussions with him?

Lathan: No.

Q: Are you aware of whether or not he has communicated with anybody else on the staff, any of the inspectors, by e-mail or text or otherwise?

Lathan: Yes. He sent a letter. Ah, umm. I don't remember the content of the letter, but it was something to the effect of, umm, I'm sorry it took me so long to let you know that I'm no longer with the commission. Umm. Something about stand up and do your job. I don't really know verbatim what it was. It was kind of a pep talk, I think. It sounded like that to me.

Q: Just for clarity's sake, you have had no discussions or communications with Mr. Paz of any kind regarding any job slowdown.

Lathan: Absolutely not.

Q: Has Mr. Paz griped to you at any point about Mr. Petrillo being let go?

Lathan: Griped? Well, I mean, he questioned it. He asked why, which, again, is natural. That's normal. Why did that happen. My response was, "I don't know."

Q: Did he in any way, theoretically, hypothetically, suggest something on the order of, "What if we did something? What if we took some kind of action?" Do you recall him saying anything like that?

Lathan: No. No, I don't. No. He was disappointed, obviously.

Paz was interrogated about the proposed job action on two occasions. The first was on May 30, 2014, at his home in Orange County, New

York. Chief investigator Robert Werner (a retired New York City police detective) took the lead.

Q: One of the concerns we have is, we received information that there has been talk of conducting a job slowdown or a no-show or a sick-out, however you want to describe it, in connection with ongoing events. Do you have any knowledge at all about that?

Paz: No, sir.

Q: Has anyone spoken to you or have you spoken to anyone about engaging in this type of activity?

Paz: No.

Q: Has there been any talk amongst any inspectors or from anyone about a slowdown?

Paz: No.

Q: When was the last time you spoke with Melvina?

Paz: The 17th of May [at a fight card in Brooklyn].

Q: So there's been no discussion among any of the inspectors that you're aware of about having either some type of rulebook slowdown or sick-out or doing anything to disrupt the athletic commission's ability to oversee an event?

Paz: No. To my knowledge, no.

Q: Has there been any talk at all to your knowledge about disrupting the activities of the athletic commission?

Paz: No.

Q: Have you spoken to Ralph recently?

Paz: The day before yesterday.

Q: As we know, Ralph is no longer with the commission.

Paz: Um-hmm.

Q: Has there been any conversation between you and Ralph about the circumstances that led to him no longer having that position?

Paz: No comment.

Q: So this was a conversation you may have had with Mr. Petrillo, but you do not want to answer any questions?

Paz: The conversation I had was just a personal conversation.

Q: So any conversation you had with Mr. Petrillo since he left the commission has been of a personal nature and not related to your commission work. Is that correct?

Paz: Most of it, yes.

Q: Well, it's like being pregnant. You have to either be pregnant or not pregnant. I just want to make sure again—because we are under oath— and be very very clear. Have you had any conversations with anyone —and this would include Mr. Petrillo—regarding what I described as a rulebook slowdown and/or sick-out? Because this is very important.

Paz: Well, I don't understand. Is this a target or something? Is this being a target?

Q: We had heard that there were plans by certain inspectors to participate in either a rulebook slowdown and/or a sick-out, and that that had been discussed by the inspectors. I asked you previously if you had knowledge of any of those conversations, and you said no.

Paz: No.

Q: So this is the first time you're hearing about any plans to disrupt the commission?

Paz: No. Did not.

Five days later, Werner met again with Paz. This time, the investigator appeared unannounced at Paz's place of work and began the session as follows.

Q: Just listen to what I have to say now as opposed to my asking you any questions. Based on my investigation, based on my conversations with other people, it's clear that what you told me was not entirely the truth. Now just listen to me for a moment. You were under oath. Before we make a determination on whether or not you actually committed perjury, I'm going to give you one chance, and only one chance, to correct what you told me. And it's really really important, because I can back it up with other people that I've spoken to. So the questions are this. Did you ever reach out to anyone or have a conversation with any inspector regarding the possibility of a job action or slowdown or something along those lines?

Paz: After I spoke to you, I sat and talked to my wife because she was upset about the whole thing. So we talked. She says, "Well, you know, you might hear from him again." I said, "If I do, I'll speak to them." Everything that you threw at me is all new to me. After reviewing it, and my wife was asking me, "Did you say something at any of the shows? Did you talk to anybody?" Because I had inspectors that called me. "Hey, what the hell happened [to Petrillo]?" I said, "I don't know. I don't know. They released him, and I don't know." And then we got into a conversation that, "This ain't right." And then we were talking about, "How would they feel if we didn't show up at shows? Then what?"

Q: That's, to me, the definition of a job action.

Paz: But as far as me saying, "Let's go rally the troops and let's go rah-rah; let's stick it to them." No. I did express I was upset.

Q: How did you express it? What did you suggest?

Paz: I said, "Well, you know, how would they feel if we didn't show up for shows because of the way we're being treated? Then what? Then what? Okay?" I said, "We'll talk about it sometime. You know? But right now, we're committed to shows, and that's where we're at."

Q: Here's the second and very important question. Did you have any conversations regarding that with Melvina? Think long and hard before you answer because what we're talking about is you and what potentially could happen to you if you weren't being truthful. Did you ever use a term such as "We have Melvina's support" or words to that effect?

Werner then referenced a specific show that Paz had attended with Lathan.

Paz [after a pause of about ten seconds]: I'm gonna be honest on this one. I don't know. I mean, we [Lathan and Paz] did grumble about how things are going. I did express about Ralph being let go. Okay. Did I tell her that we were planning on doing a walkout? I'm gonna say no.

Q: What prompted these discussions? Was it Ralph's termination?

Paz: I think that's the straw that broke the camel's back. There are changes going on. They bring in Dave Berlin, and it's like who is this guy? A lot of guys are left in limbo. When we found out that Ralph was terminated, okay, we were very upset because he was like our guiding force and to not know why, what happened, what's going on; that really just like set us off.

Q: You may feel that you have an allegiance to Ralph. You may feel that you have an allegiance to Melvina. But I'm going to tell you; we drove a long way to come see you last Friday. You were under oath. You've got to understand what that means. We are here now again to clarify this. This is your opportunity to be truthful with us. Listen, some people have nothing to lose by talking to us. So you got to keep in the back of your mind that maybe we talked to Melvina. Maybe we talked to Ralph. Maybe we talked to this one. Maybe we talked to that one. So I want to know. I want you to think real hard before you answer this. Did you speak to Melvina about this? And I get it. Everybody's pissed. What would happen now if we just said fuck you and we took our time doing this or we took our time doing that? You need to let us know who you spoke to.

Paz: I spoke to inspectors in general. You know, we just talked.

Q: When you say inspectors, Michael, what inspectors?

Paz: Uhhh, there's quite a few that worked the shows.

Q: Was Melvina around when you were having these discussions?

Paz: No.

Q: Continue.

Paz: And I said, "We're pissed. How would it feel if we didn't start showing up for shows? Then what? We're not getting paid. And look what they did to Ralph. Who's next?" So everybody's running gun-shy. I might have said some things out of emotion. But to follow through, no. I would not do something like that.

Q: Did you make any phone calls to any inspectors?

Paz: Yes.

Q: How many inspectors? Keep in mind, it's a very simple matter for me to get your phone records.

Paz: Maybe four.

Q: And how did that conversation go when you spoke to them on the phone?

Paz: I said, "Look, they let Ralph go. I don't know why." And then we got in a conversation about . . . Ummm . . . I said, "Guys are talking about, you know, maybe if we don't start showing up for shows, we'll see what happens from there." But we didn't commit for any shows for this to happen.

Q: Did you make any statement about Melvina having your back or showing you support in this? And if so, how did you determine that Melvina was supporting this? This is the 64-dollar question.

Paz: I got to be honest. I can't remember.

Q: Did you have any conversation with Melvina, exhibiting the same type of frustration?

Paz: I did mention [to] Melvina about the fact, she knows we're upset about Ralph being released. But the most sticking point is the money that we get paid. And I said to her, "Guys are upset. Some of them are looking to throw the hat in. Some of them just don't know what they're gonna do."

Q: Did you mention to Melvina, "How would they like it if we didn't show up?" And did she respond to you?

Paz: I can't remember. I'll be honest with you. I can't remember that.

Q: Do you recall any of the words that you spoke to Melvina about this potential—and I'm going to use my term—job action? Did you have any conversation with Melvina? Did she have any conversation with you? Did she indicate she was supportive of this? Not supportive? Did she say that wouldn't be a good idea?

Paz: I'm going to probably say she wasn't going to support it if there was any action. I'm gonna say she did not give, at least to me, whether she was supporting it or not. Okay? Because she was upset because of the fact, she doesn't know what her stance is. So she was more focused on what's gonna happen to her. She said to me, "If they got Ralph, they're probably going to be looking at me now." She did not give an indication to us—at least to me; I'm gonna speak for me—that she was supporting it or not supporting it. She was more worried about her fate.

Q: Okay. I'm going to re-say the 64-dollar question again. Did you have any conversation with Melvina regarding a possible job action, slow-down, stand-down, however you want to describe it, and did she respond either pro or con or try to talk you out of it or just acknowledge the fact that you guys were frustrated?

Paz: I think she acknowledged that guys were frustrated. But—umm—she did not tell me whether I support you on it or against it. She was upset more about what's happening to her.

Q: Did you tell Melvina that you were going to be reaching out to other inspectors?

Paz: I don't know if I told her that. I may. I don't know.

Q: And you made several calls to several inspectors? This is on the phone, I'm talking about.

Paz: Yeah. It was only like three or four guys I spoke to.

Q: Did you talk to Ralph about this?

Paz: About you guys?

Q: No. About this job action or discussions of the job action.

Paz: I had mentioned that we were thinking about doing it. And he says, not a good idea.

This contradicted Paz's earlier statements regarding his conversations with Petrillo. And at the end of Paz's second interrogation, there was a contradiction regarding his conversations with Lathan.

Q: Our main concern in coming here today is to make sure that we got the truth from you. Had you continued down this road and not corrected your testimony on what you told us about on Friday, you could have very seriously jeopardized yourself. We wanted to give you an opportunity to correct. We have a job to do. We take our notes. We listen to the recording. And we spoke to other people. And it's not the same set of circumstances that we got when we spoke to you. So we came here today to give you a chance. If there is anything else that you're holding back, now is the time to tell us. That's why I'm asking you again for the last time; did Melvina know about this conversation regarding a possible job action or slowdown?

Paz: I did mention it to her briefly. But like I said, she did not say, "I support you" or "don't do it."

Q: So she was non-commital?

Paz: Yes.

Q: But she heard what you were saying?

Paz: But it didn't happen as far as us taking any action.

It should be noted here that evidence of Paz telephoning more than "three or four" inspectors was presented to the inspector general's office. Also, one inspector's contemporaneous written notes on Paz's comments during a May 23, 2014, call that Paz made to the inspector read in part: "Ralph gave list of who to call / who not to call . . . Blow commission open."

Petrillo had been interviewed by the inspector general's office prior to the issue of a proposed job action arising and was not questioned by the inspector general's office on the subject.

Soon after being interviewed by the inspector general's office, Mike Paz was relieved of his duties as an inspector for the New York State Athletic Commission.

And Melvina Lathan's days as chairperson were numbered.

PART FIVE

Once David Berlin's authority as executive director of the New York State Athletic Commission was clarified, a number of pressing issues were addressed and the process of professionalizing the NYSAC began.

One of Berlin's first acts was to appoint the much-respected George Ward and Tim Duffy as co-chief inspectors. More personnel changes followed. Berlin also pushed successfully for an increase in the per diem fee paid to inspectors from $52 to $100 per fight card.

More importantly, Berlin began the much-needed process of developing clear protocols for commission personnel across the board; training a new generation of ring doctors, inspectors, referees, and judges; and ensuring that relevant information is given to fighters and their respective teams in a timely manner.

A new sense of professionalism began to pervade the commission.

On January 12, 2015, New York governor Andrew Cuomo announced that Tom Hoover would replace Melvina Lathan as NYSAC chairperson. Hoover had served as chief inspector and an assistant deputy commissioner for the commission in the 1980s and 1990s. Before that, he'd been an All-American basketball player at Villanova and a first-round NBA draft choice. After retiring from basketball, he'd served in a variety of public service and private sector jobs.

Hoover was confirmed as NYSAC chairman by the New York State Senate and took office on June 16, 2015.

Meanwhile, something strange was happening. Or to be more precise, it was strange that something was not happening. The report of the inspector general's office on its investigation of the New York State Athletic Commission wasn't released.

In some respects, the administration of New York governor Andrew Cuomo has been a model of effective governance. But at times, it has fallen short of the mark.

On July 2, 2013, pursuant to the Moreland Act and Executive Law, Governor Cuomo, with great fanfare, announced the creation of a "Commission to Investigate Public Corruption" in New York State. Then, on March 31, 2014, the governor announced that he had decided to dismantle the commission, saying that the reforms he wanted would be accomplished by the passage of new legislation.

Thereafter, in a July 23, 2014, article headlined, "Cuomo's Office Hobbled Ethics Inquiries by Moreland Commission," the *New York Times* reported, "A three-month examination by the *New York Times* found that the governor's office deeply compromised the panel's work, objecting whenever the commission focused on groups with ties to Mr. Cuomo or on issues that might reflect poorly on him."

At that point, federal authorities stepped into the fray. The three most powerful men in Albany were Cuomo, speaker of the New York State Assembly Sheldon Silver, and majority leader of the New York State Senate Dean Skelos. Silver and Skelos were each indicted by a federal grand jury. On November 30, 2015, Silver was found guilty on seven counts of abusing his office for more than $4,000,000 in personal gain. On December 11, 2015, Skelos and his son were found guilty on eight counts of bribery, extortion, and conspiracy.

With that as background, it's no surprise that politics sometimes interferes with the effective operation of the New York State Athletic Commission. The previously referenced title fight between Miguel Cotto and Antonio Margarito is a case in point.

Melvina Lathan contributed to the crisis by her delay in confronting the issue of Margarito's medical condition. But when the NYSAC medical staff sought to deny Margarito a license to box because of the condition of his eye, the political machine weighed in.

Many of the redactions from interview transcripts released by the inspector general's office pursuant to the New York State Freedom of Information Law appear to deal with political pressure exerted upon the NYSAC with regard to Cotto-Margarito. But even with these redactions, a picture emerges.

Q [asked of Dr. Barry Jordan]: Do you know if any pressure was put on anybody, political pressure or economic pressure of any kind?

Dr. Jordan: I don't know. I mean, you hear things. It was hearsay.

Q: What's the hearsay?

Dr. Jordan: I don't know how true it is. I just heard Albany wanted the—somebody said Albany wanted the fight to go through.

Dr. Anthony Curreri told investigators, "The promoters wanted Margarito to fight in New York, and myself and the rest of the medical team saw him unfit to box.

Q: What was the basis for overturning the initial finding that he shouldn't be allowed to box?

Dr. Curreri: I never could find out. I asked Ralph Petrillo. I asked Melvina Lathan. And I did not get an answer.

Q: When you asked Melvina Lathan, what did she say if she didn't give an answer?

Dr. Curreri: The exact words, I cannot recall, but that it was something beyond control.

The inspector general's office also questioned Lathan on the issue and asked, "Were there any other outside influences that tried to influence you personally on this fight to get the decision to allow Margarito to fight?"

Most of the next three pages in Lathan's testimony have been redacted. Then:

Q: Do you feel like Albany was trying to place any undue pressure on you?

Lathan: I questioned it. I questioned it.

Lathan testified next to receiving an e-mail from someone in the Department of State, whose name she didn't remember:

Lathan: It had a list of reasons for—you know, the Garden was all sold out. I don't remember each specific line.

Q: There were people's concern on why [the fight] should go forward, correct?

Lathan: Yes.

Secretary of State Cesar Perales was also questioned about the matter.

Q: I'm going to shift gears on you totally now and ask you about a fight that occurred in 2011, and see if you have any recollection of this. This was the Cotto-Margarito fight.

Perales: Yes, I do have a recollection.

Q: What is your recollection?

Cesar Perales: That [was] just a few months after I had become Secretary. I thought it was kind of messy. And I thought [there] was something wrong with the way it had been handled, which incidentally led to my asking my audit people to give me a thorough review of how the commission operated.

Q: With respect to that particular fight, did you have any communications with the Governor's office or any of the secretaries or deputy secretaries?

Perales: My executive deputy would have been the person who would have received a communication or spoken to somebody. I didn't.

Q: Are you aware of any type of, I don't want to say pressure, but that any kind of suggestion was made that efforts should be made to license Margarito?

Perales: I don't know how to answer that question. Let me say that I was personally disappointed when that fight was being canceled. We looked pretty silly in the media because, as I recall, Melvina herself had made a big deal of this bout coming to New York. And suddenly, there is an announcement that, based on the medical reports of the boxer, he couldn't fight. So I wanted to make sure that this was not being done arbitrarily. I think that it would have embarrassed everybody, including me. So I was personally concerned. I may have very well been told by somebody in my office that the Governor's office was equally concerned.

Q: I will tell you that Chairlady Lathan told us that she received an e-mail—she thought it might have been from you; she tried to retrieve it but is so far unable to—concerning the cancellation of the fight and making certain suggestions to—

Perales: It wasn't me. I'm positive of that.

Q: But it may have been somebody on your staff?

Perales: If that's what she says. I don't know what that e-mail might have said. You're not telling me exactly what it said.

Q: There was a suggestion to her, apparently in the e-mail, that every effort be made that this fight proceed.

Perales: Oh, I'm sure she received—I wouldn't have sent her an e-mail, but I wouldn't be surprised if I said to her, "Are you sure this has got to be cancelled? You're looking pretty silly."

Madeline Brady was more direct in her testimony to the inspector general's office.

Brady: Melvina went to a press conference announcing this fight, and she was all for it. Gave it a big thumbs up. Pictures of her all over the Internet saying how awesome this fight is going to be. And she hadn't looked at the whole picture. Then it was brought to the chief medical officer, at the time it was Dr. Osric King's attention. Dr. King was not going to allow Mr. Margarito to fight. From there on, things got crazy. The Secretary of State's office on behalf of the Governor intervened. The commission was being handled by the Governor's public relations people.

It was not a good two or three days in the commission. I firmly believe that Melvina [by then] wanted to not let the fight happen. But she was being pushed because it was a public relations nightmare.

Q: Who was Melvina being pushed by?

Brady: The three PR people that were, I'm going to say literally following her around for a two-day period, going into these public meetings. I remember Melvina saying, "The Governor wants this to happen and told the Secretary of State this has got to happen, so we've got to find a way to have it happen."

Q: Did she say that to you?

Brady: Oh, yeah. When she wasn't in meetings and when she wasn't with these people who were advising her, she was in Ralph's office with me like on the verge of tears. I think a lot of the tears were, she had created this monster and now she wanted to get out and she didn't know how to do it. She didn't know how to undo this mess.

At its best, the political process improves people's lives. At its worst, it destroys them.

When chief investigator Robert Werner interrogated Mike Paz for the second time, Werner told him, "Just to explain to you how things work. Although this most recent investigation started as a result of the November 2nd [Abdusalamov-Perez] fight, you start looking at policies, procedures. We start looking at the old IG reports. It's a very small agency, the athletic commission. You guys have been investigated five times. And when you start looking at that type of stat, what's wrong with this picture?"

Two of the three NYSAC commissioners at the time of the Magomed Adbusalamov vs. Mike Perez fight (Melvina Lathan and John Signorile) have been discussed previously in this report. The third commissioner was Edwin Torres.

Torres, who still sits on the commission, was nominated to his post by Governor David Paterson in 2008. He's now eighty-five years old, a retired New York State Supreme Court judge, and the author of *Carlito's Way*, which was made into a feature film starring Al Pacino.

The interview with Torres by the inspector general's office is enlightening.

Torres: I took this job as a fun thing.

Q: Were you told, or did you find out in any way, what your responsibilities would be as a commissioner for the athletic commission?

Torres: I don't have an independent recollection of those instructions. But obviously, the safety of the fighters, the integrity of the sport, those are the overarching principles that guide us.

Q: Is there anything other than the fun to the appearance at the actual boxing events?

Torres: No.

Q: Is there any kind of responsibility for you to direct any of the people who are deputy commissioners or inspectors or anything like that?

Torres: No, none of that.

Q: Any other responsibilities that are involved in being a Commissioner that we haven't discussed?

Torres: Not that comes to me.

Q: With respect to training that's given at the athletic commission, do you participate in that in any way?

Torres: What?

Q: Training?

Torres: Training who? The fighters? No.

Q: Do you have any interaction with the inspectors or the judges?

Torres: No. Say about the fights, it's social and so forth.

Q: What about the deputy commissioners?

Torres: No.

Q: On any particular fight event that you attend, do you have any responsibilities vis-à-vis any of the athletic commission personnel who are in attendance?

Torres: No, not that I know.

One might argue that it made sense to delay release of the inspector general's report until after Melvina Lathan was replaced as NYSAC chairperson. That way, she wouldn't be the one commenting on it on behalf of the commission. But the delay in releasing the report—and it still hasn't been released—is helping to perpetuate a system in which old mistakes are now being repeated.

Once again, there's friction between the chairman of the New York State Athletic Commission (Tom Hoover) and its executive director

(David Berlin). Once again, protocols are breaking down. A lot of the good work that Berlin did is being undone.

Multiple sources say that the inspector general's office has resumed its inquiry to look at some of the difficulties that have arisen since Hoover assumed the chairmanship last year.

If the inspector general's report had been released in a timely manner and its recommendations acted upon, the current extension of its investigation might not have been necessary.

Despite its faults, the NYSAC is one of the better-run state athletic commissions in the country. It has many dedicated, conscientious, knowledgeable employees.

But the NYSAC can and should do a better job. And that job is about to get tougher because the state legislature, after years of debate, seems poised to legalize mixed martial arts (MMA) in New York. That will add new responsibilities to a commission that is still coming to grips with how to best regulate boxing and has few, if any, personnel qualified to deal with MMA.

The proposed legislation would also increase the number of NYSAC commissioners from three to five. Whether these openings will be filled by qualified professionals or political patronage employees is an open issue.

Keith Sullivan (an attorney with a full-time legal practice) serves as a deputy commissioner for the New York State Athletic Commission. Talking with investigators from the inspector general's office about the Abdusalamov tragedy, Sullivan said, "You can criticize the ref, the doctor, the inspector, the cornermen. I think this is going to happen in the sport of boxing from time to time. It's boxing, it's not ballet. You're agreeing to let somebody punch you repeatedly in the head. It happens."

But Sullivan, who has long been an advocate for fighters, was moved by the horror of it all.

"I didn't think I was going to get emotional," Sullivan told investigators at one point when his voice broke. "It was a good tough fight. Ten rounds. We sat there being entertained. Those who watched and those who cheered. They were entertained. It's just hard to—it's just sad. I'm embarrassed to say that it was a good fight. It was an entertaining fight. You think of the Romans and people dying in colosseums, and it's sick that people cheered and got entertained by that. And that's sort of a little bit about how I feel about this fight."

It's unfortunate that more people in leadership roles in boxing don't show the same emotional investment regarding the welfare of fighters that Keith Sullivan does.

Meanwhile, it would be fantasy to imagine that New York governor Andrew Cuomo pays much attention to the New York State Athletic Commission. Perhaps he should. The lives of fighters are at risk.

"We know that Al likes boxers," I said to promoter Richard Schaefer. "Does he like boxing?" There was a long pause. Then Schaefer answered, "That's a very interesting question. I think that Al likes boxers far more than he likes boxing."

What We Know about Al Haymon

PART ONE

Shortly before a March 7, 2015, fight card in Las Vegas, Al Haymon did something that was totally out of character. He made a speech.

For months on end, the boxing community had buzzed with rumors: Haymon was amassing a war chest totaling hundreds of millions of dollars with the help of a venture capital fund in an effort to take over boxing . . . Haymon was signing hundreds of fighters to managerial and advisory contracts . . . Haymon was planning some sort of TV series . . . Time buys on multiple networks for an entity called Premier Boxing Champions (PBC) were confirmed.

March 7 marked the rollout of Haymon's plan. NBC was televising the inaugural PBC offering; a fight card featuring Keith Thurman vs. Robert Guerrero and Adrien Broner vs. John Molina Jr.

Haymon had poured an enormous amount of money into TV production for the event. There was a huge floor set augmented by giant video screens. Twenty-seven cameras had been set up to capture the action from every possible angle under enhanced lighting.

Three iconic sports personalities formed the core of the NBC announcing team. Al Michaels would host the telecast from a glitzy in-arena set, while Marv Albert handled blow-by-blow chores and Sugar Ray Leonard served as an expert analyst. Laila Ali, B. J. Flores, Kenny Rice, and Steve Smoger were also in the mix.

Academy Award winner Hans Zimmer, who had written screen scores for *The Lion King, Gladiator,* and *The Dark Night Trilogy* (as well as the signature music for *The Contender*) had composed special ring-walk music for the fighters.

Al Haymon was challenging the established order of boxing.

The final production meeting for the telecast was held in a meeting room at the MGM Grand.

"Al came in," a member of the production team recalls, "There were fifteen or twenty people there. He talked to us about the importance of boxing and his desire to revive interest in the sport. He said that everyone in the room should think of themselves as part of a team. He didn't talk for long, only a couple of minutes. But he seemed sincere, like this really mattered to him."

The NBC telecast averaged 3.37 million viewers, including 554,000 in the 18-to-34-year-old age group and 1.38 million in the 18-to-49 demographic. It was an encouraging start for an audacious plan. Backed by an estimated half billion dollars in venture capital, Haymon was planning to revolutionize boxing.

Boxing people were excited or terrified depending on where their interests lay. To some, Haymon was a savior who would rejuvenate the sport and bring big fights back to "free" television on a regular basis. At the other end of the spectrum, the reaction ranged from denial to panic.

Haymon was creating a sense of inevitability. PBC would dominate boxing for years.

Except it hasn't happened. And in all likelihood, it won't happen.

Winston Churchill once said of Russia, "It is a riddle wrapped in a mystery inside an enigma."

The same words could be used to describe Al Haymon. This series is an attempt to shed some light on who he is and his journey through boxing. Dozens of people who know Haymon in one way or another were interviewed in conjunction with these articles. Some were willing to talk on the understanding that they could be quoted but not for attribution. A refrain often heard from others was, "I'd like to talk with you, but I don't want to get in trouble with Al." Haymon, as is his custom, declined to be interviewed.

Haymon was born on April 21, 1955, grew up in Cleveland, and graduated from John Adams High School in 1973. Don King graduated from the same school in 1951. King recalls that Haymon's father was a clergyman and that the promoter made occasional financial contributions to the latter's church programs.

Haymon's mother was an accountant. In a rare 1994 interview with *Ebony Men*, Al recalled, "She was a role model for me to follow because she had built a small business, an accounting practice. It was very successful, and it was hers."

Haymon excelled in high school and went to college at Harvard, where he was on the freshman basketball and varsity rifle teams. He majored in economics and was president of North House (one of twelve undergraduate residences). He was also active in the Afro-American Cultural Center. He promoted his first concert in 1976 during his junior year at Harvard.

Recounting that experience for *Ebony Men*, Haymon recalled, "I saw a concert that featured Minnie Riperton and Herb Hancock in 1975 between my sophomore and junior years. It seemed like something a person like myself, who had absolutely no money at the time and a lot of ideas, could venture into. So I started calling record companies, calling buildings around town, and trying to introduce myself as a promoter so I could learn about the business and try to find out what was going to be my strategy to enter it. My original plan was to go after acts that weren't hotly pursued by much bigger competitors. I started with jazz artists. It was difficult because I didn't have any money. I was basically hustling, pulling money together for these events, and learning at the same time."

Haymon graduated from Harvard College in 1977. He took a year off from school and, with the help of his mother, continued to build his concert-promotion business. Then he returned to Harvard and, in 1980, graduated from Harvard Business School with a master's degree in business administration.

In the years that followed, Haymon created more than a dozen companies to coordinate production, advertising, marketing, and virtually every other facet of live concert promotion. He made his mark with national tours for superstars like Whitney Houston, Janet Jackson, M. C. Hammer, and Boyz II Men and co-promoted "Eddie Murphy Raw," which was the highest-grossing comedy tour and centerpiece of the highest-grossing comedy film ever up until that time. In 1992, he told *USA Today* that, during the previous year, he'd promoted approximately five hundred shows that had grossed $60 million.

Haymon is a complex man. People who've done business with him for years know next to nothing about his personal life (which is even more under the radar than his professional one).

"I have no idea how Al processes emotion," one business associate says. "His tone of voice changes when he's angry, but that's the only sign I've seen."

By all accounts, Haymon is devoted to his mother, who still lives in Cleveland. He visits her often and treats her well. When one talks with people who've done business with him, the following portrait emerges.

"Brilliant . . . Ambitious . . . Driven . . . A good listener and observer . . . He soaks things up and synthesizes information well . . . Always two or three steps ahead of everyone else."

"Persuasive . . . Patient . . . Calculating . . . Manipulative . . . Extremely well guarded."

"Sophisticated . . . Charismatic . . . Gracious and charming when he wants to be . . . Good at complimenting people in the little time he spends with them and making them feel good about themselves."

Haymon is health conscious, eats a lot of chicken and vegetables, and drinks cranberry juice mixed with club soda. "He isn't a let's go out for dinner together kind of guy," says someone who has done business with him for years.

He likes classic old movies and good contemporary ones.

In 2002, he established a non-profit corporation called The Black College Scholarship Fund.

Federal election records list Haymon as having contributed money to several Democratic candidates.

He sold the bulk of his concert promotion business to SFX Entertainment in 1999. Then he cast an eye toward boxing.

Haymon's business plan for Premier Boxing Champions is as tightly guarded as a nation's nuclear codes. What's known is that he now conducts his boxing business through a web of corporate entities with different assets, liabilities, and functions. These entities include Haymon Boxing LLC, Haymon Sports LLC, Haymon Holdings LLC, and Alan Haymon Development Inc.

He has a talent for making people he does business with feel that they're close to him at a given point in time. But except for a core group—Sylvia Browne, Brad Owens, Sam Watson, and Mike Ring—they aren't.

Browne has been with Haymon since he was in business school in the late 1970s. She's smart, loyal, and does much of his administrative work. "Al trusts Sylvia more than he trusts any other person on earth outside of his mother," one business associate says.

Owens is Browne's husband and handles myriad logistical chores for Haymon.

Watson interacts with Haymon's fighters on a regular basis and does what he can as Al's representative to keep them happy.

Ring, an attorney, functions as Haymon's de facto chief of staff and interfaces with providers of venture capital, televison networks, and other business allies.

When Haymon has a target in the crosshairs of his mind, he's incredibly focused. He pushes relationships to the brink when negotiating and has a way of leaving people afraid that, if they don't do what he wants, they're out. But he knows how to close a deal.

Brian Kweder ran ESPN's boxing program as senior director of programming and acquisitions from late 2013 through January 2016. He's now a part-time consultant for Haymon.

"Boxing has its share of swindlers, liars, and thieves," Kweder says. "Al's word might be hard to get out of him. But once he gives it, he lives up to it. He always kept his word with me."

There's a marked contrast between Haymon's enormous influence in boxing and his studied ghostlike presence. It would be wrong to say that he stays in the background. In most instances, he's not even in the picture.

Haymon has an aversion to being interviewed by the media and operates largely out of public view. Like a master puppeteer, he pulls strings but seldom allows himself to be seen. He never wanted to be a public figure. Decades ago, he told *Ebony Men*, "I'm not trying to be a star. I'm trying to be a businessman."

Tim Struby noted in a recent profile for *Playboy* that Haymon "shuns publicity and attention like a vampire avoids sunlight." Very few photographs of him are available. On those rare occasions when someone gets close enough to ask for a selfie, Haymon's standard response is, "It's nice to meet you, but I don't take pictures."

As for the fights themselves, Haymon rarely watches from ringside, preferring to view the action from a private box or in an office inside the arena on a TV monitor.

Leon Margules, who promotes fights for Haymon, acknowledges, "Sometimes I see Al onsite when I promote one of his shows; sometimes I don't. I know he's there."

"Al values his privacy," Margules adds. "He doesn't even like it when people tell nice stories about him."

Haymon's aversion to publicity feeds into a collateral issue. He often seems scornful of and even hostile toward the media, particularly the boxing media.

Haymon has an absolute right to not give interviews. But he has gone beyond that. For example, very few members of the boxing media were invited to the January 14, 2015, press conference at NBC that launched Premier Boxing Champions.

Dan Rafael, perhaps the most widely read boxing journalist in the world, was among the uninvited. "I know Al doesn't like me," Rafael says. "And that's fine. There are people I don't like either. But I do my job as best I can and expect that basic professional courtesy will be extended to me. And I don't get that from Al."

Greg Bishop, now with *Sports Illustrated*, was on staff at the *New York Times* when he began researching a story on Haymon in 2011. "I tried to introduce myself to him twice," Bishop recalls. "Each time, he said, 'Hey, nice to see you,' and turned away to talk to someone else."

Dozens of people whom Bishop called either declined comment or failed to return his telephone calls. An attorney for Haymon sent a cease-and-desist letter to the *Times* while Bishop was researching his article.

But it's not just the media that finds Haymon elusive. He often pulls people in and pushes them away as serves his purposes.

Jim Thomas is best known in boxing circles as the attorney who guided Evander Holyfield through the most profitable years of Holyfield's ring career.

"I had one dealing with Al," Thomas recalls. "I called him. He answered his cell phone. I said, 'Hi, this is Jim Thomas. I don't know if you know who I am.' And before I could get another word out, Al said,

'How could anyone in boxing not know who Jim Thomas is?' He was very gracious. I told him what I was interested in. Al said, 'Let me look at that and get back to you.' And that was it. I never heard from him again. Al never answered his phone when I called again and none of my calls were ever returned."

Greg Cohen was Austin Trout's promoter when Trout brought Haymon in as an advisor.

"At the beginning, it was good," Cohen says. "Al opened a lot of doors for us at the premium cable networks. Speaking from personal experience, he made me feel as though I was on his team. We only met in person once. That was at the W hotel in Times Square before Austin fought Miguel Cotto at Madison Square Garden [on December 1, 2012]. But we spoke on the phone regularly. Al is accessible when he wants to be. And then it got ugly. The moment Al didn't need me anymore, he cut me off."

"When Al wants you to, you can talk with him," says Gary Shaw, who, in the past, promoted some of Haymon's fighters. "But you can't reach Al when he doesn't want to be reached, and that's extremely frustrating when you're doing business together. You can't even e-mail Al directly. You e-mail Sylvia Browne, who presumably gives the message to Al. But Al can always say he never got it. He makes you feel like a million dollars until he doesn't."

Haymon's unavailability is an instrument of control. He seems to prefer control to equal partnerships.

"Even when I was the promoter of record," Greg Cohen says, "there were times when I felt like a spectator."

"Al is a control freak," says another promoter who has worked extensively with Haymon. "He hates the unexpected, doesn't like to delegate authority, and micromanages every detail. He gets what he wants and does things the way he wants. More than a few times—and I'm paraphrasing now—Al has said to me, 'Look, that's the way it has to be.'"

Given the industries that Haymon is in (television and boxing), there's remarkably little transparency in the way he conducts business. A source with knowledge of the relationship between Haymon and NBC says that NBC executives asked to see the PBC business plan and he declined to show it to them. One NBC executive complained, "He won't give us simple information that two people transacting business together would normally exchange with one another."

Promoters who have worked with Haymon—and in some instances still work with him—voice similar sentiments:

★ "Al doesn't tell you what he doesn't want you to know. And if he doesn't want you to know something, he's pretty good at keeping you from finding out."

★ "In the end, it's Al who puts the pieces together. And the way he sets things up, we don't even know what the pieces are."

★ "Sometimes the only person who knows what Al is doing is Al. And he leaves surprisingly few fingerprints for a man of his influence and power."

★ "If Al's plane went down tomorrow, it would be a mess beyond belief."

Also, there's an interesting contradiction between Haymon's low-profile persona and another aspect of his personality.

"For a guy who obsesses about flying under the radar, Al has a huge ego," one business associate notes. "It's not about what other people think of him. Al couldn't care less what the rest of the world thinks except for the handful of people he respects. It's about what he thinks of himself."

And one more thought to contemplate.

Bela Szilagyi was a concert pianist who loved boxing. He and his wife amassed a video archive of fights that were televised between 1979 and 2015. To supplement their income, they sold copies of the videos to TV networks, promoters, managers, and others who needed to study a particular fighter or fight.

Sylvia Browne and Brad Owens often ordered videos from the Szilagyis. Many of these videos were of prospective opponents for Haymon's fighters. But they also ordered a highlight reel of knockouts followed by victorious fighters proclaiming, "I want to thank Al Haymon."

PART TWO

Al Haymon's first view of boxing was through the eyes of his older brother.

Bobby Haymon was a journeyman welterweight who fought from 1969 through 1978 and compiled a record of 20 wins, 8 losses, and 1 draw with 8 knockouts. In the last fight of his career, he was stopped in three rounds by a young prospect named Sugar Ray Leonard. Al is said to still be resentful over the way his brother was treated by the lords of boxing.

The first fighter that Haymon managed was Vernon Forrest.

It's a long way from those early days to where Al Haymon is today.

The cornerstone of Haymon's empire in boxing was a relationship that evolved with HBO and, in particular, with Kery Davis (the network's point person on boxing from the turn of the millennium until June 2013). Through Davis, Haymon received lucrative paydays for his fighters, sometimes against overmatched opponents. And equally important, HBO allowed Haymon to control the promotional process for many of these fights.

Haymon worked with a half dozen different promoters. But despite their involvement, he often dealt directly with HBO Sports president Ross Greenburg and Davis during contract negotiations while the promoter of record was limited to doing basic nuts-and-bolts work on the fight. Because of his relationship with HBO, Haymon rarely had to give a promoter long-term contractual rights to one of his fighters. The promoter had little more than a handshake and Haymon's word that he had a future with a particular fighter. That gave Haymon enormous leverage over promoters in terms of how income generated from each fight was split. Promoters put up with this arrangement because, over the years, HBO was remarkably generous when giving out dates and paying license fees for fights involving Haymon's fighters.

"The big money in boxing is at the top," says promoter Gary Shaw. "I stood in line like everyone else. Al would say, 'You're my guy on this fighter. No, you can't have that one; someone else is my guy with him.' Then Al would negotiate the deal with HBO and tell the promoter what the promoter was getting paid. And we bought into it because we needed the dates. Meanwhile, I wasn't making money. Al kept telling me, 'Next time, next time.' And next time never came."

Then Haymon settled on a favored promoter (Richard Schaefer of Golden Boy). And Floyd Mayweather, who was a Haymon client, became a superstar. That took things to a new level. Haymon leveraged his Mayweather power to exact further concessions from the premium cable television networks. And he was able to sign fighters from

135 to 154 pounds by telling them, "You're in the Floyd Mayweather sweepstakes."

But Haymon's success wasn't inextricably tied to Mayweather. He was building for a future after "Money" and kept the corporate entities that he controlled largely free of obligations to Floyd. Even today, most things Mayweather are separate and apart from the PBC brand.

The first indication that Haymon was planning to challenge the established order in boxing came when he began signing managerial and advisory contracts with a massive number of fighters. Ironically, when Haymon first aligned with Golden Boy and the promotional company was stepping up efforts to add to its own roster of fighters, Haymon had quipped, "Sometimes Richard and Oscar get that Pac-Man mentality where they have to gobble everything up."

Now Haymon was gobbling everything up; an estimated two hundred fighters.

That was far beyond anything HBO and Showtime could accommodate.

Then Haymon's master plan began to take shape.

On January 14, 2015, NBC announced that it had entered into an agreement providing for twenty Premier Boxing Champions telecasts in 2015 (five on NBC on Saturday nights, six on NBC on Saturday afternoons, and nine in prime time on NBC Sports Network). But it wasn't a traditional licensing-fee deal. Instead, Haymon was buying the time from the network, would be responsible for most costs associated with the telecasts, and would recoup his expenditures as best he could by selling advertising himself.

On January 22, a similar agreement with Spike was announced; only here, Spike was to cover approximately $350,000 in expenses in conjunction with each telecast.

The announcement of time buys on CBS (February 17), Bounce TV (March 2), and ESPN (March 18) followed.

The ESPN deal was a $16 million time buy that ran over a two-year period with Haymon having an option to extend the contract for another six months for an additional $4 million. The shows were to run in prime time on ESPN with at least two Saturday afternoon shows on ABC. ESPN would foot the bill for production.

The ESPN deal was particularly significant for two reasons. First, ESPN is a pipeline to the brain of virtually every sports fan in America. And second, it meant that the long-running *ESPN2 Friday Night Fights* series would end.

On August 4, Fox Sports announced an agreement pursuant to which Premier Boxing Champions would be the exclusive boxing provider for Fox Sports 1. There were to be twenty-one Tuesday-night shows from September 8 through June 28, 2016, with the shows being simulcast on Fox Deportes. On October 18, 2015, Fox announced that there would be three prime-time Premier Boxing Champions telecasts on its broadcast network in 2016 (January 23, March 12, and July 16).

At this point, Haymon had more networks than some promoters have fighters. And he'd established a sweetheart relationship with Showtime, which was continuing to pay substantial license fees for Haymon fights (although without PBC branding).

The time buys allowed Haymon to bypass normal media filters in delivering his boxing programming to the public. He no longer had to cajole network television executives into giving him dates. He simply bought them.

Meanwhile, Haymon was also spending on other fronts.

On March 10, 2015, Warriors Boxing (a stand-in for Haymon) won a purse bid for the IBF 168-pound title fight between James DeGale and Andre Dirrell for a far-above-market bid of $3.1 million. That signaled PBC's intention to control title bouts for its fighters whenever possible.

At the same time, Haymon reached out through an intermediary to make a two-year contract offer to Michael Buffer. The proposed deal would have been exclusive insofar as Buffer's boxing work was concerned. The Hall of Fame ring announcer would attend approximately twenty-four Premier Boxing Champions shows per year, tape announcements for others, and allow Haymon to use his "let's get ready to rumble" trademark in conjunction with the promotion of PBC telecasts. In return, Buffer would receive $1 million for the first year of the contract and $1.1 million for the second.

Then the offer was withdrawn. A source close to the situation says that the idea was nixed in deference to Showtime, which felt Buffer was too closely associated in the public mind with HBO and that the deal would marginalize Jimmy Lennon (Showtime's own ring announcer).

Haymon signs fighters to an "Exclusive Management Agreement" that gives him the exclusive right to render services in securing the boxer's participation in professional boxing matches, exhibitions, entertainment performances, personal appearances, endorsements, and sponsorship opportunities that arise out of the fighter's boxing career.

In return, Haymon is required to (a) use his "best efforts" to secure remunerative boxing matches for the boxer; (b) advise and counsel the boxer in the overall development of his career; (c) secure proper training facilities and equipment for the boxer; (d) publicize and promote the talents and abilities of the boxer in the media; and (e) attempt to secure commercial endorsements, personal appearances, and entertainment opportunites for the boxer.

Haymon often charges 10 or 15 percent of a fighter's purse for his services. That's less than the standard manager's share. Sometimes, he'll pay an advance (or interest-free loan) to a fighter and only cut the fighter's purse after the purse reaches a certain level. The advance (or loan) is paid back only when the purses reach a still-higher number.

Many of Haymon's recent contracts purport to be for a five-year term with Haymon having the option to extend the contract for two more years if the fighter competes in a WBC, WBA, IBF, or WBO world championship fight. The contract further provides that the term may be "additionally" extended if the fighter becomes one of the five highest-rated contenders for a championship sanctioned by the WBC, WBA, IBF, or WBO. Another clause provides for one more two-year extension if the fighter "enters into a multifight agreement with any television network." The contract concedes that some or all of these extensions can be invalidated if they're found to be in violation of state or federal law.

Haymon is widely regarded as "pro-fighter." His fighters are paid well, often above market value.

"Al puts his fighters first," says Paulie Malignaggi. "No one puts the fighters first like Al. I don't know a single fighter who's unhappy with Al. I know I have no complaints with the way Al has treated me."

As earlier noted, Haymon has approximately two hundred boxers under contract. Fighters can be difficult to satisfy. No matter how good a job a manager or promoter does, there are complaints. But there have been virtually no complaints regarding Haymon's stewardship from the fighters he controls.

"Acts want to be promoted properly," Haymon told *Ebony Men* in 1994. "They want to be exposed to the masses. They want professional productions and proper presentation. I always focused on making sure the artists got what they needed and that they were satisfied and sufficiently taken care of to go out and represent to other artists that I had done a good job because that's the best reference."

"Everything that Al promised to me, he delivered," Floyd Mayweather said last year.

Don King and 50 Cent each took runs at separating Mayweather from Haymon and failed.

"If I was one of Haymon's fighters," says a rival promoter, "I'd think he's Santa Claus. I understand why the fighters love him."

It's nice that a capable businessman is representing the best interests of fighters. But it would be wrong to think that Haymon is Mother Teresa. The truth is more nuanced than that.

"I hear all the time that Al is an advocate for what's best for fighters," Greg Bishop of *Sports Illustrated* says. "What happened to Lamon Brewster stands in stark contrast to that."

On April 10, 2004, Brewster knocked out Wladimir Klitschko to become WBO heavyweight champion. His manager at the time was Sam Simon. Then Haymon came calling.

"Haymon wasn't the power in boxing then that he would become," Simon said several years ago. "But his modus operandi was pretty much the same. He sought Lamon out and told him, 'Hey, brother. You look like you could use some good representation from someone who cares about you.'"

Before long, Brewster had left Simon. His initial contract with Haymon called for Alan Haymon Development Inc. to receive 7 percent of the first $2 million of each purse and 5 percent thereafter.

Simon was independently wealthy. He had provided Brewster with a house to live in rent-free during the time that he was Lamon's manager. And he intended to be supportive of Brewster when the fighter's ring career was done.

On Haymon's watch, Brewster suffered a detached retina in his left eye in the first round of an unsuccessful April 1, 2006, title defense against Sergei Liakhovich in Cleveland. But that doesn't tell the whole story. Yes, Brewster suffered a detached retina during the fight. But his eye had been injured before the bout. He'd undergone laser eye surgery several weeks prior to the fight, and the eye had continued to trouble him.

Boxers who compete in Ohio are required to have an ophthalmic examination prior to the fight. "I have the form right in front of me," Bernie Profato (executive director of the Ohio State Athletic Commission) told this writer five days after Brewster-Liakhovich.

The form revealed that, on March 24, 2006, Brewster was given an ophthalmic examination by Dr. Thomas Anthony Baudo in Vero Beach, Florida. Baudo filled out a form entitled "Ophthalmological Exam for Professional Boxer." On that form, under a heading that read "specify abnormalities," he wrote that Brewster had undergone surgery for a ret- inal tear and detachment but that his eye was now "stable." Baudo also wrote, "Mr. Brewster understands the increased risk of RD [retinal dam- age] when boxing."

In accordance with Ohio law, Brewster also underwent a general pre- fight physical examination prior to receiving his license. The "Physical Examination Report" for that exam included three questions under the heading "Eye History." It asked if the applicant (1) had ever experienced blurred vision or (2) ever had a surgical procedure on his eyes or the tissue around his eyes other than simple sutures to the skin around the eyes. And it specifically asked (3), "Has applicant ever been informed by a physician that he had significant eye problems such as a retinal detachment, retinal tear, or dislocated lens?"

In each instance, the answer Brewster gave on this examination form was "no." His history of retinal surgery was covered up.

Haymon, as noted in Part One of this series, is known for microman- aging. It strains credibility to believe that he wasn't aware of Brewster's eye problems. Yet one year later, Haymon sent Brewster to Germany for his next bout to fight a July 7, 2007, rematch against Wladimir Klitschko while Lamon was still on medical suspension in the United States. Two of Brewster's sparring partners told Keith Idec of the *New Jersey Herald News* that, prior to fighting Klitschko, Brewster was having difficulty seeing out of his left eye.

Brewster lost every minute of the Klitschko rematch, which was stopped after six rounds. He ended his career as a punching bag for the likes of Gbenga Okoukon and Robert Helenius. He's now in financial difficulty and legally blind in one eye.

As Haymon's power has grown, his adversaries have alleged with increasing frequency that his conduct violates federal and state law. The first statute cited in that regard is often the Muhammad Ali Boxing Reform Act.

The Ali Act creates a firewall between managers and promoters. A manager is defined by the act as "a person who receives compensation for service as an agent or representative of a boxer." A promoter is defined as "the person primarily responsible for organizing, promoting, and producing a professional boxing match." The act makes it "unlawful for a manager (i) to have a direct or indirect financial interest in the promotion of a boxer; or (ii) to be employed or receive compensation or other benefits from a promoter, except for amounts received as consideration under the manager's contract with the boxer."

Haymon purports to be a manager. But he functions as the de facto promoter for virtually all of the shows on which his fighters appear. He negotiates with the television networks, selects most of the fighters who appear on the card, determines purses for the featured fighters, and tells the promoter of record how much the promoter will be paid.

"I don't know how much money was raised; I don't know how much money was spent; and I don't care," Leon Margules said of a recent PBC card for which he was the promoter of record. "That's Al's job."

One can argue that the Ali Act was designed to protect fighters and thus, Haymon's blurring of the line between managing and promoting is inconsequential. Other legal issues are more problematic.

Haymon seems to be engaging in some of the same questionable practices as other managers and promoters.

For example, Keith Thurman's purse as reported to the Florida State Athletic Commission in conjunction with his July 11, 2015, PBC fight against Luis Collazo was $1,500,000. But Thurman told Dan Rafael of ESPN.com that Haymon gave him a check for an additional $1,200,000.

The purses filed with the New Jersey State Athletic Control Board for the August 15, 2015, PBC fight between Antonio Tarver and Steve Cunningham were listed as $250,000 for each fighter. But Tarver is said to have received a total of $500,000. And a source close to Cunningham says that the fighter was paid an additional $100,000 as an advance.

Haymon isn't the first person in boxing to be mentioned in conjunction with differing sets of contracts and inaccurate filings with state athletic commissions. But if an inaccurate filing occurs, the tax consequences can be significant. And it might affect payments to third parties based on contract percentage splits.

The antitrust issues that surround Premier Boxing Champions are more consequential.

Talking about the American economy in 1960, John F. Kennedy declared, "A rising tide lifts all boats." But the PBC tide is threatening to sink many of them.

Haymon's time buys have changed boxing's economic model and made it increasingly difficult for mid-level promoters to survive. They can develop a prospect to the point where he's 12-and-0, and then there's virtually nowhere they can go to get him on television. Even larger promoters like Main Events lack the resources to buy time on attractive platforms. In the United States, only HBO and Showtime are paying significant license fees for fights. And Showtime does business primarily with Haymon.

In sum, Haymon is changing the structure of the marketplace in a way that's threatening to drive out competing promoters.

He has also been poaching fighters.

Cameron Dunkin manages Terence Crawford. He has lost several fighters to Haymon, including Leo Santa Cruz and Mikey Garcia.

"It's a constant battle to hold onto your fighters," Dunkin says. "Haymon has his guys whispering in their ear, 'Danny Garcia is making more money than you are because he's with Al, and you're better than Danny Garcia. Al is flying his fighters around in a private jet.' All I can tell my guys is, 'Stay with me. If you do your job in the ring, I'll get you on HBO. HBO isn't going to disappear and Haymon might.'"

"Haymon is screwing up the marketplace," Pat English (the attorney for Main Events) says. "That's for sure."

On July 1, 2015, Top Rank (Bob Arum's promotional company) filed suit in the United States District Court for the Central District of California against Haymon, three companies controlled by Haymon, Waddell & Reed (which has supplied the venture capital for Haymon), and one of Waddell & Reed's affiliated companies. The suit alleged violations of the Sherman Antitrust Act, Clayton Antitrust Act, Muhammad Ali Boxing Reform Act, and various California state statutes.

An October 16, 2015, court order dropped the Waddell & Reed defendants from the lawsuit and dismissed many of the claims against the Haymon defendants with leave to amend. On January 6, 2015, the court ruled that Top Rank's amended complaint was sufficient to survive a motion to dismiss and ordered that the litigation proceed to the discovery stage.

On May 5, 2015, Golden Boy and Bernard Hopkins filed a separate lawsuit, also in the United States District Court for the Central District of California, against Haymon, various companies that Haymon controls, Waddell & Reed, and Ryan Caldwell (a former Waddell & Reed fund manager). In late June 2015, Golden Boy dropped Waddell & Reed as a defendant in its lawsuit.

Counsel for Top Rank and Golden Boy have been coordinating their efforts.

Top Rank has served discovery demands on the Haymon defendants and close to a dozen other individuals and corporate entities including Waddell & Reed, Ryan Caldwell, Richard Schaefer, and several local promoters that Haymon has been using to promote PBC events. Similar requests for discovery from the television networks that Haymon has been doing business with are expected shortly. To date, Top Rank's discovery demands (and those of Golden Boy) have been met by a laundry list of objections with the apparent aim of delaying, if not outright obstructing, discovery.

A source close to Haymon says, "So far, Al is resisting discovery. But if discovery really goes forward, he's going to go after every piece of paper that involves Top Rank's relationship with Manny Pacquiao. Al takes pride in the fact that his representation of Mayweather is the antithesis of the way Arum has dealt with Pacquiao. And yes, I know that Arum is Pacquiao's promoter, not his manager, so he has a different fiduciary duty.

But that doesn't relieve him of the obligation to give Pacquiao an honest accounting. And by the way; why should Michael Koncz [Pacquiao's business advisor] get a free pass?"

This could get ugly.[1]

Meanwhile, the reaction of many in boxing to the ghostlike presence of Al Haymon brings to mind words written by Hughes Mearns more than a century ago:

> Yesterday upon the stair
> I met a man who wasn't there
> He wasn't there again today
> I wish, I wish he'd go away

PART THREE

The consensus is that Al Haymon is pro-fighter. Whether he's pro-investor is a separate issue.

Haymon has gotten to where he is in boxing by making alliances with bankers. His first banker was HBO Sports. Showtime filled the void when that relationship ended. Now he has found venture capitalists who are willing to underwrite his plans on an extravagant scale.

Haymon believed that, unlike most sports, boxing can be transformed by a drop in the ocean of water that flows through the venture capital market every day. His plan is based on the premise that there's a hidden audience for boxing that will watch fights on "free" television in numbers large enough to generate profitable ad sales. In furtherance of this idea, he pursued venture capital from myriad sources and got it from an asset management company called Waddell & Reed.

Bill King of *Sports Business Journal* began the process of publicly fleshing out the financial muscle behind Haymon's plans with an analysis of Premier Boxing Champions that was posted on April 20, 2015.

"The struggle began with finding out who to contact in the first place," King recalls. "You can't just call Al. I went to the first PBC press

---

[1] The Top Rank and Golden Boy lawsuits against the Haymon entities were subsequently dismissed; Top Rank's pursuant to a settlement with Haymon and Golden Boy's by court order.

conference in New York [on January 14, 2015] which was for a show on NBC. There was a guy from Chicago who was listed as a PR contact, so I e-mailed him. And Ryan Caldwell [of Waddell & Reed] was at the press conference, so I started doing research on him."

"My pitch to them," King explains, "was if PBC is going to be on network TV, we're a vehicle for you to improve your credibility with network executives and advertisers. And we have a reputation for splitting things down the middle rather than taking sides. Finally, I was told, 'Come to the first PBC event [in Las Vegas on March 7, 2015] and someone will talk with you.' My request was to talk with Al, but they said that was unlikely. And Al wouldn't talk with me. All I got from him was a hello and a handshake to acknowledge that he knew who I was."

"I had to do a lot of digging to get the financials," King continues. "There's a lot more available now than there was then. Ryan Caldwell agreed to discuss the venture with me but declined to reveal financials."

King based some of his research on quarterly filings with the Securities Exchange Commission made by an entity called the Ivy Asset Strategy Fund that Caldwell co-managed for Waddell & Reed. The Ivy Asset Strategy Fund included among its holdings an investment designated as "Media Group Holdings LLC, Series H" that King confirmed was with Haymon.

"Ivy Asset Strategy's holdings list," King wrote in *Sports Business Journal*, "included a $371.3 million investment in the company. A second Waddell fund, WRA Asset Strategy, listed an investment of $42.2 million. A third fund, Ivy Funds VIP Asset Strategy, showed holdings of $18.5 million. Together they invested $432 million. It is likely other funds run by Waddell also have invested, although their positions likely would be smaller."

King also revealed, "While Caldwell would not discuss funding specifically, he said that Waddell & Reed invested considerably more than Haymon requested in the initial business plan to build a brand and an audience, a proof-of-concept phase that would then enable him to cash in on the rights fees that continue to trend upward across sports."

"Al said, 'I think I can pull this off for X,'" Caldwell told King. "And I turned around and said, 'Absolutely not. It's X-plus or we don't do it.' You have to be capitalized for three to five years to do this, to weather the storm. Because in some regards, you're going to be the irrational player for a while. You're turning the model completely upside down."

Haymon is paying unusually large purses to fighters. That in and of itself is not a problem. HBO paid above-market license fees to promoters for years to lure fights away from ABC, CBS, and NBC. George Steinbrenner paid above-market salaries to free agents to reestablish the New York Yankees dynasty. You spend money to make money.

That said, a conflict of interest seems to be built into Haymon's methodology. He has a fiduciary duty to the fighters he manages to get them the most money possible. But he also has a fiduciary duty to his investors to cap expenses and maximize their return on investment. After all, this isn't business as usual, but it is business. The idea is to make money for the investors. And right now, Premier Boxing Champions appears to be hemorrhaging money, not making it.

Haymon assumed that income from Premier Boxing Champions telecasts would come initially from multiple sources, including advertising, ticket sales, sponsorships, and license fees for foreign rights. His managerial fee is also believed to be part of the revenue stream for investors.

More importantly, Haymon predicted that, after the time buys end, television networks will pay significant license fees for PBC fights. At the moment, that prospect looks bleak.

On May 11, 1977, 48 million viewers watched Ken Norton defeat Duane Bobick in a fight televised by NBC. Four months later, Muhammad Ali triumped over Earnie Shavers in a bout seen by almost 100 million people. Those days are long gone. But even in today's fractured digital environment, PBC's ratings have been a disappointment.

PBC's March 7, 2015, debut telecast on NBC headlined by Keith Thurman vs. Robert Guerrero averaged 3.37 million viewers. That's a good number, but it soon tapered off. When Deontay Wilder fought Johann Duhaupas on NBC in prime time on September 26, 2015, there were 2.18 million viewers. *Sports Media Watch* noted that this was the smallest audience for a prime-time boxing or MMA event on network television since 2008, a period that included twenty-five telecasts.

Carlos Acevedo further analyzed the numbers and suggested, "Compare that to *American Ninja Warrior*, which aired on NBC two weeks earlier and drew over six million viewers."

Ratings for Premier Boxing Champions telecasts on CBS, ESPN, Spike, Bounce, and Fox have also disappointed.

CBS has yet to match the 1.6 million average viewership that Adonis Stevenson vs. Sakio Bika engendered in its initial PBC telecast on April 4, 2015.

When Keith Thurman returned to the airwaves against Luis Collazo on July 11, 2015, to inaugurate PBC boxing on ESPN, the telecast averaged 799,000 viewers.

Spike's first PBC telecast (Andre Berto vs. Josesito Lopez on March 13, 2015) was also its highest rated, drawing an average of 869,000 viewers. The eight PBC telecasts on Spike since then have fallen short of that mark, hitting bottom with Andrzej Fonfara vs. Nathan Cleverly (315,000 viewers) on October 16, 2015. The *Los Angeles Times* reported that Spike's PBC numbers were below the numbers for the same Friday-evening slot in 2014, when the network televised Bellator mixed martial arts and reruns of *Cops*.

The ratings for PBC telecasts on Fox Sports 1 have been mediocre, cratering with a February 2, 2016, telecast that averaged 76,000 viewers.

Broadcast television networks and most cable channels are in the business of selling advertising. They contract for time buys when their marketing department says it can't sell enough ads to make particular programming profitable. In a sense, the time buys are a substitute for bulk ad sales.

As noted by Bill King, the most logical way for Haymon to sell ad time across so many networks is to have one group coordinate the selling. That way, there aren't six different networks competing against one another to sell the same product.

In that regard, King reported, "To approach the broader sports sponsorship community, PBC hired SJX Partners to create integrated packages that include spots during fights, branding on the ring, digital assets, tickets, and hospitality, a package rare in boxing because it has been off advertiser-supported TV for so long. PBC also brought in Bruce Binkow, former chief operating officer of Golden Boy Promotions, to advise it on operational matters and maintain relationships with brands already in the sport."

But it has been a hard sell.

Sports seasons have expanded and are continuing to expand. The Super Bowl is now played in February. The World Series routinely extends into November. If the 2016 NBA finals go the distance, the final game will be contested on June 19. And the TV calendar is filled with other high-profile events in sports like tennis and golf. That means there's no time when boxing is alone on the stage. And advertisers have limited budgets.

It's easy for TV networks to sell advertising for NFL programming. Ditto for other major sports and events like the Masters and Wimbledon. Advertising for boxing is a hard sell. Ratings are low. Many advertisers don't want their product associated with the less savory aspects of the sport. And there's another problem. In most sports, advertisers don't have to worry about two-minute knockouts. In boxing, at any moment— BOOM—the fight might end. This contingency makes boxing compelling programming for premium cable networks that are built on subscriptions. But it's a problem for networks that rely on advertising.

Haymon now has the burden of selling advertising for programming that advertisers have resisted for decades. On February 3, 2016, the *Los Angeles Times* reported, "Television advertising tracking firm Kantar Media said [PBC] collected $12.5 million in total ad revenue from 27 fight telecasts from March through September [2015], an average of $462,963 per show."

That's a low number.

Moreover, every successful sport sells tickets for its live events and makes good money from those sales. For PBC, on-site ticket sales seem to be an afterthought. PBC sometimes even loses money on the venue once the cost of opening the arena is set against ticket receipts.

"'PBC' could stand for 'Premier Boxing Comps,'" Steve Kim wrote last year in commenting on Haymon's practice of giving away tickets to paper the house and employing seat-filling services.

To that, promoter Gary Shaw adds, "They've given away so many free tickets to paper the house that it's become increasingly hard for the rest of us to sell tickets because people are waiting for freebies."

Meanwhile, the value of Waddell & Reed's investment in Haymon's boxing entities is shrinking.

Filings with the Securities Exchange Commission suggest that a total of $528,481,000 was made available to Haymon. As of December 31,

2015, that investment was valued at $82,354,000—a drop of 84 percent in investment value.

Richard Schaefer understands venture capital and boxing. Also, the former Swiss banker and one-time CEO of Golden Boy Enterprises has worked closely with Haymon in the past.

"I see the numbers," Schaefer acknowledges. "People say, 'Al has spent three hundred million dollars. Al has spent four hundred million dollars.' But those numbers don't mean the money has been spent. Those numbers are valuations of the assets. Assets can be valued in different ways. Assets can be written down for tax purposes. The value of a [non-monetary] asset like good will can change over time. Come on; four hundred million dollars? You can't spend that kind of money, not even in boxing."

In other words, the initial $528 million number could have included non-monetary assets such as fighter contracts and the value of the PBC brand. And the $82 million figure could reflect a downward evaluation of these non-monetary assets in addition to a lessening of cash on hand.

That said, the $82 million valuation as of December 31, 2015, is presumed to be less than what Haymon has spent so far. There has been a significant cash burn. A war chest that was intended to underwrite PBC's operation for three or four years has dramatically diminished. And there are no offsetting revenue streams in sight.

Meanwhile, as reported by the *Wall Street Journal,* Waddell & Reed has "hit a rough patch." Investors have withdrawn billions of dollars from its funds, and Waddell & Reed stock has dropped from a twelve-month high of $51.23 to $25.79 a share as of March 17, 2016.

Bob Arum calls Premier Boxing Champions "boxing's version of a Bernard Madoff Ponzi scheme" and has bemoaned the "fact" that "widows and orphans are losing their life savings in this horrible horrible scheme."

That characterization seems a bit extreme. Moreover, it's likely that Haymon's business plan warned investors that the venture was highly speculative and that they could lose all of their investment.

Still, if hundreds of millions of dollars disappear, not all of the investors will go quietly. An investors suit against Waddell & Reed and the Haymon entities at some point in the future is possible.

Neither Haymon nor any of the companies under his control have stated publicly how he is compensated for his work.

The role of Ryan Caldwell, who left Waddell & Reed last year to join Haymon as chief operating officer of PBC and then departed from PBC soon after to form his own asset management company is also subject to conjecture.

On February 5, 2016, a New York lawyer named Jake Zamansky sent out a press release announcing that his law firm was "investigating the departure of Mr. Caldwell [from Waddell & Reed] and whether the funds breached duties owed to shareholders."

Zamansky sounds like a lawyer looking for a plaintiff for a possible class action lawsuit.

It's not uncommon for an innovative entrepreneur to believe that the prevailing logic in an industry is wrong and should be challenged. Sometimes the entrepreneur is right in that thinking, is wildly successful under a new set of rules, and makes hundreds of millions of dollars. And sometimes the entrepreneur fails.

Meanwhile, it's worth considering the thoughts of a promoter who has been watching Haymon for years:

"I'm not an investment analyst, but I know how to count. And so far, the numbers don't add up. Forget about making a profit. I don't think Haymon's investors will get their money back. Everyone agrees that Al isn't stupid. He's very smart; a lot smarter than I am. So why is this happening? Follow the money."

PART FOUR

On May 20, 2015, NBC Sports Group chairman Mark Lazarus, CBS Sports president Sean McManus, Fox Sports president Eric Shank, and ESPN president John Skipper discussed the future of broadcast sports in a forum moderated by Richard Deitsch of *Sports Illustrated*. During the Q&A portion of the program, Richard Sandomir of the *New York Times* asked, "For those of you who do and those of you who don't associate with Al Haymon on the PBC, how do you think that strategy is going to play out in terms of building interest for boxing?"

Skipper's answer was direct and to the point: "Last time I checked my XY-axis quadrant, it's not in the right quadrant."

Sports entities are valued as businesses in significant measure based on their television contracts. Right now, PBC's television contracts are showing a lot of red ink. Al Haymon is demonstrating that it's easier to spend money than it is to make it.

As noted earlier, Premier Boxing Champions was built on the premise that there's a much broader audience for boxing than the people who watch it on HBO and Showtime. But so far, PBC has failed to find it. Whatever Haymon's master plan was, it's not working. As Bart Barry recently wrote, "Suddenly boxing is ubiquitous on free television, the last era's Promised Land. And nobody cares."

Why is PBC foundering?

For starters, Haymon has created an environment in which there are few checks and balances on his power. That means, when he makes a mistake, it often goes uncorrected.

Seth Abraham, the architect of HBO Sports, put together a leadership team that included Ross Greenburg, Lou DiBella, and Mark Taffet. There were occasions when Abraham thought one thing and they thought another.

"When that happened," Abraham recalled several years ago, "I'd go into Bryant Park, sit down with a cup of cappucino, and ask myself, 'Why do these very intelligent people have a view that's different than mine?' And often—not always, but often—I'd come around to their view."

"Just because you're the head of a department doesn't mean that you have a monopoly on brains," Abraham continued. "Sometimes you have a monopoly on shortsightedness and stupidity. Leadership is about consensus. If you're the boss, everybody knows that you're in charge and that you have the final vote. But you don't effectively manage an organization by fiat or by ignoring the opinions of the people you've chosen to work with you."

The scheduling of PBC's fights has also been a problem. There's no continuity. The date, time, and network for telecasts are often a mystery until late in the process. "Even boxing people don't know when or where Al's guys are fighting," says promoter Gary Shaw.

Haymon's attitude toward the media has further damaged his cause. He has an absolute right to not talk with the media. But his dismissive stance has been counterproductive.

"Most people in sports who don't communicate with the press have someone who does it for them," ESPN boxing writer Dan Rafael observes. "Al doesn't. You can't get basic facts from PBC, like what weight a fight will be at or how many rounds it will be until they get around to sending it out in some kind of press release. And forget about their communicating with you when you have questions about the larger picture."

Richard Schaefer, who has been one of Haymon's staunchest allies over the years, is in accord.

"I would have dealt more openly with the media," Schaefer says. "A lot of people choose not to talk to the press. Kirk Kerkorian didn't talk to the press. Jerry Perenchio doesn't talk to the press. But they have someone who does it for them. If you don't want to talk to the media and the rest of the outside world, that's fine. But then you should have someone you trust do it for you."

Then Schaefer points to another problem.

"I have great respect for Al," the former Golden Boy CEO says. "He's a friend of mine, and I admire the way he cares about his fighters. But someone who can put together big TV deals is not necessarily a promoter. I would have promoted much more on site than Al has. He hasn't done a lot of that, and I think that's one reason there hasn't been more of a buzz for his fights."

During the past year, Haymon has worked with a handful of promoters; Lou DiBella, Leon Margules, Yvon Michel, Tom Brown, Mike Battah, and Marshall Kauffman among them.

"Because of the promotional situation," Schaefer says, "there hasn't been much continuity and it becomes harder to build the fighters. When Danny Garcia fights at Barclays Center, the promoter is Lou DiBella. Then he fights at Staples Center, and the promoter is Tom Brown. Neither promoter feels that he has a long-term interest in Danny. And who should the media call when they want to talk about Danny's next fight? Lou DiBella? Tom Brown? It's a problem."

And there's another problem.

"When you're working with Al to promote a fight," says a promoter who has worked with him, "he micromanages so much that you can't do your job. And the secrecy kills you. You're watching things unfold, and you don't know how they're unfolding."

Despite all the money that Haymon has spent on the production of PBC telecasts, that area too has been wanting. There have been some positive innovations. Haymon eliminated the mob that pours into the ring before and after fights. There are no people inside the ropes shouting, "You da man." No sanctioning body officials draping T-shirts and phony belts over the combatants. No promoters, managers, commissioners, or mistresses jockeying for position in front of the camera.

But many of the gimmicks that PBC experimented with to jazz up its telecasts have fallen flat. The "ref-cam" didn't show viewers "what the referee sees" because it followed the referee's forehead, not his eyes. The 36-still-camera-over-the-ring video rig that was supposed to give viewers a moving panoramic view of the action produced visuals that had the feel of a not-very-good video game from the 1980s.

Also, the announcing has been uneven with no continuity from show to show. And for the most part, as noted by Bart Barry, "PBC broadcasting crews have the journalistic integrity of Billy Mays pitching GatorBlade bug bazookas at 3:00 a.m. Their commentary works more like a celebrity endorsement of a product than a description of what happens in the boxing ring. None of them offers commentary to invite even the softest inference of disloyalty to Al Haymon."

In some respects, the May 2, 2015, megafight between Floyd Mayweather and Manny Pacquiao also undermined Premier Boxing Champions. There was no PBC branding during fight week. And PBC didn't have a direct financial interest in the bout. But Haymon was counting on the fight to give his vision a boost. It was an important piece of the puzzle that he was putting together.

On the plus side, some powerful people and institutions made a lot of money off Mayweather-Pacquiao and feel beholden to Haymon. Also, Haymon had thousands of tickets and rooms at the MGM Grand that he could give to PBC investors, sponsors, television executives, and fighters. And most important, Haymon could tell investors, "This fight is grossing a half billion dollars. We might be losing millions of dollars now. But stay the course and there will be paydays like this for us in the future."

But there was a downside for Haymon in the way that Mayweather-Pacquiao unfolded. The fight was mediocre and soured a lot of people on boxing. Viewers felt suckered after buying the pay-per-view telecast, and many people became aware for the first time that boxing's poster boy had a penchant for physically abusing women. That made it more difficult for Haymon to attract advertisers for Premier Boxing Champions and, in some ways, left boxing less well off than before.

Haymon's plans also hit a snag when he lost the ability to work with Richard Schaefer and Golden Boy as the primary promotional vehicle for his fighters. Haymon appears to have coordinated with Schaefer in an effort to buy out Oscar De La Hoya and Golden Boy's other major share-holders (AEG and the Brener family). But that plan fell apart when De La Hoya refused to sell. After buy-out negotiations failed, Schaefer resigned from Golden Boy. Then, on June 16, 2014, the company instituted an arbitration proceeding against him, claiming $50 million in damages. The suit was settled for an undisclosed amount—reportedly in excess of $20 million—and, per terms of the settlement, Schaefer was precluded from working with Haymon on boxing matters for an undisclosed period of time.

In 2015, Bruce Binkow, Raul Jaimes, Nicole Sparks, Armando Gaytan, and Araceli Villegas (each of whom had worked previously with Schaefer at Golden Boy) formed a company called Integrated Sports Marketing LLC to coordinate sponsorships, foreign sales, on-site setups, and drug testing for Haymon. None of them has Schaefer's skills.

In the end though, the primary reason that Premier Boxing Champions has fallen short of expectations is the quality of the fights that Haymon has given the public.

One of the benefits that fight fans expected as PBC took shape was that Haymon's control over an extensive fighter roster would guarantee good fights. The PBC website promises "today's best and brightest stars in their toughest, most anticipated bouts."

Brian Kweder, who ran ESPN's boxing program as it transitioned to PBC, says, "Ending *Friday Night Fights* was bittersweet. We'd had a long run and a loyal fan base. But ESPN is a top sports site, and it didn't compute that we had what was essentially minor league boxing."

But to date, too many PBC fights have been minor league. Bart Barry puts the matter in perspective when he says, "The PBC telecasts have had every ingredient imaginable. Special ringwalk music, rotating cameras, monster display boards. It's like they're making a cake. Flour, sugar, butter, chocolate. Wait! Here's a chili pepper. Let's throw that in too. The only ingredient they haven't thrown in is good fights."

Looking at year one, the Premier Boxing Champions website lists fifty-five televised fight cards that were contested between March 7, 2015, and March 5, 2016. Virtually none of these were "must see viewing" or "water-cooler fights." Some weren't even credible match-ups.

Haymon has a well-deserved reputation for putting his favored fighters in soft. To be entertaining over the long run, boxing needs competitive fights. In that regard, one promoter associated with PBC notes, "Al's biggest problem isn't that he's acting like a promoter. It's that he's not acting enough like a promoter. He has all the control and he's protecting too many of his guys by putting them in easy. He's making the fights that he wants to make rather than the fights that people want to see."

Overall, Haymon's PBC match-ups have been disappointing on paper and, where it counts most, in the ring.

Matchmaking isn't rocket science. Fans were looking forward to Leo Santa Cruz vs. Abner Mares. It was the kind of fight that viewers once saw regularly on *Boxing After Dark* when Lou DiBella was HBO's boxing guru. And there have been other anticipated PBC match-ups. Danny Garcia vs. Lamont Peterson, Amir Khan vs. Chris Algeri, and Adrien Broner vs. Shawn Porter come to mind. Sometimes an underdog surprises, as Krzysztof Glowacki did against Marco Huck.

But Haymon has diluted his own product. In Greg Bishop's words, "He's saturating the market with borderline unwatchable fights."

Hall of Fame matchmaker Teddy Brenner once proclaimed, "Fights make fights."

But on PBC, each fight seems like a one-off. There's no continuity from show to show and no natural progression toward fights of greater importance. Viewers are consigned to watching what seems like the endless first round of what could have been an exciting tournament.

In sum, for all the money that Haymon has spent, he has delivered an ordinary product. And with multiple fight cards on television week after week, boxing fans have become more discriminating about what they watch. PBC fighters have had a lot of air time over the past year. By and large, they've failed to impress.

Years ago, I received an e-mail from a reader. I'll paraphrase what he wrote:

"I work in a marketing department. And one of the things I've learned is that you can package things and market them as good quality whether they are or not. You can sell perfume that smells bad. You can sell clothes that are ugly. The one thing you can not sell is bad sports programming. Sports fans know whether they're being entertained or not."

Premier Boxing Champions isn't entertaining the public. Certainly not the general public. Too many of its telecasts are like concert warm-up acts. If Al Haymon had promoted concerts that were of the same quality as his fights, he never would have become a giant in the music business.

PART FIVE

Richard Schaefer once observed, "In boxing, money alone doesn't bring success."

Al Haymon is still boxing's most influential power broker. But he's learning that trying to control and restructure the sweet science is like nation building in Iraq. Early victories are no guarantee of long-term progress.

Haymon had the means to shape the presentation of Premier Boxing Champions any way he wanted to in building a brand. But PBC has failed to make new fans or energize old ones. It lacks an identity in the public mind.

The initial curiosity of boxing fans with regard to PBC has turned to indifference. "I'm on social media every day," ESPN boxing writer Dan Rafael says. "And let me tell you, there's no buzz now for PBC. There was at the start, but it's gone."

As previously noted, Haymon has approximately two hundred fighters under contract. But very few of them are A-list guys. Not a single fighter on ESPN's top-ten pound-for-pound list is a PBC fighter. Outside of Deontay Wilder, it's hard to think of a PBC fighter who has a greater following or is more marketable now than he was a year ago. That might change with Errol Spence Jr. But the rest of Haymon's "stars" are trading on the interest that was engendered in them when they fought on HBO or Showtime.

Haymon's grand plan is turning out to be not so grand. There are times when PBC evokes the image of a giant elephant lumbering down-hill toward a pit of quicksand.

"We know it can't go on like this," says a rival promoter. "Al is skating on thin ice, and some of us wouldn't mind if it breaks."

"It's an uphill battle for Al now," Richard Schaefer acknowledges. "A lot of things will have to change for PBC to work. But you learn from your mistakes. You keep doing what worked and cut back on what didn't work. I believe in Al, and I believe that PBC can still be successful."

But what's the fallback plan? And what is Haymon's current mindset? Confidence? Crisis?

PBC appears to be cutting back on expenses. The days when Haymon Sports purchased two airplanes (an eleven-seat Learjet and a twenty-two-seat Gulfstream Areospace G-IV) are gone.

Dan Rafael says that Haymon's contract with NBC and his contract with ESPN called for him to pay each network in advance on a yearly basis ($20 million per year for NBC and $8 million per year for ESPN). But when Haymon closed a deal with Fox Sports 1 in mid-2015, it called for monthly payments, and he declined to give them a letter of credit for the full amount.

The first few months of 2016 were slower than expected. The "monthly" PBC shows on Spike turned out to be not monthly.

On March 1, 2016, Rafael reported, "ESPN's first Premier Boxing Champions card of 2016 was initially scheduled for January. Then the card was delayed until April 2, when it was to be televised in the afternoon on ABC with a second card scheduled for April 30 in prime time on ESPN. Two more shows were scheduled for ESPN in May. PBC, however, has pushed back the start until June. In all, there are seven PBC shows on ESPN to end the first season, even though the series was announced last year as a monthly series [twelve shows a year for two years]. The last PBC on ESPN card was on November 25."

And there was no public explanation for the change in plans, which might lead one to believe that PBC is tightening the purse strings because it has been losing an alarming amount of money.

PBC is also cutting back on TV production expenses. The staging has become less elaborate. Fewer people are traveling to the shows. Less money is being spent on on-air talent than at the start.

And Haymon has started sending PBC fighters outside of the PBC universe. Dominic Wade and Amir Khan (both under contract to Haymon) have been offered up as presumptive sacrificial lambs for Gennady Golovkin and Canelo Alvarez on April 23, 2016 (*HBO World Championship Boxing*) and May 7, 2016 (HBO-PPV) respectively. Should Wade or Khan win, it would be good for them and good for Haymon. But the move takes the burden of paying for their fights off of Haymon's shoulders.

Still, at the end of the day, Haymon doesn't want to be dependent on networks and promoters that he doesn't control. So what might he do within his own universe?

Let's start with the understanding that Haymon can't change what he ate for dinner last night, let alone undo the past year. But he can change direction in the future.

Premier Boxing Champions needs more continuity in scheduling than it has had during the past year. Right now, many prospective viewers don't know when or where to find PBC fights.

There should be more emphasis on ESPN, which is a portal to mainstream sports fans in a way that the other PBC networks aren't.

Richard Schaefer's absence from the mix has been curious. It was widely expected that he would join forces with Haymon when the contractual limitations imposed by his settlement with Golden Boy expired last summer. That hasn't happened, perhaps because Schaefer's involvement with PBC at the present time is considered too risky in light of the ongoing lawsuits against Haymon.

Schaefer recently told this writer, "There are a number of things, including some real estate deals, that I'm working on now. But I'd be interested in coming back into boxing some day. I'm observing what's going on to see if, when, and how I want to come back; not to come back for a year or two, but to build something for the long term."

Schaefer also made the point, "Al is the captain of the ship. But for a ship this big, you have to delegate responsibility for the ship to be run right."

But most important, Haymon has to give the public better fights. In some respects, he has been remarkably tone-deaf. And nowhere has that been more evident than in the fights he has made.

The ratings show that sports fans haven't bought into Premier Boxing Champions as a brand. Whether or not they watch a given PBC telecast depends on who's fighting.

Boxing After Dark, in its early years, had the buzz and brand that PBC should be trying to duplicate. Before HBO started using *BAD* as a favor bank for promoters and as a vehicle to "build" fighters through one-sided match-ups, it featured the most competitive risky entertaining fights that the network could buy.

"You can't reinvent boxing," promoter Gary Shaw says. "Boxing is two guys in the ring putting on what you hope is a great fight. Everything else, all the bells and whistles, is secondary to that."

Schaefer concurs, acknowledging, "One thing Oscar always said that I agree with is the best should fight the best. If I were Al, I would make fewer fights. The schedule is too cluttered now. And I would try to make bigger fights with the best fighting the best."

It's not rocket science. Schedule a fight that shapes up as an entertaining match-up and more people will watch.

The indications are that Haymon still has tens of millions of dollars in his war chest. He should use that money to make the best, most exciting fights he can make. If a fighter goes in tough and loses, PBC can bring him back any way it wants.

Two upcoming PBC telecasts offer a contrast in programming philosophy.

Keith Thurman vs. Shawn Porter is scheduled for June 25, 2016, on CBS. That shapes up as an entertaining fight. At the other end of the spectrum, an April 29 telecast on Spike features Anthony Dirrell vs. Caleb Truax and Andre Dirrell vs. Blake Caparello in what are expected to be unattractive lopsided matches.

There have been—and continue to be—too many "people don't care" PBC fights.

And wouldn't Thurman-Porter be even more exciting if viewers knew that the winner was slated to fight the winner of an equally high-profile match-up? Tournaments and playoffs work in every other sport. Why can't PBC match winners against winners and its best against its best?

Also, it's worth noting that Thurman vs. Porter will be labeled "Showtime Boxing on CBS." The Showtime commentating team will call the action, and Jimmy Lennon will be the ring announcer. That's because the Showtime brand is expected to attract more advertisers and viewers than the PBC brand. That exemplifies the failure of the PBC brand to date.

Meanwhile, all of the issues discussed above should be viewed within the framework of the overriding question: Is Al Haymon good for boxing?

Boxing is a sport ruled by predators who follow no rules except those that are in their own self-interest. At their worst, they're like pirates on an ocean where fate is determined by the survival of the fittest. The powers that be in the sport created the conditions that made Haymon's rise possible. In many instances, their incompetence has been breathtaking and their greed shortsighted.

When Premier Boxing Champions was launched, boxing fans gave Haymon the benefit of the doubt and wanted to believe in him. He positioned himself as a reformer who was going to make the sweet science more popular and more equitable. He was looking at problems that other people only complained about and trying to solve them. He challenged the status quo and the sense of entitlement that too many promoters, sanctioning body officials, network executives, and others have.

"The people who want Al to fail," says Lou DiBella, "aren't rooting for boxing."

But to date, Haymon has done nothing to improve the entertainment value of the sport. And his time-buy model (which he says is transitional) is not self-sustaining.

When one looks at Haymon's history in boxing, he left HBO worse off than when he found it. He left Golden Boy worse off than when he found it. Promoters like Lou DiBella are less powerful now than when they began doing business with him.

Haymon is in the spotlight now whether he likes it or not. He's said to be looking at an initial term of three to four years before evaluating the overall success of Premier Boxing Champions. He might not get that far. And even if PBC survives, it's unlikely to achieve the UFC-type domination that Haymon once envisioned.

Fox wanted to say, "We have all the UFC that's on free television." No one will pay hundreds of millions of dollars to say, "We have all the PBC that's on free television."

Mike Borao (the manager of record for Charles Martin) likens evaluating Premier Boxing Champions to critiquing a painting by

Picasso: "You evaluate it when the work is done, not halfway through its creation."

Richard Schaefer also cautions that time is necessary, saying, "When you start a new business like this with plans that are as ambitious as Al has, you need time to succeed. If someone had judged Golden Boy after one year, we weren't nearly as good as we became later on."

But a television executive who has been involved with sports for decades says, "If a transition to advertiser-supported networks paying large license fees was Al's plan, then Al was delusional. Those networks aren't interested in building boxing. If lightning strikes, fine. But right now, they're selling a time buy; that's all. The only reason they're carrying Al's boxing programming is that he's paying them to do it."

If the advertiser-supported networks that Haymon is doing business with now decide to license fights in the future, Haymon is likely to hear, "We're not paying you what you were paying us." And even then, there's no guarantee that they'll buy fights from Haymon as opposed to another promoter.

If Premier Boxing Champions fails to live up to expectations, Haymon will still have the wherewithal to be a force in boxing. But he doesn't just want a place at the table. He already has that. He wants to dominate. Maybe he'll pull a rabbit out of a hat. But right now, it looks as though he was wiser in raising money than he has been in spending it. And if Haymon's fallback plan is some sort of subscription channel or pay-per-view model, that won't be good for fans.

There may come a time when the money gets tight. If that day comes, will PBC be like musical chairs with some fighters being thrown out of the game? Or will the band stop playing altogether?

If Haymon's grand plan falls apart, how will the pieces realign?

One or more of the companies that comprise Haymon's corporate organizational chart could survive in some form if he wants them to survive. Meanwhile, HBO and Showtime could continue doing what they already do. *ESPN2 Friday Night Fights* could be revived. Other cable networks might be drawn to the sweet science on a small scale, as they have been in the past. The broadcast networks might utilize inexpensive boxing telecasts as cost-efficient counter-programming against major events on other networks.

Also, let's not forget; the broadcast networks got out of boxing a long time ago. If PBC fails, Haymon isn't chasing the networks out of something that they were in before he came on the scene.

So let's close for now with a final thought on Al Haymon.

"Al is smart, very smart," says someone who has done business with him for years. "But the rest of us aren't all stupid. And I'll tell you something else. Maybe Al isn't as smart as people think he is. And when it comes to boxing, maybe Al doesn't know as much as he thinks he knows."

★ ★ ★

Who we are when we're young shapes who we are as we grow older.

Dr. Enrico Melson graduated from the University of California at Irvine with a medical degree in 1982. Since then, he has served in a variety of positions, drawing in particular on his expertise in holistic medicine and other indigenous healing practices.

Dr. Melson was a young man with a dream when he began his journey from the mean streets of Los Angeles to a different world. In September 1973, he arrived at Harvard, where he was assigned to room with another freshman who had a background similar to his own: Alan Haymon.

Dr. Melson's memories of Al Haymon follow.

Let me start with how I met Alan. It was freshman week, and we were assigned to be roommates in Comstock dormitory, room 310, in Radcliffe Yard. It was an experiment in coed education with young men and women living in the same dorm. Being the guy that I was—a burgeoning ladies' man coming out of the Los Angeles ghetto—that was fine with me. Alan and I had that in common to start with. He came out of Cleveland. I came out of Watts and Compton, so we could relate on that level.

I met Alan as we were moving in. He and his family were bringing in his belongings. I had a cousin who was also attending Harvard as a freshman, and my cousin and I thought maybe we could get Alan to switch. Alan was cool with the idea if he could get a single room instead of a double. As luck would have it, there was an available single room about the size of a lady's closet down the hall.

I helped Alan carry his belongings down the hall, and it was an experience. He looked like Superfly with a big Afro. And he had platform shoes of all types. Green glitter platform shoes, silver platform shoes, boxes and boxes of platform shoes. And I found out later that he had a blue Cadillac de Ville with an off-white top that he'd drive around looking for a parking space. It was always a challenge to find parking in Cambridge. But there must have been some money in the family if he had a car of his own. I know, when I got my first financial aid check, I sent it home to my family. And I stayed in the dorms over Christmas my freshman year to save the money it would have cost to fly back to California.

I met Alan's family the day we moved in. They seemed like a strong upright cohesive family unit. His parents were proud of him, but they were proud of his brother and sister too. I remember, his brother was a professional boxer. His sister was kind of quiet, but that could have been the circumstances. So Alan had something that I'd never had—an intact family that brought him to Harvard, figuratively and literally. My father didn't get to Harvard until I graduated four years later. And my mother couldn't make it to my graduation because she was in an intensive care unit with a gunshot wound.

Alan had gifts as an athlete. He liked to party. He was a good dancer. He was brilliant.

The fight against apartheid in South Africa and the struggle to free Nelson Mandela were issues at the time. Alan wasn't a political activist, but he was clear in his support. He was at Harvard to learn how to do business, and I was there to save the world. But we got along.

There was a lot of polarization at Harvard in those days, black versus white. There were young black men who were predicted by the conventionalists as being unlikely to make it through Harvard because they refused to assimilate. Alan was one of those who refused to assimilate. So was I. The issue wasn't whether we were smart enough to make it. It was whether we would fold ourselves into the assimilation pool. We could hold onto our blackness or we could swing over to the establishment side. A lot of the black students wanted to join the elite. They wanted to become the next generation of bankers and politicians and rulers of the system. And believe me, when you're coming from the underclass and an oppressed minority, survival in that cultural environment is an issue; not just in the classroom but emotionally too.

Alan wanted to succeed in the business world and keep his identity. He was a brother who stood in both worlds and never sold out. He had a strong personality that enabled him to survive at Harvard and stay true to himself. He chose not to abandon his cultural identity. He never sacrificed his core. He was at Harvard but he had his own style and lifestyle. "Look at me. This is who I am. The streets of Cleveland are in me." He was bold. He had a strong will. Like the rest of us, he was wrestling with the issue of who he was and what kind of person he wanted to be. But he was never arrogant or unkind.

Even then, he was driven. In our junior year, I started to hear the term "an Alan Haymon production" on the radio. I thought that was pretty cool. By Alan's senior year, he was mentoring some of the younger students like George Jackson [who later produced *New Jack City*]. I remember George telling me during my last year at Harvard that his role model was Alan Haymon.

None of it came easily. About fifteen years ago, I heard from a classmate that Alan was going through some hard times emotionally and battling depression. That comes sometimes with the pressures of fame and success on the level that Alan has had. From what I was told, it was a dark time and he had to rebuild emotionally. But he seems to have done that successfully, and it's to his credit that he did.

So that's what I remember about Alan. He had a sense of destiny about what he wanted to do, and he did it. It's remarkable to actualize that kind of ambition. I respect and admire who he is and everything that he has accomplished.

Blood Brothers was a welcome addition to the literature on Muhammad Ali
and Malcolm X.

"Blood Brothers": Muhammad Ali and Malcolm X

Blood Brothers by Randy Roberts and Johnny Smith (Basic Books)
focuses on the thirty-two months between June 1962 when Cassius Clay
and Malcolm X met and February 21, 1965, when Malcolm was assassi-
nated at the Audobon Ballroom in Harlem.

In the authors' words, it's "the story of how Cassius Clay became
Muhammad Ali and the central role Malcolm X played in his life. It is
a tale of friendship and brotherhood, love and deep affection. It is also a
story of deceit, betrayal, and violence during a troubled time."

Blood Brothers contains some interesting insights into Cassius Clay's
early home life; most notably, the recounting of an incident when Cassius
Clay Sr. stabbed his fifteen-year-old son in the thigh after Cassius Jr.
sought to protect his mother against an alcohol-fueled assault. That's followed by a recounting of Clay's early ring career that offers no new
insights, although there's an interesting quote from Angelo Dundee.

Dundee, who trained Clay from his second pro fight on, believed that
every fighter has his own unique style.

"There's not two alike," Angelo declared. "You don't say, 'This guy
fights like this guy.' They don't. They're all individuals. They all got their
own idiosyncracies, got their own rhythm."Thus, Dundee told Clay, "You
are neither Sugar Ray Robinson nor Archie Moore. Who you are is
Cassius Marcellus Clay Jr., and that's the man I'm going to teach you to
fight like. A guy is never going to get anywhere thinking he's somebody
else."

Blood Brothers gathers steam when Malcolm and twenty-year-old
Cassius Clay meet.

"For about two years," the authors recount, "Malcolm X counseled
and spiritually guided the young boxer, instructing him on the evil ways

of the world but also, more importantly, convincing him to love himself
and his people. They were like blood brothers, and briefly it must have
seemed as if the world was theirs. In the year and a half before Cassius
won the heavyweight crown, Malcolm consciously molded him into
Muhammad Ali. But after Cassius defeated Sonny Liston for the title,
at the instant when his political value to Malcolm was the highest, the
preacher lost his convert."

Blood Brothers comes alive and crackles with tension once Malcolm
falls out of favor with Elijah Muhammad (who had founded and, at that
time, still led the Nation of Islam). From that point on, the story is grip-
ping and told with particular drama.

Malcolm was now dependent on Clay as a way of maintaining his
influence within the Nation of Islam.

"When Malcolm's life was in danger," Roberts and Smith write,
"when Elijah Muhammad threatened to cast him outside the Nation of
Islam, Clay became the central figure in his world. As long as they were
together, Malcolm figured, he was safe. Cassius was the perfect shield.
However, only ten days after they celebrated the boxer's championship
victory over Sonny Liston, Cassius stopped taking Malcolm's phone calls.
Malcolm's mistake was that he believed Cassius would see the world
through his eyes and perhaps their brotherhood would become stronger
than Clay's allegiance to Elijah."

"Cassius," *Blood Brothers* continues, "knew that the internecine fighting between Elijah and Malcolm had escalated to a critical violent stage.
He had heard stories about Muslims who crossed Muhammad and paid
severely for it. Now he had a choice to make. Ultimately, he submitted
to Elijah. Cassius Clay had said, 'I don't have to be what you want me
to be. I'm free to be what I want to be.' Yet that was never really true.
There were limits to his new freedom. Submitting to Elijah, the champ
accepted a new name and the Supreme Minister's edict that all Muslims
cease contact with Malcolm. When Malcolm lost the contest for Clay's
loyalty, he had no more moves. At that moment, his life was in jeopardy."

A particularly dramatic accounting of events culminating in Malcolm's
assassination follows. Meanwhile, according to multiple sources cited by
Roberts and Smith, the newly named Muhammad Ali came to fear that,
if he stepped out of line, he might meet the same fate as Malcolm.

Blood Brothers is the most thorough and compelling book yet on the relationship between Cassius Clay and Malcolm X. "That it ended violently and tragically," Roberts and Smith conclude, "does not diminish what they once had. Elijah Muhammad anointed Cassius as Muhammad Ali. [But] without Malcolm X, he never would have become Muhammad Ali."

For those who believe that the world's holy books are the word of God, there is still a question as to who should interpret them.

The Bible and Manny Pacquiao

At a January 21, 2016, press conference in New York to promote his upcoming fight against Tim Bradley, Manny Pacquiao was asked what he thought about Republican presidential candidate Donald Trump.

Trump seems to be patterning his campaign on the Floyd Mayweather model: Rub how much money you have in people's faces and talk incessantly about how great you are.

Further to that point, the Trump electoral phenomenon can be analogized to an election for homecoming queen on a college campus where a John-Belushi-like character dresses in drag and enters the competition. People might enjoy the spectacle. But at the end of the day, most of them don't want Belushi in drag as their significant other.

In addition to readying for the Bradley fight, Pacquiao is running for the Senate in his native Philippines. The election will be held on May 9. Weighing the plusses and minuses of commenting on Trump, Pacquiao responded, "I don't want to get into politics here. We have our own politics."

They do indeed. And last month in conjunction with those politics, Pacquiao was interviewed by TV5. When asked about his views on gay marriage, candidate Pacquiao declared, "It's common sense. Will you see any animals where male is to male and female is to female? The animals are better. They know how to distinguish male from female. If we approve male on male, female on female, then man is worse than animals."

Next came a post on Instagram from Pacquiao that read, "I'd rather obey the Lord's command than obey the desires of the flesh. I'm not condemning anyone, but I'm just telling the truth of what the Bible says. The truth from the Bible is what changed me from my old ways." [Quoting I *Corinthians* 6:9]: "Do you not know that wrongdoers will not inherit the kingdom of God? Do not be deceived, neither the sexually immoral nor idolaters nor adulterers nor men who have sex with men."

Faced with a storm of protest over his remarks, Pacquiao issued a non-apologetic apology on Twitter: "I'm sorry for everyone who got hurt due to my comparison of gay people to animals. It was my mistake. Please forgive me for those who I've hurt. But this does not change my position against same sex marriage. That's what I believe. My only mistake is comparing gay people to animals."

But that pretense of an apology was shortlived. One day later, Pacquiao posted another Bible verse on Instagram: "If a man has sexual relations with a man as one does with a woman, both of them have done what is detestable. They are to be put to death; their blood will be on their own heads" [*Leviticus* 20:13].

Finally, on February 19, Pacquiao met with reporters at his training camp in General Santos City and was asked about the controversy that had erupted over his remarks.

"I'm happy," Pacquiao answered. "I'm always happy because God is with me. What I am saying is right. I am just stating the truth, what the Bible says. You know what I am telling is the truth."

On February 17, Nike (which had enjoyed a ten-year commercial relationship with Pacquiao) issued a statement saying, "We find Manny Pacquiao's comments abhorrent. Nike strongly opposes discrimination of any kind and has a long history of supporting and standing up for the rights of the LGBT community. We no longer have a relationship with Manny Pacquiao."

That was followed by a March 2 statement from HBO that read, "Next month, Manny Pacquiao and Timothy Bradley Jr. are scheduled to meet in a pay-per-view bout. We have an obligation to both fighters and, therefore, will proceed to produce and distribute that event. However, we felt it important to leave no uncertainty about our position on Mr. Pacquiao's recent comments toward the LGBTQ community. We consider them insensitive, offensive and deplorable. HBO has been a proud home to many LGBTQ stories and couldn't approach this event without clearly voicing our opinion."

Pacquiao isn't alone in the boxing world when it comes to making homophobic statements. Tyson Fury caused a stir with remarks that he made last November. But Fury is widely regarded as a madman and is not a candidate for public office (although these days, the two often seem to coincide). Pacquiao, on the other hand, is seeking a position that would empower him to translate his prejudices into public policy.

So it's worth asking: Does Manny Pacquiao really believe that gay men should be put to death?

And while we're on the subject, there's another biblical verse that should be scrutinized. *Leviticus* chapter 25, verse 44 states, "Both thy bondmen and thy bondmaids which thou shalt have, shall be of the heathen that are around you; of them shall ye buy bondmen and bondmaids."

Does Pacquiao countenance slavery?

The current Pacquiao controversy is focused on his interpretation of the Bible and gay marriage. So what does Pacquiao think about other biblical dictates regarding marriage:

1. Marriage shall consist of a union between a man and one or more women (Genesis 29:17–28, II Samuel 3:2–5).

2. Marriage shall not impede a man's right to take concubines in addition to his wife or wives (II Samuel 5:13, I Kings 11:3, II Chronicles 11:21).

3. A marriage shall be considered valid only if the wife is a virgin. If the wife is not a virgin, she shall be executed (Deuteronomy 22:13–21).

4. The marriage of a believer and a non-believer is forbidden (Genesis 24:3, Numbers 25:1–9, Ezra 9:12, Nehemiah 10:30).

5. Divorce shall not be allowed (Deuteronomy 22:19, Mark 10:9).

6. If a married man dies without children, his brother shall marry his widow. If the brother refuses to marry the widow or deliberately does not give her children, he shall pay a fine of one shoe and be otherwise punished in a manner to be determined by law (Genesis 38:6–10, Deuteronomy 25:5–10).

Veteran sportswriter Bill Dwyre recently observed, "Pacquiao is a decent, hard-working, rise-from-the-ashes person who is generous and caring and the last person on the face of the Earth you would expect to verbalize himself into this corner of public hell. I have covered most of his important fights, admired his patience and work ethic, even stood within feet of him that night in May of 2010, when the key precinct result came in for the Congressional spot he sought in the Philippines' Sarangani province. He had been an urchin on the streets less than two decades before and now he was a Congressman."

That said, some people get wiser when they get older. Pacquiao seems to be just getting older.

Ezzard Charles is #1 at 175 pounds.

Ranking the Modern Light-Heavyweight Greats

Ranking great fighters from different eras, when done seriously, is a daunting task. It's easy to sit down and put together a shoot-from-the-hip list. But that doesn't do justice to the fighters.

In recent years, I've sought to quantify ring greatness in a credible way. I've compiled lists of great champions who reigned at 135, 147, and 160 pounds and matched them against each other in round-robin tournaments with the results of each fight being predicted by a panel of boxing industry experts.

This time, it's modern 175-pound greats.

The light-heavyweights chosen for the tournament in alphabetical order are Ezzard Charles, Billy Conn, Bob Foster, Roy Jones, Sergey Kovalev, Archie Moore, Matthew Saad Muhammad, and Michael Spinks.

Six of these fighters tested the heavyweight waters in a meaningful way. Charles and Spinks claimed the legitimate heavyweight championship of the world. Jones bested John Ruiz for the WBA belt. Conn fought Joe Louis twice. Moore vied for the title against Rocky Marciano and Floyd Patterson. Foster fought Joe Frazier and Muhammad Ali.

Charles never won the light-heavyweight title. But he's included in this tournament because many people believe he was at his best at 175 pounds. Here, I should note that Charles fought Archie Moore three times and won each time.

I didn't include fighters who plied their trade prior to the mid-1930s because there's not enough film footage available to properly evaluate them. Where Sergey Kovalev is concerned, he has yet to face inquisitors against whom he could demonstrate greatness. Now is his chance.

The panelists were asked to assume for each hypothetical fight that both fighters were at the point in their respective careers when they were able to make 175 pounds and capable of duplicating their best 175-pound performance. One can look to side issues such as same-day weigh-ins versus day-before weigh-ins. And there's a difference between going twelve rounds as opposed to fifteen. But at the end of the day, either a fighter is very good, great, or the greatest.

Twenty-six experts participated in the rankings process. Listed alphabetically, the panelists were:

Trainers: Teddy Atlas, Pat Burns, Naazim Richardson, and Don Turner

Media: Al Bernstein, Ron Borges, Norm Frauenheim, Jerry Izenberg, Harold Lederman, Paulie Malignaggi, Dan Rafael, and Michael Rosenthal

Matchmakers: Eric Bottjer, Don Elbaum, Bobby Goodman, Brad Goodman, Ron Katz, Mike Marchionte, Russell Peltz, and Bruce Trampler

Historians: Craig Hamilton, Bob Mee, Clay Moyle, Adam Pollack, Randy Roberts, and Mike Tyson

If each of the eight fighters in the tournament had fought the other seven, there would have been twenty-eight fights. And there were twenty-six panelists. Thus, 728 fight predictions were entered into the database. Fighters were awarded one point for each predicted win and a half point for each predicted draw (too close to call). A perfect score would have been 182 points.

One matchmaker said that he never saw Moore, Charles, or Conn fight and didn't feel comfortable predicting outcomes for their matches based on film footage. A weighted average from the other electors was used to fill in the fights at issue in his tournament grid.

In the end, Ezzard Charles was the clear choice for #1.

The final rankings and point totals are:

Ezzard Charles	156 points
Archie Moore	120
Roy Jones	104.5
Bob Foster	103.5
Michael Spinks	88
Billy Conn	66
Sergey Kovalev	48
Matthew Saad Muhammad	42

Sixteen of the twenty-six panelists thought that Bob Foster would have beaten Roy Jones. Nine picked Jones, while one said the match-up was too close to call. But Jones's record against four of the other six fighters in the tournament was superior to Foster's. That gave Roy a one-point edge in the final rankings.

Thirteen of the twenty-six panelists thought that Charles would have won all of his fights. Four thought that Jones would have prevailed in all seven of his bouts. Three awarded similar accolades to Foster. One elector gave Michael Spinks a perfect score.

Among the comments made by electors were:

"The old guys were better boxers. The new guys are better athletes. It's called boxing, isn't it?"

"There are some big punchers in this tournament. But it took Rocky Marciano twenty-three rounds to knock Ezzard Charles out, so I don't think any of these guys would have done it . . . Moore had a greater career at 175 pounds than Charles did. But Charles had his number . . . I hate to pick against Archie Moore at 175 pounds. But I can't rewrite history, so I'll pick Charles over Moore."

"Archie Moore didn't have the best chin in the world, but he knew how to protect it and he knew how to disarm punchers . . . No modern-day fighter beats Archie Moore at 175 pounds. He knew all the tricks, and fighters today don't know those tricks . . . I know Charles beat Moore three times. But a fighter has to prove himself every time. On Moore's best night, I'm going with Moore."

"Jones is the most athletically gifted one in the group. He would have given all of the others trouble . . . The question about Roy is his chin. He'd be beating a lot of these guys until he got hit. Then, who knows?"

"Some of these fighters—especially Jones and Foster—had questionable chins. And all of them could whack. So the guys with questionable chins could have gotten knocked out at any point."

"I don't care who you were. If you weighed 175 pounds and Bob Foster hit you on the chin, you were in trouble . . . Foster lost to some great fighters. How many great fighters did he beat?"

"People don't realize how clever Michael Spinks was. He was old-school in a lot of ways."

"Billy Conn fought seventy-six times. He got stopped by some guy right after he turned pro. And the only fighter who knocked him out after that was Joe Louis. Most of the guys on your list could punch. But none of them could punch as hard as Joe Louis . . . Billy Conn had great footwork. He knew how to control distance with his legs, and his legs were great. Styles make fights, and Conn had the style to beat a lot of these guys . . . Conn weighed in at 169 pounds and was ahead of Joe Louis on the scorecards after twelve rounds."

"Kovalev hasn't shown that he's ready for this level of competition yet."

"I love Matthew Saad Muhammad. He was the most courageous fighter I've ever seen, but I don't see him doing well in this tournament. He took what he had to take and always came back punching. But he was too easy to hit, and I don't think he could have taken the punishment that these guys were capable of handing out . . . Saad Muhammad was life and death with opponents who weren't nearly as good as the fighters on this list."

"They're in good company; all of them."

Charts 1 and 2 contain underlying statistical data from the tournament. Chart 1 shows that the trainers, matchmakers, media representatives, and historians all ranked Charles in the #1 slot. There was a divergence of opinion after that. Chart 2 shows how the panelists thought each fighter would have fared against the other seven.

CHART 1

Name Points	Overall Rank	Matchmaker Rank	Trainer Rank	Media Rank	Historian Rank
Charles 156	1	1	1	1	1
Moore 120	2	2	2	3	3
Jones 104.5	3	5	7	2	2
Foster 103.5	4	3	3	4	5
Spinks 88	5	4	6	5	4
Conn 66	6	6	5	8	6
Kovalev 48	7	8	4	6	7
Muhammad 42	8	7	8	7	8

CHART 2

-	Ezzard Charles	Billy Conn	Bob Foster	Roy Jones	Sergey Kovalev	Archie Moore	Matthew S. Muhammad	Michael Spinks
Charles 154-24-4	-	23	19	18	25	25	23	23
Conn 63-113-6	3	-	8	4.5	14	8.5	17	11
Foster 101-76-5	7	18	-	16.5	18	7.5	22.5	14
Jones 100-73-9	8	21.5	9.5	-	22.5	9.5	20	13.5
Kovalev 44-130-8	1	12	8	3.5	-	2.5	13	8
Moore 116-58-8	1	17.5	18.5	16.5	23,5	-	25.5	17.5
Muhammad 39-137-6	3	9	3.5	6	13	.5	-	7
Spinks 84-90-8	3	15	12	12.5	18	8.5	19	-

This article was part of my "More Important Than Boxing" series.

Instead of Kneeling:
Slow Down, Don't Play, Vote

Being a good police officer is one of the most difficult, dangerous, idealistic jobs in the world. The nature of police work is such that innocent people, including law enforcement officials, will sometimes be killed.

Within that framework, America has a problem. Some shootings by police officers are unjustified. And a disproportionate number of these unjustified shootings have involved white police officers and black victims.

San Francisco 49ers quarterback Colin Kaepernick has intensified the national debate on this issue. His first open act of protest was to sit while the national anthem was played prior to an August 26, 2016, pre-season game against the Green Bay Packers. Thereafter, Kaepernick told NFL.com, "I am not going to stand up to show pride in a flag for a country that oppresses black people and people of color. To me, this is bigger than football, and it would be selfish on my part to look the other way. There are bodies in the street and people getting paid leave and getting away with murder."

Kaepernick later modified his protest by kneeling on one knee instead of sitting while the national anthem is played. His protest is now being emulated by other athletes, in other leagues, and in other sports.

I'm conversant with the issues involved. Years ago, I wrote a book about Thomas Shea, a New York City cop who shot and killed a ten-year-old African American named Clifford Glover. Shot him in the back. Later, as Muhammad Ali's biographer, I saw what one man can accomplish by standing up for his beliefs in the face of an unjust system. I was tangentially involved as an attorney in litigation against state authorities after two Jackson State College students were shot and killed by members of the Mississippi Highway Patrol in 1970. And in 1971, I experienced the criminal justice system in Selma, Alabama, firsthand.

Something bothered me when Colin Kaepernick began his protest. At first, I couldn't put my finger on it. Then I read what Jim Brown (one of the greatest football players of all time and an outspoken civil rights activist for decades) had to say.

"I would not challenge our flag," Brown declared. "I would not do anything that has to do with [dis]respecting the flag or the national anthem. I don't think it's appropriate."

I'm inclined to agree with Brown. Part of that sentiment springs from the belief that we need more unifying symbols in this country, not fewer. The national anthem, like the flag, has the potential to be one of these symbols.

I felt more comfortable with Kaepernick's protest when he chose to kneel rather than sit while the anthem is played. Sitting seems too dismissive, whereas kneeling is more respectful. And I can see the benefit in standing at attention with an upraised fist in the manner of Tommie Smith and John Carlos with its powerful imagery of speaking out for what is right.

Why is Kaepernick doing this? His detractors say that he's an unpatriotic second-string quarterback who's trying to draw attention to himself. But it's easier to attack Kaepernick than it is to constructively address the issues that he has raised. People who protested against the invasion of Iraq were attacked as unpatriotic too.

One might also question why playing the national anthem before sports events has become all but mandatory in the United States. We don't play the anthem before theatrical performances or concerts. And I haven't heard anyone question the patriotism of fans who start shouting halfway through the anthem. Does it bother Kaepernick's detractors when, around the time the vocalist gets to the rockets' red glare, fans are screaming, "Go, Cowboys! Fuckin' go!" And are they concerned that most telecasts cut to a commercial rather than televise the playing of the anthem?

That said, kneeling during the playing of the national anthem—like burning one's draft card in an earlier era as a protest against the war in Vietnam—is only a symbolic act. Players who kneel and do nothing more have, in the words of Khizr Khan (the father of slain war hero Humayun Khan), "sacrificed nothing."

Also, while kneeling during the national anthem might draw attention to the issue of unjustified police shootings, it doesn't apply real
pressure on the powers that be. Like wearing a hoodie in solidarity with
Trayvon Martin, it accomplishes next to nothing unless more is done.

It doesn't interrupt corporate America's cash flow.

So here's a suggestion.

Suppose Colin Kaepernick and the San Francisco 49ers took the field
a half hour late for their nationally televised Thursday night game against
the Arizona Cardinals on October 6?

Suppose Michael Jordan's Charlotte Hornets took the court a half hour
late for their home opener against the Boston Celtics on October 29?

There's strength in numbers. Team players who stand together have
less to fear in the way of retaliation than athletes in individual sports.

If an entire team is thirty minutes late for the start of a game, would
NFL commissioner Roger Goodell or NBA commissioner Adam Silver
fine all of the players and risk a widespread rebellion from their workforce? I don't think so. Goodell has enough image problems at the
moment. And Silver isn't about to risk the gains he achieved when he
brought the guillotine down on Los Angeles Clippers owner Donald
Sterling following revelation of Sterling's over-the-top bigoted remarks.
Neither league wants that confrontation with its workforce.

And there's a more radical alternative that the players can pursue.

Suppose the two teams that make it to the next Super Bowl threaten
a work slowdown or the possibility of a last-minute refusal to play the
game? Do you think that FOX Broadcasting Company, which is slated to
televise Super Bowl 51, might take a second look at its institutional stance
on the issue of police shootings if its telecast of the game were threatened?

Muhammad Ali gave up the heavyweight championship of the world
for what he believed in. Professional athletes in team sports can give up
a day's pay.

It might also be noted that the anti-war movement of the 1960s
was fueled by outrage on college campuses. That outrage wasn't entirely
selfless. College students in those days were afraid of being drafted. And I
don't mean by the NFL.

College campuses have been relatively quiet in recent years because
no one is being drafted to fight in Afghanistan or Iraq. But that doesn't

mean college students should sit on their butts. It would certainly get the attention of the powers that be if ESPN's telecast of the semi-finals and finals in the upcoming College Football Playoff were threatened.

What's the NCAA going to do about it? It can't fine the players.

Presidential election campaigns offer a unique opportunity to educate the public and engage in an intelligent dialogue on issues of national importance. That process has been sorely lacking this year, so other forms of expression (such as kneeling for the national anthem) have filled the void.

This leads to the most important thing that Colin Kaepernick and everyone else who's concerned about the road our country is taking can do.

Vote.

I'm old enough to have lived through a time when Martin Luther King Jr., Medgar Evers, Viola Liuzzo, Andrew Goodman, Michael Schwerner, James Chaney, and others died so people of color could vote.

People who think there's "no real difference" between Hillary Clinton and Donald Trump are as ignorant as the people who thought there was no real difference between George W. Bush and Al Gore sixteen years ago.

Not voting is disrespecting the best of what this nation stands for.

Moreover, there are local elections across the country that will determine who appoints police commissioners, which cases are prosecuted, and who makes policy on law enforcement matters for years to come.

North Carolina is a crucial swing state. Is Carolina Panthers quarterback Cam Newton registered to vote?

Ohio is a crucial swing state. Cleveland Cavaliers superstar LeBron James is urging people to vote.

Colin Kaepernick should be telling people to register to vote.

The beauty of voting is that one doesn't have to be an elite athlete to do it.

As a contrast to "Fistic Nuggets," these "Notes" were on the serious side.

Fistic Notes

Promoters have always wrestled with the challenge of how to build interest in a fight from the time it's announced until the opening bell. In days of old, the "tale of the tape" was part of that process.

Adam Pollack (who has written a series of excellent biographies about boxing's early gloved heavyweight champions) says that the September 23, 1880, edition of the *Boston Daily Globe* listed John L. Sullivan's measurements as 6' tall, 43" chest, 16" bicep, 14" forearm, 26" thigh, and 17" calf. Details like that became part of what would evolve into a national fascination with Sullivan.

On April 22, 1904, when Jack Johnson fought Sam McVey in San Francisco, local newspapers carried what eventually became the traditional tale of the tape. Five months later, on September 16, 1904, the *Seattle Daily Times* listed similar measurements for Tommy Burns vs. Billy Woods.

Boxing historian and memorabilia dealer Craig Hamilton says that the tale of the tape became common for big fights in California in the first decade of the twentieth century. By 1910, it was a regular part of newspaper reporting in advance of big fights.

"By the time Joe Louis was champion," Hamilton recounts, "8-by-10-inch photographs of the 'tale of the tape' were distributed regularly to newspapers to use in their pre-fight stories."

A typical "tale of the tape" layout consisted of three columns. The center column, from top to bottom, read, "height, weight, reach, neck, chest normal, chest expanded, waist, biceps, forearm, thigh, calf, wrist, ankle." The champion's (or A-side fighter's) measurements were listed in the column to the left and the challenger's on the right.

Pollack says that early versions of the tale of the tape were often inaccurate and inconsistent from fight to fight.

So were later versions. In 1964, much was made of the fact that Sonny Liston's fist measured 15 1/2 inches around (as opposed to the 12-inch fist of Cassius Clay). But when Liston fought Floyd Patterson seven months earlier, Sonny's fist had been listed as 14 inches.

The tale of the tape sprang from the misbegotten idea that physical measurements could quantify greatness in a fighter. Obviously, weight is significant in terms of the competitive nature of a fight. But other tale-of-the-tape measurements have always been of limited use.

"Reach" actually measured wingspan and was dependent in part on how broad a fighter's back was. The size of a fighter's ankle was totally irrelevant.

More importantly, the tale of the tape didn't say a thing about a fighter's quickness, ring savvy, power, technique, heart, or his ability to take a punch.

Fights fans and the media began ignoring the tale of the tape in the 1970s. The "tale" still appears in the build-up to big fights from time to time, but no one pays much attention to it.

★ ★ ★

The home of an internationally renowed concert pianist and his talented pianist wife is not where one expects to come across a large piece of boxing history. But that's what one finds in a spacious Riverside Drive apartment several blocks from the City College of New York in a gentrified part of Harlem.

Bela Szilagyi was born on March 11, 1934. As a footnote to his birth, he was the first baby born at New York Hospital to weigh two pounds or less and survive.

Bela's parents were Hungarian immigrants. His father played first violin in a Gypsy orchestra that, depending on the occasion, consisted of six to nine players. His mother worked at Governor's Cafeteria across the street from the Metropolitan Opera House.

When Bela was three, his father started teaching him to play the violin. Six years later, piano was added to his repertoire. Bela was gifted. At age twelve, he performed at Carnegie Hall as a soloist pianist. In his late teens, he was awarded a full scholarship to study music at Juilliard.

During his career, Bela performed throughout the United States and Europe with orchestras and as a solo pianist. He also taught. During the

1964–1965 academic year, he was a visiting artist in residence at the University of North Carolina at Greensboro. One of his students was a young women named Elizabeth Brett, who was eight years his junior and had started playing piano at age four.

Bela was married with five children (ages five, four, and three, in addition to one-year-old twins). After the school year ended, he sent a letter to Elizabeth, confiding, "Something has happened to me. I've fallen in love with you."

One year after graduating from college, Elizabeth moved to New York. In 1968, she and Bela were married.

What does all of this have to do with boxing?

When Bela was a boy, his father listened to Friday night fights on the radio. If Bela had practiced piano conscientiously that week, he was allowed to listen to the fights with his father. Over time, he became a passionate boxing fan.

Fast forward to 1979. Home VCRs were becoming widely available. Bela began recording fights as a hobby. Then it became an obsession. He recorded every fight that was televised live and added old fights that were shown on ESPN Classic and other networks to his archive. He received tapes of fights from overseas. News of his collection spread. Before long, television networks, promoters, managers, trainers, fighters, and fans were asking him for copies.

Thus, a business—"Captain Video Boxing"—was born.

Captain Video Boxing skirted the boundaries of copyright law. Recording the fights off of television was legal. Selling tapes of the fights was a different matter. But the copyright holders (TV networks, promoters, and a few others) frequently did business with Bela. They needed tapes from him to evaluate proposed match-ups.

Szilagyi's concert career ended in 1997, when doctors discovered an inoperable aortic aneurysm. At that point, the boxing archive became even more important to him. The venture was never cost-efficient, given the thousands of hours that he poured into it. But it was a labor of love.

Bela died in 2012. Since then, Elizabeth has maintained the collection. It contains more than 50,000 fights collected on 8,000 VHS tapes and 4,000 DVDs.

The VHS tapes are a stunning sight. Entering the Szilagyi home, one sees an immense eighty-foot-long, floor-to-ceiling bookshelf that stretches down and around a long hallway. Another room houses dozens of multicolored plastic containers, each one holding one hundred DVDs.

"Bela was obsessive," Elizabeth says. "Thank God, he started cataloging the collection early so things are well organized."

That brings us to the present. Elizabeth would like to sell the collection.

"It's a living thing," she explains. "It needs to be maintained. And I don't want to do that anymore."

But there are obstacles. Given today's technology, a buyer would want to digitalize the 8,000 VHS tapes. That would take time and money.

A lot of the material on the tapes and DVDs is available now on YouTube.

"And I want the collection to be in the right hands," Elizabeth says. "Bela's sincere objective was to create a video history of boxing. I know how much this archive meant to him, and I want it to have a good home."

★ ★ ★

Ten years ago—on October 7, 2006—Nikolay Valuev emblazoned his 7-foot-1-inch, 328-pound frame on the American boxing scene with an eleventh-round knockout of Monte Barrett in a fight that was televised by HBO. Soon after, Valuev was asked, "You always step over the ring ropes instead of climbing through them like the other boxers. Do you do this to intimidate your opponents?" With impeccable logic, Valuev answered, "I do this because it is easier for me to step over the ropes than to climb through."

Valuev went on to beat the likes of Jameel McCline, Sergey Liakhovich, John Ruiz, and a badly faded Evander Holyfield. He also briefly held the WBA heavyweight title on two occasions. Chronic physical problems hampered his ring career, which ended with a November 7, 2009, majority-decision loss to David Haye.

Valuev, along with the Klitschko brothers and Kostya Tszyu, was part of a generation of fighters who came out of what had once been the Soviet Union.

And he was aware of what might follow.

"The time has come," Valuev said in 2007. "It is our turn now. Since the breakdown of the Soviet Union, many boxers have taken the opportunity to head west and have trained there. By doing so, they have gained valuable experience. We are influenced by the Russian school, but we can implement this newfound knowledge. That is the secret of our success."

Gennady Golovkin, Sergey Kovalev, Vasyl Lomachenko, and others have proven Valuev right. Their time has come.

★ ★ ★

It's often said that boxing, despite the duplicity that surrounds it outside the ring, is the most honest sport. That contention stands what might be called the test of time.

In theory, a football game contains sixty minutes of action. But a *Wall Street Journal* study determined that, in an average National Football League contest, the ball is in play for only eleven minutes.

A similar study by the *WSJ* concluded that the average Major League Baseball game contains seventeen minutes and fifty-eight seconds of action.

NBA basketball delivers forty-eight minutes of actual play plus free-throw shooting while the clock is stopped. But the last two minutes of a basketball game can take twenty minutes if the team that's losing intentionally fouls to stop the clock.

In boxing, a fighter who's behind late in a fight and fouls intentionally is penalized and sometimes disqualified. In basketball, the transgressor is sometimes rewarded.

Meanwhile, boxing's clock is constant. Three minutes of action in every round with a one-minute rest period in between. Unless of course, a fight ends early because of a knockout.

Baseball doesn't have first-inning knockouts.

★ ★ ★

PBC's boxing telecasts have highlighted a troubling trend. The men on the commentating teams come in all shapes and sizes from Marv

Albert to Teddy Atlas. The women, for the most part, are packaged like models on assignment.

This phenomenon isn't limited to boxing. Savvy women sideline reporters like fifty-year-old NBA expert Doris Burke (who has everyday looks and outstanding journalistic skills) are few and far between. Many of Burke's sister commentators are better known for their appearance than their knowledge of the sports they cover. *Bleacher Report* once ran a feature entitled "The 50 Hottest Female Sports Broadcasters from Around the World."

But the problem is particularly acute in boxing, where many women hosts and reporters seem as though they've been prepped for a modeling assignment that involves little more than reading scripted lines and asking scripted questions.

Why is it that a certain type of look is a prerequisite for women to be behind a microphone in boxing but the same requirement doesn't exist for men?

Just asking.

★ ★ ★

Last month, the WBC released its ranking of the top ten WBC middleweight champions of all time.

Ray Leonard is #1, which is a stretch. As great as Leonard was, he had only two wins at middleweight; one against Marvin Hagler and the other in his long-forgotten third bout against Roberto Duran.

Bernard Hopkins is ranked #2 by the WBC. Then things get truly idiotic.

The WBC lists Joey Giardello as its third-greatest middleweight champion. That places Giardello (a marginal champion) ahead of Carlos Monzon (#4), Marvin Hagler (#5), Nino Benvenuti (#6), and Gennady Golovkin (#7).

Boxing fans should keep these rankings in mind the next time the WBC tries to defend the credibility of its contemporary rankings.

★ ★ ★

Some Thoughts on Boxing

Carlo Rotella: "Boxing is brutal and corrupt, which is part of what makes it worth writing about."

Carlos Acevedo: "Boxing is the most serious of all sports; a sport where participants actively forge their own destinies from moment to moment."

Hamilton Nolan: "Boxing, unlike a job that involves spending hours wasting time on the Internet each day, is unforgiving of even the smallest amount of slacking."

Matt Wells: "Boxing is a tough sport to wrap your head around. A fighter has to maintain a certain level of aggression without letting it get out of control."

Robert Ecksel: "Boxing is all things to all people. For some of us, for the exceptionally delusional, it's the noble art, the sweet science, the sport of sports, the gentlemanly art of self-defense, and the fight game. For others, perhaps more discerning or less, it's just two guys punching each other in the face."

★ ★ ★

Word that forty-three-year-old Nigerian heavyweight Ike Ibeabuchi has been released from prison and plans a return to boxing has prompted a flood of memories.

Ibeabuchi posted a 20-0 (15 KOs) record highlighted by victories over David Tua and Chris Byrd. He was a force in the heavyweight division and had the look of a future champion. But there were problems. Ibeabuchi's personality was—shall we say—mercurial. There were wild mood swings and outbursts of temper leading to unacceptable conduct.

In July 1999, Ibeabuchi telephoned a sex-industry service and asked that a lap dancer be sent to his room at the Mirage Hotel and Casino in Las Vegas. According to testimony, the dancer insisted on cash payment in advance, at which point the 245-pound fighter became enraged and raped her. This came on the heels of similar allegations against Ibeabuchi made by two other outcall dancers in Nevada and Arizona. Ibeabuchi was sentenced to five to thirty years in prison as the result of a plea deal with prosecutors.

Cedric Kushner promoted Ibeabuchi for much of the boxer's career and was frustrated by his erratic behavior.

Kushner once had lunch at The Palm in New York with Ideabuchi, Steve Munisteri (Ibeabuchi's manager), and Lou DiBella (then with HBO). At one point during the conversation, Ibeabuchi became enraged, grabbed a steak knife, and jammed it into the table.

On another cccasion, Kushner told associates, "Ike telephoned me at three o'clock in the morning and complained that he was seeing demons. I understand why Ike was seeing demons. What I don't understand is why he called me."

★ ★ ★

The Association of Boxing Commissions (ABC) has been in existence since 1985 and currently has sixty-eight state and Native American member commissions. Thirty-eight commissions from outside of the United States have joined as associate members but do not have voting rights.

In July 2015, Mike Mazzulli (director of the Department of Athletic Regulation for the Mohegan Tribe) defeated Bernie Profato (director of the Ohio Athletic Commission) in an election to determine the new ABC president. Mazzulli succeeded Tim Lueckenhoff (executive director of the Missouri Office of Athletics), who had served six 2-year terms as ABC president and was barred from seeking reelection last year by a recent term-limits initiative.

It was a contentious election with Lueckenhoff backing Profato. And the split widened after Mazzulli's victory when he named new chairpeople for each ABC committee.

Mazzulli's backers say that he's entitled to bring in a new team with a philosophy that matches his own. They also point to areas where the ABC can, and should, be doing a better job. His opponents claim that qualified chairpeople were removed from their positions simply because they supported Lueckenhoff and Profato.

Now the other shoe has dropped.

On February 5, 2016, Lueckenhoff sent out a press release announcing formation of the Association of Combative Sports Commissions

(ACSC), which he described as "a newly-formed non-profit organization comprised of athletic commissions" that will "move in a new direction in working to protect the health, safety and welfare of combative sports contestants."

The press release further stated, "Any athletic commission or similar government entity [in the United States or elsewhere] is invited to be a ACSC member regardless of whether or not is it affiliated with [the ABC]. All athletic commissions will be granted full membership and accompanying full voting rights."

Lueckenhoff subsequently announced that the ACSC will hold its inaugural conference from July 9 through July 12, 2016, in New Orleans. That's three weeks before the ABC convenes in Las Vegas for its annual meeting.

In response, Pat Reid (executive director of the Edmonton Combative Sports Association) sent an e-mail to Lueckenhoff with a copy to everyone on the ABC distribution list.

Reid's e-mail read in part, "My disappointment is that you were ABC president for six consecutive terms, and I would have thought you would have had more allegiance to the organization you headed up for such a long period of time. The optics do not look good. After twelve years, as soon as you lose an election, you appear to have gone off and formed a rival organization. It's unfortunate you could not find it in yourself to continue to work within the ABC rather than going in this direction. I don't understand why you wanted to destroy your legacy with the ABC rather than continue to contribute to its ongoing success."

Contacted by *The Ring*, Lueckenhoff said that Missouri would retain its membership in the ABC and that he hoped the ACSC would be more global in nature than the ABC has been.

Boxing needs two associations of state and Native American boxing commissions even less than it needs another world sanctioning body.

★ ★ ★

Writer Tom Gerbasi has a nice ear for quotes. And he put it to good use recently in recounting a sitdown with George Foreman. Among the thoughts that Big George voiced were:

★ "Boxing is an easy sport to get into, probably the easiest of all. But it's the hardest one to get out of. The person most responsible for over-seeing his welfare is the fighter himself. And I had never thought about that in my life, how I really wanted to leave. Most people aren't given that kind of advice. And we're failures, all of us, because we can't see that we want to get out the way we came in, feeling good about ourselves."

★ [On Sonny Liston as his role model]: "He'd been heavyweight champion of the world. I'd see that title belt sitting there in his luxurious home and the way he treated people. I said I guess that's the way you ought to be when you're champion. And I started being the same way. As a matter of fact, I think I became worse. I picked up a lot of bad habits because I didn't know they were bad habits. I thought they were just traits of being champion of the world."

★ [On Muhammad Ali, Joe Frazier, Ken Norton, and too many of the other men he fought dying in recent years]: "I never did visualize a world without them. And when they started passing, it hurt. It's like a part of me died."

It's also worth mentioning something that Foreman said to me in 2014 after undergoing a knee replacement: "I'm happy with my life. The only thing I'd change today is, I would have done my roadwork on grass, not concrete."

★ ★ ★

Once upon a time, there were no clearly defined weight classes in boxing. Combatants who were referred to as "lightweights" entertained crowds prior to some championship bouts. But fighters of average size weren't taken seriously until the early 1800s when English fighters weigh-ing 154 pounds or less became known as "middleweights."

In 1853, Nat Langham became the first widely acknowledged cham-pion in a weight division below heavyweight, when he knocked out Tom Sayers in a middleweight title bout that lasted sixty-one rounds. Then, in 1909, the London-based National Sporting Club established the eight weight classes that remained the backbone of championship boxing for the better part of a century: heavyweight, light-heavyweight, middleweight, welterweight, lightweight, featherweight, bantamweight, and flyweight.

Boxing now has seventeen weight divisions. The primary rationale for this proliferation is that fighters should not be forced to choose between dehydrating to make weight and facing opponents who are significantly heavier than they are. But that rationale has been undermined by day-before weigh-ins, which have increased the practice of "drying out" and, in some instances, increased the disparity in fight-night weight.

For the better part of a century, fighters weighed in on the day of a fight, and sometimes in the ring immediately before they fought. Day-before weigh-ins were instituted to accommodate the desire of promoters for television sound bites that helped market fights. For mega-fights, the weigh-in is now an attraction in and of itself.

This gives rise to two issues. The first is the health and safety of the fighter. The second is how day-before weigh-ins affect the competitive balance of fights.

The medical rationale for early weigh-ins is that it's dangerous for a fighter to compete in a dehydrated state where his body is deprived of fluid and essential minerals and that a fighter needs at least twenty-four hours to recover from drying out. But gaining sixteen pounds in a day isn't so healthy either. And while a fighter who dries out for a weigh-in thirty hours before a fight has time to recover, early weigh-ins are unfair to fighters who can make weight on the day of a fight. In many instances, they force fighters who might otherwise legitimately make weight to dry out and drop down a division in order to face comparably sized adversaries.

Let's look at the situation in reverse. No one would suggest that jockeys in the Kentucky Derby be allowed to weigh in thirty hours before the race and then dry out to lessen their horse's load. Yet in principle, that's what boxing allows today.

Tradition alone isn't a valid reason to return to same-day weigh-ins any more than it's a valid reason to return to fifteen-round title fights. But boxing needs a serious study of the issue from a medical and competitive point of view. And one state can't do it alone. Because if one state bans same-day weigh-ins, it would lose big fights to other jurisdictions.

Let's start by gathering a statistical base. The ABC should ask its member commissions to weigh all fighters in the dressing room before they fight. Then its medical committee should evaluate the data with an eye toward fighter safety and competitive balance.

★ ★ ★

Recent negotiations for the fight between Gennady Golovkin and Canelo Alvarez highlighted some of the idiocies that undermine boxing today.

Golovkin, as of this writing, is the WBA "super world middleweight champion," IBF "world middleweight champion," and WBC "world middleweight champion," having been recently elevated by the WBC from its "interim world middleweight champion" throne.

Alvarez is the former WBC and current "lineal world middleweight champion" despite the fact that he never fought a fight in which the contract weight was 160 pounds.

It's a given that boxing has too many champions. But the Golovkin-Alvarez negotiations put the spotlight on another problem. Fighters with economic leverage now often use their clout to gain an unfair competitive edge through the imposition of "catchweights."

I have no problem with fighters agreeing to fight at whatever weight they choose when a championship isn't at stake. Last year, Danny Garcia and Lamont Peterson contracted to face each other at 143 pounds despite the fact that each man held a 140-pound belt. That's okay. There was no title at stake and both men were comfortable at the weight.

But in recent years, Floyd Mayweather, Manny Pacquiao, Oscar De La Hoya, Miguel Cotto, and others have imposed strength-draining catchweights on opponents in so-called championship fights. The world sanctioning organizations have been reluctant to end the practice because they want the sanctioning fees that elite fighters contribute to their coffers. And state athletic commissions have no say in the matter because they regulate fights, not belts.

Alvarez himself was the victim of a catchweight squeeze when he challenged Mayweather for a 154-pound belt while not being allowed to weigh-in above 152 pounds. Then Canelo sought to impose a similar inequity on Golovkin. More specifically, he said that he would only defend his 160-pound title if Gennady agreed to weigh-in at 155 pounds.

If a fight is for a championship, both fighters should be permitted to weigh in at the maximum weight allowable in that division.

★ ★ ★

Craig Hamilton, one of boxing's foremost memorabilia dealers, estimates that he has close to ten thousand photographs. His favorite dates to August 29, 1885, and is the only known photo of John L. Sullivan in action in one of his fights.

In the photo, Sullivan, who is clearly out of shape, can be seen standing over Dominick McCaffery, whom he knocked down several times. The bout was originally scheduled for six rounds but lasted seven, after which the referee declared Sullivan the winner by decision. In a harbinger of things to come, both combatants wore gloves.

The photo is known in the trade as an original first-generation image. Hamilton didn't know it existed until 2014 when he acquired it from a collector. He estimates that, because of its historical significance and rarity, it's worth between $3,000 and $4,000.

"Nothing preserves a sport more vividly than visual images," Hamilton says. "Maybe someday we'll find more photos of John L. Sullivan in action. But for now, this is the only one that's known to have survived."

★ ★ ★

On June 3, 2014, I had a conversation with Mauricio Sulaiman, who, several months earlier, had succeeded his father as president of the World Boxing Council. Sulaiman told me he intended to introduce a mandatory testing program that would require all WBC champions and fighters ranked by the organization in the top fifteen to submit to mandatory PED testing by VADA on a year-round basis. A champion who refused to be tested would be stripped of his title. Contenders who refused would be removed from the rankings.

VADA (the Voluntary Anti-Doping Agency) is run by Dr. Margaret Goodman, who served previously as chief ringside physician and chairperson of the medical advisory board for the Nevada State Athletic Commission. It's the most credible of the entities that test for the use of illegal performance-enhancing drugs in boxing today.

My response to Sulaiman reflected my skepticism: "It would be great if you did it, but I don't think you will. Whatever drug-testing program you put in place will have loopholes because the WBC won't give up the sanctioning fees that elite fighters engender."

"We will do it," Mauricio assured me.

"If you do, I'll sing your praises to the sky."

There have been jiggles and bumps along the way. But on July 1, 2016, the WBC sent out an advisory that reads as follows: "To all promoters, managers, trainers, and boxers . . . The WBC announced the official registration period for the Clean Boxing Program on May 5 in Las Vegas, Nevada. Every champion and any top-15-rated fighter in the WBC is eligible for out-of-competition and in-competition random testing. The Voluntary Anti-Doping Association (VADA) is responsible to administer the program, including the system, which randomly selects eligible boxers for collection of samples. This section of the Clean Boxing Program, which is random testing, has no cost to the boxer, their representatives or anyone else, as it is paid in full by the Clean Boxing Program. All eligible fighters must submit their paperwork to enroll in the program immediately, as the 90-day grace period will expire August 9, 2016. Any fighter who is not enrolled in the Clean Boxing Program will be removed from the WBC ratings."

Will the WBC really enforce its newly announced PED-testing program and sanction elite fighters who refuse to submit to random testing?

I hope that, in the near future, I have occasion to sing Mauricio Sulaiman's praises to the sky.

★ ★ ★

Boxing is a rude sport and business. But the people who oversee world amateur boxing are taking things to a new level.

International Boxing Association president Cing-Kuo Wu recently suggested that professional boxers be allowed to compete in the 2016 Rio de Janeiro Olympics.

The proposal is part of an effort by IBA to expand its power base and regain its following in parts of the world (most notably, the United States) where interest in amateur boxing has waned. It's absurd.

Lennox Lewis won a gold medal in the super-heavyweight division at the 1988 Seoul Olympics. Ever a fount of common sense, Lewis had this to say to the BBC about IBA's proposal:

"It's preposterous. The amateur system is for amateurs. They have a lack of experience and they are not that primed as a professional. Now, all of a sudden, you get a world champion or somebody in the top ten as a professional going against an amateur, somebody with a lack of experience. I don't look at that as being fair. It's a different type of boxing altogether. So for them to marry the two, I don't think they marry well."

"Anthony Joshua went to the Olympics," Lewis continued. "If he had boxed Wladimir Klitschko at the Olympics, it wouldn't have been fair for him because Wladimir has seventy fights as a professional. I don't really understand it."

Patrick English, who has long had an interest in fighter safety and serves as the attorney for Main Events, concurs.

"If anyone thinks an amateur can compete with an elite professional, they are deluded," English says. "The punching power of an elite professional and the ring generalship learned over many professional bouts is simply too great. This is a death or brain trauma waiting to happen."

Professionals are allowed to compete in most Olympic sports. But this isn't a question of young competitors being outrun by Usain Bolt or flummoxed by Stephen Curry. Does IBA really want eighteen-year-old amateurs being hit in the head by the likes of Sergey Kovalev and Gennady Golovkin?

The remedy for what ails amateur boxing is a better scoring system (one that weighs debilitating punches more heavily than jabs) coupled with judges who are competent and honest.

★ ★ ★

Big fights in Las Vegas are marked by myriad promotional activities. Two days before Canelo Alvarez vs. Amir Khan, Golden Boy arranged for a panel discussion featuring Lennox Lewis, Evander Holyfield, Oscar De La Hoya, and Bernard Hopkins.

Evander stole the show. Among the thoughts he offered were:

★ "I became heavyweight champion of the world. And the next day, they told me, 'But you didn't beat Tyson.' I said, 'I beat the guy [Buster Douglas] that beat Tyson.' And they said, 'That don't matter.'"

★ "When I fought George Foreman, he was throwing boulders and I was throwing rocks. But I threw a lot of them."

★ "You get hit and it hurts. But you got to act like it don't."

★ "I was a 20-to-1 underdog when I fought Mike Tyson. But Mike didn't think that."

★ ★ ★

Sugar Ray Leonard is enshrined in boxing lore because of his victories over Thomas Hearns, Roberto Duran, Marvin Hagler, and Wilfredo Benetiz. But two of his other triumphs provide an interesting footnote to ring history.

Leonard fought eleven times in 1978. One of those fights was an April 13 third-round knockout of Bobby Haymon at the Capitol Centre in Landover, Maryland. Then, on September 9, Leonard stopped Floyd Joy Mayweather in the tenth round at the Civic Center in Providence, Rhode Island.

For the uninitiated, that's knockout victories over Al Haymon's brother and Floyd Mayweather's father in the same year.

★ ★ ★

June 18, 2016, marks the diamond anniversary of one of the most memorable fights in ring history. Seventy-five years ago, Joe Louis and Billy Conn did battle at the Polo Grounds in New York in one of the most storied bouts in boxing lore.

Louis was heavyweight champion of the world with a 49-and-1 record and 42 knockouts. His first-round stoppage of Max Schmeling in 1938 had redefined what it meant to be black in America and fixed the Brown Bomber firmly in the consciousness of the free world. Now, in 1941, England was at war. Six months later, in Winston Churchill's words, the new world would come to the rescue of the old.

Louis had seventeen successful heavyweight championship defenses to his credit before weighing in at 199 1/2 pounds to face Conn.

Conn, who had relinquished the light-heavyweight crown to campaign as a heavyweight, sported a 59-9-1 ledger and had been on the canvas only twice in his ring career. But he lacked big-punch power, having scored only 13 knockouts in sixty-nine fights.

More ominously, Conn officially weighed in to fight Louis at 174 pounds. And it was reliably said that his actual weight that night was 169.

Conn had a way with words. Before the bout, he told reporters, "Joe's a nice guy. I ain't mad at him. I just want that title of his."

He almost got it.

Louis scored well in the early going but couldn't put away the challenger. Conn, boxing masterfully, controlled the middle stanzas. After twelve rounds, Louis trailed on the scorecards by a 7-4-1, 7-5, 6-6 margin.

The time of the knockout was 2:58 of the thirteenth round. Conn said afterward that he got too brave and careless. An alternative explanation is that, eventually, the inevitable happened. A right to the jaw followed by a barrage of right hands put the challenger on the canvas. He struggled valiantly to regain his feet, but was unable to do so until just after the count of ten.

If Conn had beaten the count, he would have had a minute to recover before the start of round fourteen. But in all likelihood, Louis would still have prevailed.

In 1941, championship fights were scored on the basis of rounds, not points. That would have benefited Conn. Had round thirteen been scored, the challenger would still have led 7-5-1, 7-6, 6-7. But at that point, Conn was hurt and tiring badly. Even if Louis failed to score a knockout in round fourteen or fifteen, most likely the Brown Bomber would have dominated those six minutes. That would have given the champion a 9-6, 8-7, 7-7-1 triumph.

"Billy was great last night," Conn's manager Johnny Ray said afterward. "But Louis was just a little greater." Ray also said of his fighter, "He was swell in defeat, but we'd rather have won."

Five years later—on June 19, 1946—Louis and Conn fought again, this time at Yankee Stadium. Louis had managed to stay reasonably sharp during the intervening years by boxing exhibitions during the war. Conn hadn't fought in four years and was a shadow of his former self.

"He can run but he can't hide," Louis said of Conn before their rematch.

To that, Art Rooney (one of America's preeminent sportsmen) added, "Billy is like every guy who's been knocked out by Joe Louis. Sure, Billy was great the first time. He'd never been tagged by Joe before and he never knew how hard Joe could hit. He knows now, and it's not good. No guy going in against Louis the second time has the same confidence."

Louis knocked Conn out in the eighth round.

So on June 18, raise a glass to Joe Louis and Billy Conn. Seventy-five years after their historic first encounter, they're remembered together in history and deservedly so.

★ ★ ★

More Thoughts on Boxing

Randall "Tex" Cobb: "I hit people, but I ain't mad at them. If I want to quit, I can. If I get scared, I can sit. I don't because that's part of the game. But if this were a real fight, do you think I'd be out there with leather on my fists? I'd be out behind a bar in some alley with a bat. I'd be tearing the guy's lungs out. This ain't the real thing. It's a game."

Andre Berto: "The boxing media can make you a lot of money. They can make you bigger than what you are. If you're good enough, they can make you a superstar. But you got to be careful with the boxing media because they're up and down. If you're a superstar, they're your best friend. But if you lose in a way they don't like, they turn it around really quick."

George Chuvalo: "When you win, you feel like a lion. When you lose, you feel like a Christian."

★ ★ ★

UFC made its long-awaited New York debut at Madison Square Garden on November 12, 2016.

The star of UFC 205 was Conor McGregor, a trash-talking former plumber who stepped into the void when Ronda Rousey lost to Holly Holm on November 15 of last year. McGregor subsequently lost to Nate Diaz. But unlike Rousey, who has been out of action since losing to Holm, Conor returned quickly to the octagon and defeated Diaz on a razor-thin majority decision in a rematch this past August 20.

When UFC 205 finally arrived, McGregor disposed of Eddie Alvarez with relative ease to claim the UFC 155-pound throne. Tyron Woodley and Joanna Jedrzejczyk prevailed in other title fights.

Boxing can learn from UFC. Take the September 27 kickoff press conference for UFC 205 as an example. The curtain went up on the stage at The Theater at Madison Square Garden. UFC president Dana White was standing center stage at a podium flanked by a dozen combatants who would appear on the card and were seated on either side of him. There were no long-winded speeches from managers, trainers, television executives, athletic commission personnel, or sponsors. White and the fighters took questions for thirty minutes. Then the press conference was over.

On fight night, the attitude wasn't, "We have Conor McGregor in the main event so the undercard can be garbage." It was, "Let's give people who are buying tickets and paying for the pay-per-view a lot of exciting fights." Moreover, by and large, UFC gives its fans what they want to see when they want to see it. It doesn't "marinate" fights until the meat turns rancid.

★ ★ ★

Cleaning out old files is an adventure. I never know what I'll find. Recently, I was going through some notes on a telephone conversation I had with Dan Goossen years ago.

"I'm sitting here with Pete Rose," Goossen said proudly.

That piqued my interest because, among other things, I'd heard that Rose participated in several amateur fights when he was young. So Dan put Pete on the phone, and I asked Major League Baseball's all-time career hits leader about his ring exploits.

"I was fourteen years old," Rose told me. "I had two fights and lost them both. The second one was against a guy who had five kids at ringside watching. I didn't get knocked out. But I did say to myself, 'I better go play ball.'"

★ ★ ★

Professional boxers beat people up for a living. But some of them are among the nicest people you'll ever meet.

Alex Stewart, who died on November 16, 2016, at the much-too-young age of fifty-two, was one of the nicest people I've ever met.

Stewart was born in England on June 28, 1964. The son of Jamaican immigrants, he grew up in London and was athletically gifted as a child.

"I started boxing to please people," Stewart told me years ago. "It made me feel good to have someone come over to me after I won and say, 'Nice fight, congratulations.' Then I saw Sugar Ray Leonard at the Olympics in Montreal. From that day on, I wanted to be an Olympic fighter. I told my mum, and she laughed at me. She said, 'You're twelve years old and you're not going to any Olympics in boxing.' But when I was fifteen, my parents moved back to Jamaica and that made me more determined than ever to reach my goal."

Representing Jamaica, Stewart won a bronze medal in the 1983 Pan Am Games. Then, fighting under the Jamaican flag at the 1984 Los Angeles Olympics, he fulfilled his dream, scoring a second-round knockout in his first bout before losing by decision to a more-experienced foe.

Two years later, Stewart turned pro under the guidance of co-managers Jim Fennell and Mike Jones. He won his first twenty-four fights by knockout over the usual suspects. But he was slow, even for a heavyweight. That was painfully clear on November 4, 1989, when he stepped up the level of competition and was stopped by another undefeated fighter—Evander Holyfield—in the eighth round.

The first four losses in Stewart's career were against Holyfield, Mike Tyson, Michael Moorer, and George Foreman. He is the only man to have fought all four of them. His final ring record was 43 wins against 10 losses with 40 knockouts and 7 KOs by. He never won the big fight. But he came close.

On April 11, 1992, Stewart fought George Foreman at the Thomas & Mack Center in Las Vegas.

"George is one of the nicest people I've ever met," Alex said before the bout. "But fighting and eating hamburgers are two different things."

Foreman dropped Stewart twice in the second round and looked to be en route to an easy triumph. But Stewart fought back behind a punishing jab and beat Foreman's face into a disfigured bloody mess. The decision could have gone either way. Big George prevailed by a razor-thin 94-93, 94-93, 94-94 margin.

"This guy hurt me," Foreman acknowledged at the post-fight press conference. "When he hit me, it was like a brick going up against my bones. Such pain. I never want to go through that again as long as I live."

This from a man who had fought Muhammad Ali, Joe Frazier, Evander Holyfield, and Gerry Cooney before fighting Stewart.

Bill Caplan (who was Foreman's publicist at that time and has been his friend for years) recalls George looking at his face in the mirror after fighting Stewart and saying, "I can't go home to my wife looking like this."

Alex Stewart had a ready smile and almost musical voice.

"As far as hurting my opponent is concerned," he told me long ago, "that's not what boxing is about to me at all. I just want to win. I don't need anger or hate or the other things some fighters use to motivate themselves. In the ring, I take care of business; that's all. Some fighters, when they knock an opponent down and see him struggling to get up, they want him to make it so they can hit him again. I'm not like that. I want the guy to stay down so I can win. Hey, if I wanted him standing up, I wouldn't have knocked him down to begin with."

There was sadness in the boxing community when Stewart died last week. "He was a sweet guy," longtime boxing writer Ron Borges said. "If ever anyone was miscast as a fighter, Alex Stewart was the guy." Jerry Izenberg, the dean of American sportswriters, was in accord, noting, "Alex was a pretty good fighter and a great great guy."

And what of the man whose face Stewart beat into a swollen bloody mess? On the day I heard that Alex had died, I reached out to George Foreman.

"Meeting Alex Stewart the first time was special for me, both of us being Olympians," George said. "Our first meeting was in Houston while I was in retirement [in the mid-1980s]. It was all joy. The next time we met, it was to announce we'd be fighting. We fought, and it was a brutal night for me. I had Alex down twice. Thinking the fight was over, I eased up a bit. Alex let me know he truly was fit. It was all I could do to keep him off me. When the match was over, you'd never tell who the winner was by our faces. Alex had me looking like the Cowardly Lion from *The Wizard of Oz*. I'll never forget his will and desire to compete. Yet I will always remember him and our first meeting; just a cheerful boy who wanted to make a name for himself and his family. Going to miss him."

Alex Stewart is part of boxing history. May he be respectfully and fondly remembered.

★ ★ ★

A significant anniversary in boxing history is drawing near. Thirty years ago—on November 22, 1986—twenty-year-old Mike Tyson annihilated Trevor Berbick to claim his first championship belt. Nine months later, he was the undisputed, unified, heavyweight champion of the world.

Tyson-Berbick was contested at the Hilton Hotel in Las Vegas. Berbick (31-4-1, 23 KOs) had claimed the WBC crown with a narrow points win over Pinklon Thomas eight months earlier. Tyson entered the ring with 27 victories and 25 knockouts in twenty-seven outings.

It was a coronation rather than a competitive fight.

Don King once said of Tyson, "No fighter has ever been more committed to the knockout. And no fighter was ever better able to deliver it."

There was no feeling-out process in Tyson-Berbick. Tyson went after his foe like a pitbull tearing apart a rabbit. He dominated Berbick from the opening bell and staggered him several times in the first stanza. In round two, he pummeled Berbick around the ring, knocking him down twice. After the second knockdown, Berbick tried to rise from the canvas and fell down. Twice. It was over at 2:35 of the second round.

Tyson looks askance now at the person he was when he was heavyweight champion. The self-loathing he felt then appears to have been replaced by cautious optimism on his part regarding the future and how he has evolved as a person.

"The best decision I ever made was to retire from boxing," Tyson says. "I like the person I am now more than I did. I don't like Iron Mike. I like Mike Tyson."

That said, I hope that, on some level, Tyson understands and derives satisfaction from what a great fighter he was when he was young.

★ ★ ★

Sixteen years ago—on November 11, 2000—the eyes of the fight world were on Las Vegas when Lennox Lewis successfully defended his heavyweight throne against the challenge of David Tua. But the rest of the world was focused on the uncertainty surrounding the November 7, 2000, presidential election and whether George Bush or Al Gore would be awarded Florida's twenty-five electoral votes and become the next president of the United States. Ultimately, Bush prevailed before the United States Supreme Court by a 5-to-4 margin.

Eight years later, on November 4, 2008, Barack Obama defeated John McCain to become the forty-fourth president of the United States. The next day, Roy Jones and Joe Calzaghe met at the final prefight press conference prior to their November 8, 2008, fight at Madison Square Garden.

"Last night made us all equal," Roy told me as we chatted after the press conference.

Three nights later, I was in Jones's dressing room after he lost a lopsided decision to Calzaghe. Roy sat on a folding metal chair with his head down, his face battered and swollen. Roy Jones III, age eight, stood to the side with tears streaming down his face. Raegan Jones, as cute as a four-year-old can be, moved to her father's side and put her arms around him.

"I'm a big girl, daddy," Raegan said. "I don't cry."

Roy smiled and gave her a hug. Then I reminded Roy of what he'd said the morning after Barack Obama was elected president.

Roy's face lit up.

"God is good," he told me.

On November 19, 2016, the eyes of the fight world will once again be on Las Vegas when Andre Ward and Sergey Kovalev meet in the most significant boxing match of the year. Once again, presidential politics will provide the backdrop; this time with the reality that Donald Trump has been elected president of the United States.

★ ★ ★

Author's Note: The item below was written several months before Muhammad Ali's death.

Muhammad Ali in his prime was one of the most exciting, charismatic people who ever lived. In recent years, physical infirmities have taken a toll on "The Greatest." But the world is still drawn to Ali. And Ali watchers still take note when new insights into his character are revealed.

BoxNation will soon televise an original half-hour documentary entitled *My Life with Ali.* The show is built around a six-hour interview that I conducted with Khalilah Ali on January 26–27 of this year. Andrew Muscato directed the project.

Anyone who was alive in the 1960s and 1970s knew who Khalilah was. Her name then was Belinda Ali, and she was married to the most famous man on earth. Belinda was ten years old when she met Cassius Marcellus Clay Jr. in 1960. She was seventeen when they married in 1967. For ten years, until their marriage eroded, she was in the eye of the hurricane that was Muhammad Ali's life.

The documentary tracks Khalilah's upbringing in the Nation of Islam, Ali's ring career, his refusal to accept induction into the United States Army, and more. One of my favorite exchanges comes in response to the thought I voiced that, every time Ali looked in the mirror and said "I'm so pretty," he was saying "black is beautiful" before that phrase became fashionable.

"That's what you think?" Khalilah countered. Then she laughed. "If Ali saw himself in the mirror, he saw he was beautiful. It wasn't about no black pride or nothing like that. He was just a pretty boy thinking he cute. It wasn't a black is beautiful kind of thing. He was pretty."

Some of the most poignant portions of the documentary deal with Khalilah's growing awareness that Ali was unfaithful to her and the humiliation that his profligate womanizing caused her. It was a thread that ran through their marriage and ultimately became too much for her to live with.

But Khalilah also talked about the things that made Ali great and closed on a positive note, saying, "Overall he's a good person. I pray that he walks in paradise when he leaves and he's at peace with himself and he's at peace with God. And I thank him for the children that we were blessed to have and the children he was blessed to have other than my own."

Making a documentary involves choices. Not everything of value can survive the final cut. So it's worth noting a few exchanges that BoxNation subscribers can look forward to in future Ali programming.

Khalilah was raised in a strict Muslim home. The first time Ali kissed her was after he proposed marriage and she accepted. The following exchange between us took place as she looked back on that long-ago time.

Khalilah: "I said, 'Oh man, I can't do this. My mother did not tell me about this. This is not good.' I couldn't breathe. I said, 'Man, I'm seventeen years old and I can't even kiss a guy.'"

Q: "Had you kissed anybody before?"

Khalilah: "No, no."

Q: "So your first kiss ever was with Muhammad Ali?"

Khalilah: "That's my first kiss. It was scary as hell. When I got married, I was kind of—this just wasn't for me. This is not something that I was ready for. The first night we went to our own house, I didn't know what to do, where to go. I was scared, real scared. I wanted to go home. This was too much for me. He said, 'You can't go home anymore. You're my wife now.' But eventually I got over it."

It's also worth recounting what happened when Khalilah and Muhammad met Queen Elizabeth.

"I didn't know the customs over there," Khalilah told me. "All I know is, if you see somebody, you hug them. I did it so fast, they didn't catch me in time. I ran up and grabbed the Queen and hugged her. She says, 'Stop!' And these guards start coming. I said, 'I am so sorry; I didn't know.' She said, 'That's all right.' Then she patted me on the back like an old grandmother would pat her grandchild."

★ ★ ★

There are many iconic images of Muhammad Ali that are known the world over. The photograph on the front cover of this book isn't one of them. But it's one of my favorite Ali photos.

I met Alicia Shulman in the 1990s when she was a freelance photographer. We worked together on a photo essay for a national boxing magazine. Then Alicia went on to other things. Among her many ventures, she now designs jewelry for David Yurman.

Alicia's Ali photo was taken in February 1998. Muhammad was in New York for the NBA All-Star game. She left a letter with the concierge at the Sheraton Hotel where Ali was staying, asking if she could photograph him. At 9:30 that night, she received a telephone call.

"Hi, Alicia? This is Lonnie Ali, Muhammad Ali's wife."

An hour later, camera in hand, Alicia was in a suite at the Sheraton Hotel. Years later, she would recall, "I remember it all like it was yesterday. He's sitting at the dining table. The Greatest. A gentle giant in a Missoni-esque sweater. Myth meets reality. The magnitude of the moment shoots through me like electric current. His presence takes my breath away. Ali motions for me to sit in front of him. 'Let's take some pictures,' he says. I'm experiencing what will become the memory of a lifetime."

Alicia's photo of Ali captures the Muhammad I knew at that time in his life. He's fifty-six years old. The sad physical decline has begun. But the warmth, caring, inner strength, and love at the core of his character are still there and evident for all the world to see.

★ ★ ★

The tidal wave of commentary that washed over the world when Muhammad Ali died has receded in recent months. But some of the observations bear repeating. One of these comes from Bart Barry, who, shortly after Ali's death, wrote, "Look closely at how Ali set his mouth when he threw righthands—hurting punches thrown with every intention of bringing pain or unconsciousness or both to the men across from him. Don't dismiss this as an anomaly either. Ali had athleticism and charisma enough to make his living quite a few ways other than hurting others. But he hurt others for a living because he was great at it in a way we rightly call historic. That is an aesthetic judgment, not a moral one. It is a reminder that Ali's ascent from Olympic gold medalist to heavyweight champion of the world relied necessarily on his conversion from an athlete who boxed for points to a fighter who hurt other men. And he didn't do it reluctantly. Look at his eyes when he took other men's consciousness. Ali was all fighter."

★ ★ ★

Muhammad Ali fought fifty different opponents in his sixty-one professional fights. Twenty-nine of them predeceased him. As the world celebrate's Ali's life, let's pause to remember those who died before him: Tunney Hunsaker (2005), Herb Siler (2001), Tony Esperti (2002), Jim Robinson (date of death unknown), Donnie Fleeman (2012), Lamar Clark (2006), Duke Sabedong (2008), Willi Besmanoff (2010), Sonny Banks (1965), Alejandro Lavorante (1964), Archie Moore (1998), Charlie Powell (2014), Henry Cooper (2011), Sonny Liston (1970), Floyd Patterson (2006), Cleveland Williams (1999), Ernie Terrell (2014), Zora Folley (1972), Jerry Quarry (1999), Oscar Bonavena (1976), Joe Frazier (2011), Jimmy Ellis (2014), Buster Mathis (1995), Mac Foster (2010), Bob Foster (2015), Ken Norton (2013), Ron Lyle (2011), Jimmy Young (2005), Trever Berbick (2006).

Paul Gallico once wrote, "I have never had much respect for a sportswriter who can sit calmly and coldly in the press coop with no interest whatsoever in the outcome of the event he is watching. The bored sportswriter who doesn't root isn't a good one and never will be. It is human to take sides, to want to see someone win and his or her adversary lose. All the world roots. It merely requires tact and experience to know when to do it."

Paul Gallico: "A Farewell to Sport"

Boxing's popularity is linked to its tradition, so a trip down memory lane is in order.

Paul Gallico was born in New York in 1897, graduated from Columbia in 1919, and began work soon after as a writer for the *New York Daily News*. Ultimately, he became the paper's sports editor at a time when heroes like Babe Ruth, Jack Dempsey, Red Grange, Bobby Jones, and Bill Tilden roamed the American landscape and were creating "The Golden Age of Sports."

Gallico's introduction to the harsh realities of boxing came in August 1923 when he attended his first training camp. Jack Dempsey was in Saratoga Springs, readying to defend his championship against Luis Firpo.

"My burning curiosity got the better of prudence," the 6-foot-3-inch Gallico later wrote, "I asked Dempsey to permit me to box a round with him. I had never boxed before, but I was in good physical shape having just completed a four-year stretch as a galley slave in the Columbia eight-oared shell."

How did the sparring session go?

"I knew the sensation of being stalked and pursued by a relentless professional whose trade and business it was to injure men," Gallico recounted. "I saw the quick flash of the brown forearm that precedes the stunning shock as a bony leather-bound fist lands on cheek or mouth. I learned too that, as the soldier never hears the bullet that kills him, so does the fighter rarely, if ever, see the punch that tumbles blackness over him like a mantle with a tearing rip as though the roof of his skull were exploding and robs him of his senses. There was just that—a ripping in my head, then a sudden blackness, and the next thing I knew, I was sitting on the canvas with my legs collapsed under me. I held on to the floor with both hands because the ring and the audience outside were making a complete clockwise revolution, came to a stop, and then went back again counterclockwise. When it was over, I escaped through the ropes, shaking, bleeding a little from the mouth with a vicious throbbing in my head."

Thereafter, Gallico ruefully acknowledged, "A man who has been tapped on the chin with five fingers wrapped up in a leather boxing glove and propelled by the arm of an expert knows more about that particular sensation than one who has not."

Gallico left the *Daily News* in 1936 to become a full-time fiction writer. His good-bye to the world he'd previously known came in a series of essays published first in magazines and then in book form under the title *A Farewell to Sport* (Alfred A. Knopf, 1938). He lived for much of the next few decades in South Devonshire, England, and later in Mexico, Lichtenstein, Monaco, and France. He married and divorced four times (twice to baronesses).

Gallico's writing about boxing was on a par with the best of what he wrote. He was able to distill the sweet science to its gritty essence. Eight decades later, many of his observations still ring true:

★ "A fight is a fight, and there is rarely anything pretty about it. When the gong is struck, two men are unleashed against one another for purposes of destruction. Rules change and vary, but the basic idea remains the same. Two men are trying to do to one another as much injury and damage as they possibly can within an allotted time."

★ "I like my prizefighters mean. Cruelty and absolute lack of mercy are an essential quality in every successful prizefighter. I have never known one who wasn't ruthless and amoral. It is childish to believe that this can be put on and off like a mantle. The gentle lambs outside the ropes are never much good within. Much later, when they are older and retire from the ring, the mean streak may become more deeply submerged. But the life that a prizefighter lives is hardly conducive to softening his character. His brutality and viciousness are carefully cultivated."

★ "If there are any friendships among fighters, they manage to cease inside the ropes. Men whale away at one another with complete and unmerciful ferocity while the fight lasts, afterwards grin at one another through blood and sweat, shake hands, and that is that. I have asked many fighters how they felt about this, how they could bring themselves to cripple a friend and knock him out if they managed to get him going. None of them were able to give me an intelligent answer or any kind of answer beyond, 'I dunno. It's different when you're in the ring. We got no hard feelings afterwards.' Well, I suppose the manufacturer or merchant cuts his pal's throat just as cold-bloodedly with a 'Sorry! Business, you know.'"

★ "By the nature of your work [as a sportswriter], you know both men involved intimately. In a way, you are fond of them, perhaps fonder of one than the other. It is a dangerous business on which they are about to embark. It may result in disfigurement, blindness, even death, not to mention the financial importance to both parties. It is a good deal like having an appointment to go see a friend have an accident."

★ "The changes worked in fine-looking, clear-eyed youngsters who adopt the ring as a profession are sometimes shocking to observe. You see them at the start, fresh and unmarked, and you live through their grad-ual disintegration. The knotted ears and the smashed noses are the least of their injuries. Their lips begin to thicken and their eyes seem to sink deeper and deeper into the cavernous ridges above them, ridges that are thickened and scarred from battle. Many of them acquire little nervous tics. Their voices change to husky half-intelligible whispers. Their walk is affected. And worst of all, sometimes they cannot remember or they say queer things. The industry laughs and says: 'Don't pay any attention to him. He's punchy.'"

Gallico didn't like fight managers. He called them "the most shame-less rapacious, and unmoral crew in the world," adding, "The only pity is that the fight manager cannot be more decent and honest with his bum and content himself with cheating his rivals in business. A few of the men who own and operate stables of fighters are decent and reputable, but the majority are not. Some of the sheer cold-blooded heartlessness shown by so-called human beings who have the health, sanity, and lives of other human beings in their charge is sickening. A manager will coddle and protect a champion or money-making fighter because he is his meal-ticket and a valuable piece of property which he doesn't want to see dam-aged because he will be out-of-pocket. But he will send a run-of-the-mill club fighter out round after round, cut, dazed, semi-conscious, bleeding badly from wounds, to take a further beating or get knocked out. If there is any feeling of humanity or mercy in their dark souls, they keep it for themselves."

A Farewell to Sport also offers Gallico's take on some of the heavyweight champions of his time. Regarding Gene Tunney, he wrote, "When the typical denizen of the fight world said bitterly, 'Tunney thinks we're not good enough for him,' he was quite right. It was exactly what Tunney thought. And they weren't good enough either because it doesn't take much to be better than the average citizen of Cauliflower Alley. No one will ever get to the top of a game as essentially foul and unprincipled as prizefighting with absolutely clean hands. Tunney was in many ways an idealist. He was always ambitious and preferred the company of pleasant people to toughs. But he had the great strength of character to take that little stroll through the sewer when there was no other way."

As for Primo Carnera, who rode a trail of fixed fights to the heavyweight championship of the world, Gallico opined, "There is probably no more scandalous, pitiful, incredible story in all the record of these last mad sports years than the tale of the living giant, who was made into a prizefighter and developed into the heavyweight champion of the world by a group of American gangsters. Then, when his usefulness as a meal ticket was outlived, he was discarded. This unfortunate pituitary case was a poor simple-minded peasant by the name of Primo Carnera, the first son of a stonecutter of Sequals, Italy. He stood 6 feet 7 inches in height and weighed 268 pounds. Yet never in his life was he anything more than a freak and a fourth-rater at prizefighting. He was born far too late. He belonged to the twelfth or thirteenth century, when he would have been a man at arms and a famous fellow with mace and halberd, pike or bill. At least he would have fought nobly and to the limit of his great strength, properly armed, because Carnera was a courageous fellow to the limit of his endurance. In those days, he would have won honor afield and would have gotten himself decently killed or, surviving, would have been retired by his feudal lord to round out his days and talk over the old brave fights. The carrion birds that fed upon this poor, big, dumb man picked him clean. They left him nothing, not even his pride and his self-respect. That was probably the cruelest thing of all."

Gallico also embraced humor in his writing.

"Max Baer," he observed, "achieved something notable when he sold more than one hundred percent of himself to various parties in return for ready cash. He excused himself on grounds that he thought he owned a thousand percent of himself."

The most lyrical boxing writing in *A Farewell to Sport* is reserved for Jack Dempsey:

★ "He began as a rough tough nobody, a hard, mean, life-battered hobo, a kid with little or no education, bitter, disillusioned, restless, and vicious, digging food out of an equally hard rough world in which there was never any softness or decency, a tramp, a bum, and a misfit at heart."

★ "Dempsey looked the part [of a fighter]. He had dark eyes, blue-black hair, the wide but sharply sloping shoulders of the puncher, a slim waist, and fine symmetrical legs. His weaving shuffling style of approach was drama in itself and suggested the stalking of a jungle animal."

★ "Dempsey had a valuable and unlimited fund of natural cruelty, tremendous courage, speed and determination, and good hitting powers. He was never a good boxer and had little or no defense. His protection was aggression. Dempsey never boxed anybody. When the bell rang, he ran out and began to attack his opponent, and he never stopped attacking him, trying to batter him to the floor until the bell ended the round."

★ "Dempsey seemed to have a constant bottomless well of cold fury somewhere close to his throat. He had a smouldering truculence on his face and hatred in his eyes. He was utterly without mercy or pity, asked no quarter, gave none. He would do anything he could get away with, fair or foul, to win. He is accused by many of having been a foul fighter. Dempsey himself never denied it. Either it was a fight or it wasn't. He had no advantage or protective armor that was denied his opponent."

Gallico didn't always get things right. He couldn't shake the image of Joe Louis's twelfth-round stoppage at the hands of Max Schmeling in 1936 from his mind. Writing after The Brown Bomber dethroned James Braddock to claim the heavyweight crown (but before Louis-Schmeling II), Gallico proclaimed, "Joe Louis won the heavyweight championship of the world when he was on a downgrade. He will not hold it long."

All of us make mistakes.

A Farewell to Sport is beautifully written and a tribute to the craft of sportswriting. The athletes that Gallico wrote about meant a great deal to him, as he acknowledged in saying good-bye:

"Sportwriting has been an old and good friend and companion to me. One does not barge ruthlessly out of such a friendship. Rather, one lingers a little over the good-bye, sometimes even a little reluctant to leave, and uncertain, turning back as some old well-loved incident is remembered, calling up again the picture of vanished friends, having one's last say, lingering as long as one dares before that final irrevocable shutting of the door."

Ian Probert asks the question, "How could someone who calls himself a writer not be interested in writing about boxing?"

"Rope Burns" and "Dangerous"

In 1998, Ian Probert authored a book entitled *Rope Burns* that took readers on an autobiographical journey through the prism of boxing.

Probert had dabbled with being an artist and film-maker. There was a time when he worked the beat as a boxing writer. Eighteen years ago in *Rope Burns*, he wrote, "Ultimately, I left boxing because it was a world that I never really felt part of. Although it was easy to fall under the spell of these young men who tortured their bodies and battled each other for the right to put their hands on the most temporary of prizes, there was a large portion of me that knew that what I was witnessing was wrong."

Thereafter, Probert's journey was marked by hypothyroidism that, before it was diagnosed, rendered him morbidly obese and barely able to walk. There were periods in his life when he drank too much. He was depressed and, in his words, "lay in bed, night after night, trying to work out how I could die in a way that would cause the least distress to my wife and daughter."

Two decades after walking away from boxing, Probert was sucked back in. *Dangerous*, published this year by Pitch Publishing, picks up where *Rope Burns* left off. Pitch has also reissued *Rope Burns* with a new foreword and postscript by the author.

"What am I doing here among the broken noses and bulging scar tissue and calloused hands and knotted brows?" Probert asks in *Dangerous*. "I said goodbye to this a long time ago and tried not to look behind me. I suppose a comeback of sorts was always inevitable. I'm older, of course, not remotely wiser, and my stamina is shot to pieces. Sounds like an ideal time to try and do something that you used to do years ago but abandoned because you couldn't handle it anymore. Ring any bells, anyone?"

Dangerous recounts Probert's recent reunion with Michael Watson (who was beaten into a coma by Chris Eubank in 1991), Kellie Maloney (often referred to by the boxing media as "the former Frank Maloney"),

Herol Graham, Nigel Benn, Alan Minter, and others. But it isn't a book about boxing. Like *Rope Burns*, it's primarily a book about Probert and how boxing has impacted upon his life.

"Ninety-nine-point-nine percent of the time, boxing keeps a discreet distance from me," Probert writes. "And I try to keep as far away from it as circumstances permit. Boxing lets me get on with my life and, for a while, I even forget that it exists. But every now and then, it leaps out at me and catches me unawares."

Probert's insights into the sport and business of boxing are, for the most part, solid. That's not to say that all is right with *Rope Burns* and *Dangerous*. At one point, Probert opines, "For a fight to be considered a truly great fight, it must be resolved with a knockout." Those who remember Ali-Frazier I and Gatti-Ward I would take issue with that view. And there are several places where Probert inadvertently mischaracterizes the historical record.

That said, Probert's work is thought provoking and well written as evidenced by the following quotes:

★ "What exactly is a 'boxing man?' At its simplest level, it's a term often utilized by those who work within the sport to describe those who work within the sport. To be nominated a 'boxing man' signifies entry into an exclusive club whose membership, while comprising some of the richest and most powerful people in the world, finds room to incorporate a number of the saddest, most desperate examples of humanity that you will ever come across. All of these people have one thing in common. From the journalists who make their living writing about the exploits of boxers to the numerous courtiers with which a professional boxer will surround himself, they are all liars."

★ "Boxers are often perceived by the public as ignorant thugs who just happen to be good at fighting. In reality, the majority of boxers possess a refined form of intelligence that only those who study the sport can even begin to understand. I can honestly say that I have never met an unintelligent boxer. I have come across many who would struggle with quantum mechanics. I have also met some who would have difficulty reciting their six-times table. But I have never been in the presence of a fighter who could in any way be described as stupid. Boxers are decision makers. They are trained to reach a conclusion at speeds that would be impossible for the likes of you and I. When a boxer makes a decision, he must commit to it instantly and prepare to suffer the consequences of his actions. Moreover, the decisions that they are compelled to make are often life transforming."

★ "The next time you happen to be watching a fight on television, take a look at the faces of the two men involved. If the one with the cauliflower ears and the broken nose and the heavily-scarred eyebrows looks tough to you, think again before you attempt to pick a winner. He got those cauliflower ears and that broken nose and those heavily-scarred eyebrows because people keep hitting him around those places. It's the pretty one that you should be putting your money on."

★ "Boxing has been around in various forms since the ancient Greeks. And nobody has ever been able to find a way of stopping people from doing it; not that anybody has really wanted to. But where do you draw the line? My feelings are ambiguous. I'm one hundred percent sure that I don't want people to get fatally injured for my enjoyment. You'd have to be a psychopath to enjoy that. I get no pleasure from seeing these people bleeding, and I get no pleasure from seeing them sustain a broken nose. But I also know that the spectacle of two men standing before you, aiming punches at each other until one of them falls to the floor unconscious, can be one of the most exciting things that you will ever bear witness to in life. And perversely—and I don't want to say this—I enjoy watching people get knocked out."

★ "Now it's time to cut to the chase. Boxing is wrong. There, I've said it. There can be no place in a civilized society for an activity provided exclusively for the entertainment of the masses which places its main protagonists in clear danger of losing their lives. I am aware of all the counter-arguments. I have employed them myself on far too many occasions. I know that nobody is forcing the boxers to climb into the ring and hit each other. I know too that boxing has allowed many people to live a life that would have been unthinkable were it not for their ability to hit other people accurately and hard. However valid these arguments might appear, they fall flat on their faces when a boxer loses his life. There is simply no way that this can be defended."

★ "When I said that there can be no place in a civilized society for an activity such as boxing, I meant every word. What I didn't say was that it should be banned. Yes, in an ideal world, boxing should be consigned to the trash can that contains the remnants of other equally abhorrent pastimes such as badger baiting, bullfighting, and seal culling. Yet I would suggest that, before society elects to make an example of boxing, there are plenty of other things that it should be worrying about. Prior to ridding itself of the sport that is not a sport, which gives us all a glimpse of our species' most primitive and primal urges, society could turn its attention to more pressing and immediate problems."

The emotional climax of Probert's journey comes at the end of *Dangerous*. Talking about sessions with his therapist, Probert confides to the reader, "I seem to slip boxing into the conversation more than is healthy or coincidental."

Why is he doing that?

It has to do with the man Probert describes as "my nasty and abusive deceased father."

"So I do what I have to do," Probert writes. "I go and see my mother. I've seen her only once since my father's funeral two years ago. I turn up unannounced on a warm Saturday morning, which obviously shocks her. I've never done this before. 'What are you doing here?' she asks. For the first time ever, I tell my mother everything. I'm not going to go into detail here. Suffice it to say, he was a monster. A monster who ruled by fear—psychological and physical—when I was a child. And more of a monster when I became a teenager, who did things to me when we were alone that a father should never do to a son. A demon who stole my childhood from me in a manner that I've never really been able to get over. I spill out all the lurid details. Her face remains expressionless as she listens. She calls him a bastard. She says that she hates him. She says it like he's still alive. She asks me why I never told her it was happening. I tell her that I tried to. At least, I think I tried to. 'Well, you should have tried harder,' she says, too coldly, too callously."

"And yet," Probert concedes, "in spite of all this, I wanted him to be proud of me."

Probert's father loved boxing.

"It's absurd the lengths to which one will go to earn a father's approval," Probert confesses. "Even one who brutalized you. In retrospect, it's certainly no accident that I ended up jettisoning the career in the arts that I'd always coveted and became a boxing writer. Even though I could never admit it to myself, it's clear that I did it for him. I did it because a part of me wanted him to be impressed by something that I had achieved. And I was prepared to mould my entire life around this silly objective."

That's not as unusual as one might think. Probert's writing brought back the memory of a conversation I had years ago with Randy Neumann.

Neumann was a heavyweight contender in the 1970s, best known for a bloody ring trilogy with Chuck Wepner and a decision triumph over Jimmy Young. After retiring as an active fighter, he refereed more than three hundred bouts. More significantly perhaps, he graduated from college and went on to build a successful career as a financial planner.

I asked Neumann why he became a professional fighter, and he began by telling me about his parents.

"My father was a scholar-athlete and my mother was an incredibly beautiful woman," he recalled. "They could have been the king and queen at any high school senior prom. But my father was a tragedy of World War II. He was in the Air Force. He saw a lot of his friends killed. After he came back from the war, he had a nervous breakdown. When I was five years old, he moved away from home. My mother was a tough independent woman. She never remarried. Instead, she went to work as a model and earned enough money to raise my sister and me well."

Then Neumann broke into tears.

"I didn't know it at the time," he said. "But I was looking for the hardest thing I could do this side of the law to prove to a father who had left me that I was tough."

Joe Louis, who was one of Sonny Liston's pallbearers, arrived late for the funeral because he'd been shooting craps. "Sonny would understand," Joe said.

"The Murder of Sonny Liston"

On January 5, 1971, Sonny Liston's wife returned home from a holiday trip to St. Louis and found her husband's rotting corpse in the bedroom of their Las Vegas home. The official autopsy report concluded that Liston died of natural causes (pulmonary and lung congestion). An equally plausible view is that he died from an overdose of heroin. *The Murder of Sonny Liston* by Shaun Assael (Blue Rider Press) takes things a step further and argues that, whether or not Liston died from an overdose, he was murdered (most likely by a rogue cop in the service of the Las Vegas mob).

According to Assael, Liston worked as a collection agent for the mob in Las Vegas in the late 1960s. He was also a go-between for moving cocaine (and possibly heroin) in the Keno room at The International hotel in Las Vegas.

"Every so often," Assael writes, "a manager or a dealer would send someone over whom he would make eye contact with. At the bar or in the bathroom or in a leather chair in the lounge, the former heavyweight champion would unfurl his gigantic hand and inside would be cocaine."

At this point, a skeptic might ask, "I thought drug dealers are supposed to be inconspicuous. Do you really want a former heavyweight champion (who everyone in the room is likely to be looking at) handing out cocaine?"

Assael also writes that Liston was a heavy cocaine user and later became addicted to heroin, an escalating habit that led to the concomitant loosening of his tongue. He then speculates that Liston had taken a dive in his second fight against Muhammad Ali in exchange for a promise from the Nation of Islam that Sonny and his mob backers would receive a percentage of Ali's purses for the rest of Ali's ring career. Then, prior to Ali-Frazier I (which was contested on March 8, 1971), Liston began to talk openly about being owed money and was murdered to ensure his silence.

In that regard, Assael declares, "Here he was, hustling fifty-dollar bags of coke to support himself. And every time he heard another dollar figure thrown around about the Ali-Frazier fight, he got moodier. Some very powerful people might have started to worry that Sonny was talking too much about the money he was going to get from Ali . . . too much for his—and their—own good."

Assael writes smoothly. His tale is woven together in entertaining fashion, presents a compelling personal portrait of Liston, and offers an interesting look at Las Vegas during a time of transition from a mob-run town with corrupt law enforcement authorities to a sleeker, more corporate-like model.

There are elements of humor such as the story about a middle-aged woman who approached Liston while he was playing blackjack at the Frontier Hotel and Casino and exclaimed, "You're Sonny Liston."

"Yeah, I knew that," Liston told her.

But there are problems with *The Murder of Sonny Liston*. The book is billed as investigative reporting. The foundation for good investigative reporting is an accurate recounting of facts.

I know very little about law enforcement in Las Vegas during the period in question. Thus, the assumption I would normally make is that Assael's recitation of facts is accurate, and I'd evaluate his theories accordingly.

However, I know a great deal about Muhammad Ali and boxing. And *The Murder of Sonny Liston* is so plagued by factual errors in these areas that it erodes confidence in the factual foundation for Assael's broader conspiracy theories.

For example . . .

Assael downplays Cassius Clay's victory over Sonny Liston in their first encounter by saying that Liston "needed cortisone treatments for bursitis in both shoulders the day before the fight," and that "after the furious pounding he gave Clay, Sonny could barely raise his left arm."

I'm unaware of credible evidence regarding the above-referenced cortisone treatments. As for the "furious pounding" that Liston administered to Clay, a review of the fight (which is available on YouTube) shows that there was none.

Assael states that Ali–Liston II was contested in Lewiston, Maine, in a venue with "fifty thousand seats." In reality, St. Dominic's Arena was able to accommodate five thousand fans.

Assael also writes that Ali received a draft notice in 1963 but "showed up for his medical exam acting so crazy that he got classified as 1-Y."

That's simply wrong.

To set the record straight, on January 24, 1964, Cassius Clay reported to the Armed Forces Induction Center in Coral Gables, Florida, for a military qualifying examination. He easily passed the physical portion of the exam, but the fifty-minute mental aptitude (IQ) test was another matter. Ali had always tested poorly in school. Here, the result was an Army IQ score of 78, which put him in the sixteenth percentile, well below the passing grade of thirty. As a result, he was reclassified 1-Y ("not qualified under current standards for service in the armed forces").

Assael then writes, "As his star continued to climb, the draft board kept an eye on him. In 1967, he suddenly found himself bumped up to 1-A, which made him immediately eligible to serve."

That's misleading. In truth, in early 1966 with manpower needs for the war in Vietnam growing, the mental-aptitude percentile required for induction into the US military was lowered from thirty to fifteen, rendering Ali (and hundreds of thousands of other young men who had previously been classified 1-Y) eligible for the draft.

Writing about Ali versus Oscar Bonavena, Assael declares that Ali "gave him a thunderous straight-ahead jab" in the fifteenth round and, "before the crowd could process what had happened, Bonavena staggered like someone who'd been shot unknowingly from a distance and fallen."

It wasn't a jab. It was a classic left hook. There's a difference.

Assael also writes that Liston outweighed Leotis Martin (who dealt Sonny the final loss of his ring career) by ten pounds. Two paragraphs later, he says it was twenty pounds. This does not inspire confidence in Assael's investigative reporting.

Facts matter.

Assael also has the tendency to disregard information that interferes with his explanation of events.

For example, referring to the end of round four and round five of Liston-Clay I (when Clay was temporarily blinded by a caustic solution), Assael writes, "The cause of the burning was probably liniment oil, though where it came from was the subject of great debate. It could have accidently dripped into Clay's eyes from one of the towels that his trainers were using or, if it came from Sonny's gloves as Clay's camp suspected, it could have been the result of accidental spillage and not a dirty trick."

Let's be honest.

Jack McKinney of the *Philadelphia Daily News* is described by Assael as "one of the few reporters who was able to get close to Sonny." McKinney later said of that night, "The problems Clay had with his vision in the first Liston fight were no accident. The two toughest opponents that Liston faced prior to Clay were Eddie Machen and Cleveland Williams. Machen lost a twelve-round decision to Liston and complained afterward that he'd been bothered by an astringent in his eyes. But he'd fought so poorly that no one believed him. Everyone thought it was just an alibi. And Cleveland Williams gave Liston all kinds of trouble in the first round. I was at that fight," McKinney continued. "And after the first round there seemed to be a lot of confusion in Sonny's corner. In fact, he was late coming out for the second round because his mouthpiece wasn't in. He knocked Williams out in that round. And after the fight, Williams was obviously having trouble seeing. He kept rubbing his eyes. Later on, I kidded Sonny's cornerman, Joe Polino, who was responsible for the mouthpiece, about the confusion. Joe told me, 'Someday I'll explain it to you.' Well, I got my explanation at the first Clay-Liston fight. If you look at a film of what went on in Liston's corner between the third and fourth rounds of that fight, you'll see Polino in the ring with Willie Reddish [Liston's trainer] standing behind him, blocking everyone else's view. And Polino is at Sonny's knees, rubbing something on his gloves."

The Murder of Sonny Liston contains a lot of anecdotal material about big names from the world of politics and entertainment. But again, reliability is an issue. For example, Assael references an incident when Carl Cohen (a vice president at the Sands) punched Frank Sinatra in the mouth. But that incident is recounted differently and more reliably by James Kaplan in volume two of his definitive biography of Sinatra.

At one point, Assael references law enforcement authorities utilizing "a covert automated tracking system, a shoe-box-size device that fit in a vehicle's car." This leaves a reader wondering whether anyone proofread the manuscript.

In a similar vein, writing about Ali–Quarry I, Assael states, "Quarry had trained to anticipate Ali's ten-inch range." That's an incoherent sentence. And if Assael meant "ten-inch reach advantage," that number is wrong.

One might add that anonymous posts in chatroom threads (which are among the puzzle pieces that Assael puts together) are not reliable sources.

Is it possible that Sonny Liston was murdered? Yes. But *The Murder of Sonny Liston* doesn't prove it.

Numerous other books were also worthy of mention in 2016.

Literary Notes

One of boxing's more entertaining legends concerns an unsavory manager who brought a Latin American fighter named Marcos to New York in the 1960s, changed his name to Marcus, and began touting him in ring circles as "The Star of Zion." The Star, it was widely advertised, was of Orthodox Jewish vintage, fought to bring honor to the Jewish people, and would someday be a superb champion. He blew his cover at a B'nai B'rith luncheon when, hungrily eyeing the matzoh, he said politely, "Please pass the tortillas."

Stars in the Ring by Mike Silver (Lyons Press) recalls an era when Jewish fighters were many in number and there was no need for subterfuge of that kind. The book's focus is on the period from 1900 to 1940, which Silver calls the Golden Age of Boxing and also a Golden Age for Jewish fighters.

Silver estimates that there were more than three thousand Jewish boxers in the United States during those four decades. That equaled between 7 and 10 percent of the total number of professional boxers plying their trade at that time. During the same period, there were twenty-nine Jewish world champions. In the 1920s, fourteen of boxing's sixty-six world champions were Jewish. Putting these numbers in further perspective, only fifty-two Jews played major league baseball from 1900 to 1940.

"An unprecedented confluence of social and historic events," Silver writes, "converged to create one of the most unique and colorful chapters of the Jewish immigrant experience in America. At a time when boxing mattered to society far more than it does today, Jewish people were earning the attention and respect of their fellow citizens in the prize ring."

In some respects, *Stars in the Ring* is a social history of boxing as seen through the Jewish experience. Drawing parallels with society as a whole, Silver recounts, "The Golden Age of the Jewish boxer in America coincided with the Golden Age of the Jewish gangster. Both came from the same gritty rough-and-tumble city streets, and their worlds often intersected. In 1921, Jews represented 14 percent of New York State's prison population, and Jewish women accounted for 20 percent of all female prisoners in New York State."

Meanwhile, by the mid-1920s, Jewish boxers were so popular that some non-Jewish fighters changed their names to Jewish-sounding ones to advance their ring career. And extending Silver's "golden age" by ten years, it's worth running some numbers regarding Madison Square Garden, which was then "The Mecca of Boxing." In the first five decades of the twentieth century, the Garden hosted 866 fight cards. Two hundred forty of those cards featured at least one Jewish fighter in the main event.

The heart of *Stars in the Ring* consists of mini-biographies of 166 Jewish boxers. It's not a book to be read straight through in one or two sittings. The profiles tend to blend together. But it's a good all-in-one reference work on little-known Jewish fighters and their more-famous brethren like Abe Attell, Joe Choynski, Ted "Kid" Lewis, Jackie "Kid" Berg, Barney Ross, and "Slapsie Maxie" Rosenbloom (whom author Philip Roth called "a more miraculous Jewish phenomenon than Albert Einstein").

There are also interesting nuggets of information on Jewish boxers whose ring exploits were modest at best. For example, a Jewish adolescent growing up on Long Island won twenty-two of twenty-six amateur bouts, left the sport for good, and later looked back on his years in boxing with the thought, "I must have been out of my mind. But I really enjoyed it while I was doing it."

His name? Billy Joel.

And Silver pays special attention to the man who, mixing religious metaphors, could be labeled the patron saint of Jewish boxers: lightweight great Benny Leonard.

Silver calls Leonard "the most famous Jew in America" in the 1920s and "the gold standard to which all other Jewish boxers are compared." He also observes, "Not only was Benny Leonard one of the greatest boxers who ever lived; he was the first Jewish superstar of the mass media age and the first Jewish-American pop culture icon. Leonard's conduct in and out of the ring and his impeccable public image stood as the refutation of the immigrants' anxiety that boxing would suck their children into a criminal underworld or somehow undermine the very rationale for fleeing to the Golden Land. Leonard legitimized boxing as an acceptable Jewish pursuit."

But times change. Inevitably, social and economic progress put an end to the Golden Age of Jewish boxing. That leaves Silver to write, "As the last Jewish boxers of the Golden Age die off, it becomes even more important to document their accomplishments so that future generations can acknowledge and appreciate how a people with no athletic traditions and with so many doors closed to them used their intelligence and drive to open another door to opportunity and eventually dominate, both as athletes and entrepreneurs, what was for several decades the most popular sport in America."

★ ★ ★

"Floyd Mayweather knows boxing," Tris Dixon writes. "He knows it better than he knows anything else."

Those words ring true. And they're at the heart of Dixon's new book, *Money: The Life and Fast Times of Floyd Mayweather* (Arena Sport).

Early in *Money*, Dixon quotes writer Nigel Collins as saying, "I believe most fighters come to the sport damaged emotionally."

That certainly was true of Mayweather. Floyd's mother was a crack addict. His father was a drug dealer who spent five of his son's formative years in prison for selling cocaine.

Dixon's recounting of Mayweather's hard origins through the end of his amateur career is detailed and compelling.

Mayweather's father and two of his uncles were professional fighters. Dixon writes, "When Mayweather says, 'I knew boxing before I knew anything else,' that is probably the case because that kind of violence came before he could remember anything. Life was boxing. Boxing was life. Winning at boxing was winning at life."

When Mayweather turned pro, he moved from the fight game to the fight business. He had a vision of what his starpower could be. It was grandiose and went far beyond logic. But he made it happen.

Dixon takes readers on that journey. There's in-depth reporting on Mayweather's fights, his ongoing dysfunctional family life, his ostentatious lifestyle, and all the other outside-the-ring touchstones of the fighter's career.

Always, it comes back to boxing.

Dixon is a thorough researcher, an accurate reporter, and a good writer. But after its exceptionally good beginning, his book loses some of its luster.

The material on Mayweather's early life and amateur career is interesting in part because Dixon supplements what boxing fans already know. But the further down the road *Money* travels, the fewer new insights are offered to readers. The familiar stories are told well, but they've already been told. The fight-by-fight recitation of Floyd's career is thorough but repetitious and more detailed than necessary at times.

What's missing is something new.

The best biographies break new ground. They offer new insights and interpretations, and lead readers to reevaluate what they think they already know.

Dixon could have broken new ground with Al Haymon, who was one of the masterminds behind Mayweather's extraordinary economic success. But there's surprisingly little in *Money* about Haymon.

Nor is there in-depth evaluation of the manner in which HBO, Showtime, and others in the mainstream media enabled Mayweather for years with regard to his physical abuse of women.

For example, in 2012, HBO (which was televising Mayweather's fights on HBO-PPV at the time) aired a special in which Michael Eric Dyson (a professor at Georgetown University) interviewed Floyd regarding his impending jail sentence for physically abusing Josie Harris (the mother of three of his children). Dyson likened Mayweather to Muhammad Ali, Jim Brown, and Kareem Abdul-Jabbar as an oppressed black athlete that the system was trying to silence. Mayweather's previous convictions involving violence against women went unmentioned on the program.

We live in an age of diminished standards and accountability. Too many people at all levels of society say whatever they want without regard to truth, knowing that their enablers will support them. Mayweather is a poster boy for that phenomenon.

"Am I guilty?" Floyd asked Dyson rhetorically. "Absolutely not. I took a plea. Sometimes they put us in a no-win situation to where you don't have no choice but to take a plea."

That statement went unrebutted.

Dixon could have used the Mayweather-Dyson interview as the fulcrum for penetrating analysis of a much larger issue. Instead, he chose not to discuss it.

Money is the most thorough book about Floyd Mayweather that we're likely to see for a long time. But to repeat: the best biographies break new ground, offer new insights and interpretations, and lead readers to reevaluate what they think they already know.

It's precisely because Dixon is such a good writer with so much potential that he should be held to such a high standard.

★ ★ ★

Alfonso Theofilo Brown was born into horrendous poverty in Panama in 1902. At age twenty-one, he boarded a vessel in the Canal Zone as a stowaway, was pressed into service peeling potatoes after he was discovered, and jumped ship in New York (then the capital of the boxing world).

During the course of a twenty-year ring career, Brown compiled a record of 129 wins, 19 losses, and 13 draws. In 161 fights, he was never knocked out. He was freakishly tall (5 feet 9 inches) for a bantamweight and was boxing's first Hispanic world champion. Complicating his life, he was gay.

Black Ink by Jose Corpas (Win by KO Publications) tells the story of Brown's life.

Boxing was a different world then. As Corpas recounts, "Eyes were thumbed, kidneys were pounded, and laces were dragged across faces until blood flowed. A coddled prospect being fed a steady diet of carefully selected stiffs on the way to a 20-and-0 record was virtually non-existent and impressed no one the few times it occurred. Fighters fought whoever was available."

Social customs were different too. Brown spent most of his adult life with one foot in and one foot out of the closet. He lived for a time in Paris (where the French poet Jean Cocteau was his lover and manager), spent profligately on clothes, and developed a fondness for betting on horses.

He was often instructed to carry opponents, lest it become too difficult for him to get fights.

Brown's ring career was marred by heavy drinking that evolved to cocaine and heroin use. He contracted syphillis and, later in life, was arrested multiple times for drug-related and other criminal offenses. During his final years, he lived homeless on the streets of New York. He died in 1951 at age forty-eight.

Corpas has researched his subject extensively, particularly in online newspaper archives throughout the world. His writing is a bit sloppy at times, and Brown's many fights tend to blur together in the recounting. But the book has a powerful undercurrent.

"It wasn't just the money that drove Brown," Corpas writes. "The feeling that consumed him when the bell rang had no price. When the bell rang, he was chief, king, the boss. And everyone watching knew it. For someone who was often told that he should be ashamed of who he was, that feeling of superiority was addictive. The respect and awe his ring dominance earned him spilled out into the cabarets and streets, where Brown was often the richest, most famous, and toughest man in the room. When he couldn't box, he was a poor, skinny, gay drunk."

But the inevitable happened.

"With each work of art," Corpas observes, "he left a piece of himself in the ring. When he climbed out of the ring for the last time, there was almost nothing left."

★ ★ ★

In the Cheap Seats by Springs Toledo (Tora Book Publishing) is a collection of essays written between 2009 and 2015.

Toledo has an understanding and appreciation of boxing history. His essays join the present to the past. Occasionally, he leans a bit too far toward the lyrical and allegorical rather than the accurate. Hence, Bryant Jennings is analogized to Jack Dempsey and Wladimir Klitschko to Jess Willard.

But Toledo writes well, borrowing from *The Karate Kid* to liken Bernard Hopkins's losing effort against Roy Jones in 1993 to a man trying "to catch a hornet with chopsticks."

Gennady Golovkin's jab is described as "the cramming, not the flicking kind," one that "transformed a simple set up punch into a debilitating weapon" thrown by a fighter "who wore a mask of brutal indifference."

The crushing left hook to the body by Golovkin that dropped David Lemieux to the canvas is characterized as follows: "The worst thing about it isn't the pain. It's the cruel delay before the pain. You get just enough time to think about it; two seconds of panic that unmans the roughest and the toughest. Most guys try to muffle a bellow that sounds like a gutted steer."

In another essay—this one about the nature of boxing—Toledo writes, "Draped in a robe that feels like a shroud, the boxer's walk to the ring, trainer in tow, feels something like a condemned man's walk to the death chamber, priest in tow . . . The truth of existence has a way of coming into focus when you're flat on your back under the lights and there's nowhere to look but up. Whether those lights are in an arena, a nursing home, or on a Chicago street is beside the point. We'll all see them eventually."

Toledo also has a good ear for the quotes of others when he's not crafting his own.

There's Mikkel Kessler complaining about the difficulty of fighting Joe Calzaghe: "He ruins your boxing."

Showtime's Mauro Ranallo notes that the world sanctioning bodies "hand out belts like business cards."

Larry Merchant observes, "We know who the real fighters are. We no longer know who the real champions are."

Floyd Mayweather comes in for his share of criticism. In an essay written six years ago, Toledo proclaimed, "Floyd 'Money' Mayweather is undefeated. But so were gunfighters who shot at cans on stumps in yards. While his talent is undeniable, Floyd has been spending more time shaking his fist at his legions of critics than he has at serious challengers. Floyd would do well to avoid comparisons between himself and the fistic dieties of the past. Even the best of bronze looks dull next to polished gold."

My favorite passage in the book is Toledo's recounting of referee Roberto Ramirez Sr.'s decision to stop the March 10, 2012, beating that Juan Manuel Lopez was taking at the hands of Orlando Salido. Ramirez, Toldeo writes, "had to distinguish between pride and the very real prospect of a ring tragedy. He had a momentous decision to make and only seconds to make it. Luckily, he understood his responsibilities. He turned a deaf ear to the roaring thousands in the Coliseum and looked into the glazed eyes of a defeated fighter. Then he stopped the fight. He knew that no one enters the ring without first suppressing the instinct of self-preservation and that some go too far. The referee is there to protect boxers from their own spirits and remind us that boxing is still a sport."

★ ★ ★

Arne K. Lang has written a book entitled *The Nelson-Wolgast Fight and the San Francisco Boxing Scene, 1900–1914* (McFarland & Company).

Nelson and Wolgast fought three times, with Wolgast winning all three. The fight referenced in the book's title is their second encounter, which took place in Point Richmond, California (a thirty-five-minute ferry ride from San Francisco) on February 22, 1910.

San Francisco in 1910 was arguably the fight capital of America. Nelson was already a celebrity, having fought Joe Gans three times and beaten him twice. His victory in part 2 of the Gans-Nelson trilogy—a July 4, 1908, seventeenth-round knockout—earned him the lightweight championship of the world.

Nelson-Wolgast II was contested on George Washington's birthday, one of only five federal holidays at that time. The bout was scheduled for forty-five rounds or less and was for Nelson's lightweight crown.

The encounter, Lang writes, "tops virtually every list of the most savage fights of all time." Wolgast prevailed on a brutal forty-round beatdown.

Each man was plagued by dementia at the end of his life. Nelson stayed healthy longer. But as Lang acknowledges, few fighters as active as he was (Nelson boxed 1,254 rounds over the course of 132 fights) escape brain damage. He died in 1954 at age seventy-two after a brief stay in a psychiatric hospital.

Wolgast, who boxed 1,123 rounds over the course of 138 fights, suffered longer and spent nineteen years in psychiatric hospitals before his death in 1955.

The Nelson-Wolgast Fight and the San Francisco Boxing Scene, 1900–1914 is unlikely to appeal to a crossover audience. But hardcore fight fans will appreciate the thorough nature of Lang's research and the fact that his book fills in some blank pages regarding a significant fight and a little-known era in boxing history.

There are solid portraits of Nelson and Wolgast as well as descriptions of the major players on the 1910 San Francisco boxing scene.

To Lang's credit, he doesn't over-romanticize the era. After quoting fight manager Daniel Morgan, who proclaimed, "In those days, there was a good lightweight on every street corner," Lang observes, "The good fighters to which Morgan alluded were not always good and, in truth, many were not all that skilled. The sum of their athleticism and their science left something lacking."

Also, Lang has a nice eye for detail. Writing about the mining town of Goldfield, Nevada (where the first Gans-Nelson fight was contested), he reports, "Goldfield was a place where shops advertised remedies for gonorrhea and diamonds for sale on the same signboard."

Lang also recounts how Nelson was sent to Toledo by the *Chicago Daily News* to report on the July 4, 1919, heavyweight championship fight between Jess Willard and Jack Dempsey.

"Toledo was experiencing a terrible heat wave," Lang writes. "Late on the eve of the fight, Nelson wandered away from his tent in search of a place to cool off and was discovered taking a bath in his underwear in a giant vat of lemonade. News of the incident spread like wildfire and the vendor was stuck with a lot of unsold lemonade."

★ ★ ★

Max Baer and the Star of David by Jay Neugeboren (Mandel Vilar Press) uses the former heavyweight champion as a vehicle to tell the story of two fictitious characters.

The book takes the form of a memoir by Horace Littlejohn, a black man born into poverty in rural Louisiana in the early years of the twentieth century. Littlejohn survives a tortured childhood made worse by a horribly abusive father and moves west to become Baer's sparring partner, road buddy, and friend.

Neugeboren dresses the historical Max Baer in fiction, interpreting and imagining his persona. His Baer is a non-stop womanizer who falls in love again and again. . . . Good-hearted . . . Goofy . . . Generous . . . Sweet . . . Innocent in some ways . . . Part wise man, part fool . . . Irresponsible . . . Childlike . . . Immature . . . A decent man who cares and feels . . . A fighter in the ring but not in his heart.

This is not a book about boxing, although the significant fights in Baer's career are nicely (albeit briefly) told. Also, the title is misleading. Baer is a major character in the book. But his religion—he was one-quarter Jewish—isn't much of a factor in the story.

Max Baer and the Song of Solomon would have been a more appropriate title.

In the world that Neugeboren has created, Baer is one point of a truly incestuous triangle with Littlejohn and his sister Jolene, who contrary to how they live and appear to the world, are brother and sister, not husband and wife.

Neugeboren writes well and puts his words together with care. *Max Baer and the Star of David* is a provocative and entertaining read.

★ ★ ★

Pitch Publishing is carving out a niche for itself in the world of boxing. It's latest offering is the autobiography of Jamie Moore (written with Paul Zanon).

Mooresy offers a recounting of Moore's frequent interaction with the police when he was young, his ring career, and the horror of being shot multiple times by a would-be assassin in 2014. There's also a bit of homespun logic in Moore's feelings on the turn in his life that came sixteen days after a 2004 knockout loss to Ossie Duran: "If you are ever looking for a distraction to take your mind off a boxing loss, try getting married."

But the most interesting insight in *Mooresy* comes from novelist Andrew Vachss, whom Moore quotes as saying, "Fighting means you could lose. Bullying means you can't. A bully wants to beat somebody. He doesn't want to fight somebody."

★ ★ ★

Havana Boxing Club is a collection of photographs by Thierry Le Goues gathered together in a large-format book published by power-House. Except for the dust jacket, the photos are all in black and white.

Le Goues's photographs strip boxing down to its essence in often grainy imagery that captures the mood of the fighters and their combat. Poverty is omnipresent in makeshift rings and the dilapidated gym with cracked mirrors, corroded metal pipes, and equipment that's falling apart. The fighters are spurred on, not by dreams of wealth but by pride. There's very little joy in their faces. Each photo tells its own story.

Too many of the images are similar. And it's sometimes hard to put them in context because, other than the credits, a garbled one-page introduction is the only text. That said, *Havana Boxing Club* is an honest portrait of a hard unforgiving world where boxing is not so much a way out as a way of life and each day is a struggle to survive.

★ ★ ★

On December 11, 1981, the man who was arguably the greatest fighter in the history of boxing ended his ring career with a ten-round loss in a dilapidated ballpark adjacent to a cow pasture in the Bahamas. *Drama in the Bahamas* by Dave Hannigan (Sports Publishing) tells the story of that sad night, the events leading up to it, and the players involved.

After Muhammad Ali's listless performance in an October 21, 1980, knockout defeat at the hands of Larry Holmes, the assumption was—at last, thank God—he would never fight again. But soon, Ali was saying, "Ain't this something. One bad day on the job and they want to fire me. I'm not just some Negro off the street. I'm the most controversial fighter in history. I want to be free to make my own decisions. If I stop, it's because I want to stop. Nobody's going to make me stop."

That set the stage for thirty-nine-year-old Muhammad Ali—the conqueror of Sonny Liston, Joe Frazier, and George Foreman—versus Trevor Berbick.

Berbick, age twenty-seven, was a solid but limited fighter with an erratic persona. He'd been born in Jamaica but later moved to Montreal. Fellow Canadian George Chuvalo called him "a bit whacky."

The first obstacle Hannigan faced in writing *Drama in the Bahamas* was that it's hard to make a silk purse out of a sow's ear. And Ali-Berbick was a sow's ear. That said, Hannigan's work is a smoothly written, full account of the making and promotion of Ali-Berbick, the financial machinations surrounding the venture, and the fight itself.

Ali's deteriorating physical condition is a recurring theme throughout the book. Each of the first twelve chapters is prefaced by a quote from

Ali, spoken at various times between 1971 and 1979, announcing his retirement from boxing.

By the time Ali–Berbick rolled around, retirement was an imperative and the warning signs were flashing in red lights.

Ali's longtime ring physician Ferdie Pacheco (who refused to work with Ali subsequent to Ali versus Earnie Shavers in 1977) declared, "Ali looks smooth and unmarked on the outside. But if you look inside, you would see a terrible picture. No man can take as much punishment to his head and body as he has over the last twenty years without incurring tremendous damage."

Will Grimsley of the Associated Press reported on Ali at the kickoff press conference for Ali–Berbick as follows: "He stood on the dais, all polished and spruced up like an antique car, the relic he is. Kick his tires and the wheels shimmy. Raise the hood and the engine is a mess of pipes and tubes, bent and rusty. Turn the key and you get a labored chug."

Reporting on the same press conference, Hugh McIlvanney of *The Observer* wrote, "He continues to recite the commentary for an epic, but what we are seeing is a cruel cartoon. Muhammad Ali can still preach and philosophize, boast and charm and predict. What he can't do is fight."

Things got worse when the promotion moved to the Bahamas. Legendary trainer Eddie Futch was on site with Ernie Singletary, who was scheduled to face Thomas Hearns on the undercard. Futch watched Ali train for four rounds and declared, "It was slow motion. The jab had no snap. He didn't move. Four rounds of nothing, and he was wore out. It's like a pair of socks. When the elastic goes, it's gone. Throw the socks away. You can't fix the elastic. The reflexes are the elastic in your body. If it's gone, it's gone."

Ali's longtime publicist and jack-of-all-trades Harold Conrad likened the limousine convoy of Ali's entourage to the arena on fight night to a funeral cortege.

There was chaos at the arena. The promotion had neglected to arrange for a ring bell. One was hastily removed from around the neck of a cow that was grazing in a nearby pasture. The promotion had also forgotten to order gloves. Fortunately, several pairs were available. Undercard fighters were told not to cut the laces off at the end of a bout so their gloves could be re-used later in the evening. Four of nine scheduled undercard fights were canceled at the last minute for financial reasons.

The main event was an ugly mess. Ali was tired by the second round and took a pounding for the next eight. Only his heart and Berbick's limitations enabled Ali to survive. Afterward, Hugh McIlvanney wrote, "Graceful exits are rare in professional boxing. But few great champions have gone out more miserably."

Ali's physical condition in his final years is a matter of record. Berbick had his own sad end. In 2006, he was beaten to death by his nephew and an accomplice in an act of pre-meditated murder.

★ ★ ★

Forty-two years ago, *New Times* magazine sent a young photographer named Peter Angelo Simon to Muhammad Ali's training camp in Deer Lake just before Ali journeyed to Zaire to reclaim the heavyweight throne.

Simon spent two days at Deer Lake and shot thirty-three rolls of black-and-white film; 1,080 images in all. Some of the images were contained in a small self-published volume four years ago. Now Simon has fashioned a more ambitious undertaking, a coffee-table photo book entitled *Muhammad Ali: Fighter's Heaven 1974* (Reel Art Press).

There are no classic photos in *Fighter's Heaven*. But there are a lot of good ones. Taken together, they recreate a time, place, and mood. The book has the requisite images of Ali sparring. But my favorite photos are of Ali away from the ring. Private moments in and outside his cabin at Deer Lake; the astonishment and joy that greet him on a visit to an assisted living facility; a run through the countryside just after dawn.

One photo, in particular, caught my eye. Ali is running past a cow that's grazing in a flower-filled meadow. The meager daylight gives the image the feel of an impressionistic painting. One can imagine Ali calling out, "Hello, Mr. Cow," and throwing punches in the air as he runs by. It's harder to conjure up what the cow might have thought of Ali.

★ ★ ★

A vast marketing machine has been put in place to sell Muhammad Ali products. Two books among the first wave of publications since Ali's death have the most promotional resources behind them and thus are likely to get the most attention.

Muhammad Ali: The Tribute is a hardcover book produced by the editors of *Sports Illustrated*.

Sports Illustrated was one of the first major media outlets to understand that Ali was a great fighter and also that his importance extended well beyond boxing. The *SI* tribute book reflects that understanding in real time. It contains the complete original text of sixteen articles that appeared in the magazine and tracks Ali's life from his origins as Cassius Clay to the glory years as Muhammad Ali and, ultimately, his courageous and sad end. The articles—written by Huston Horn, Tex Maule, George Plimpton, Edwin Shrake, Mark Kram, Pat Putnam, William Nack, and Gary Smith—are supplemented by excerpts from additional Ali pieces that appeared in *Sports Illustrated* and well-chosen photographs. The production values are superb.

By contrast, *Muhammad Ali: Unfiltered* (a photo book from Jeter Publishing) falls short of the mark. The photos are loosely organized into sections entitled Ali the Fighter, Ali the Activist, Ali the Man, and Ali the Icon. But there's no coherent flow from photo to photo or tagline captions to identify the photos. Quotes from Ali are sprinkled throughout the manuscript but often bear little or no relationship to the photo they're paired with. The images themselves—particularly, the color photos—are poorly reproduced. And despite the book's title, this is a very-much-filtered version of Ali with virtually no mention of Nation of Islam doctrine or anything else that might conflict with a sanitized portrait of The Greatest.

Muhammad Ali: The Tribute is a treasure. *Muhammad Ali: Unfiltered* is a disappointment.

A state athletic commission isn't a favor bank for doling out toys to political associates, family members, and friends.

The New York State Athletic Commission Under Fire

PART ONE

The resignation of Tom Hoover as chairman of the New York State Athletic Commission, announced on July 25, 2016, is the tip of an iceberg. Multiple sources say that two separate federal investigations of events at the NYSAC are underway.

One of these investigations is being conducted by the Public Integrity Section of the United States Attorney's Office for the Eastern District of New York and is believed to be focusing on wrongdoing by NYSAC officials.

The other investigation has broader implications. Its nerve center is the United States Attorney's Office for the Southern District of New York. This investigation is exploring whether the administration of New York governor Andrew Cuomo improperly influenced the inspector general of the State of New York in conjunction with an investigation undertaken in the aftermath of the life-changing injuries suffered by Magomed Abdusalamov in a fight against Mike Perez at Madison Square Garden on November 2, 2013.

In February of this year, I authored a five-part investigative report entitled "The New York State Inspector General's Investigation." That series was based in large measure upon thousands of pages of interview transcripts that were generated as part of the inspector general's investigation and produced pursuant to the New York State Freedom of Information Law. Among the themes I explored then were:

(1) Magomed Abdusalamov was the victim of inadequate medical procedures and protocols that were in place at the time of his injury.

(2) The New York State Athletic Commission was beset by larger issues of incompetence and corruption.

Equally troubling was the fact that the inspector general's report had not been released in a timely manner. More than a year earlier, a representative of the inspector general's office had made courtesy telephone calls to several people, telling them that release of the report was "imminent." This writer received one of those calls (on December 3, 2014), as did David Berlin (executive director of the New York State Athletic Commission at that time).

But the inspector general's report wasn't released. Nineteen more months passed. During that time, Andrew Cuomo announced that Tom Hoover would replace Melvina Lathan as chairperson of the New York State Athletic Commission. Hoover was confirmed by the New York State Senate on June 16, 2015.

Finally, on July 25, 2016, the inspector general's report was made public.

The bulk of the report relates to Magomed Abdusalamov and the medical issues surrounding his fate. In part, the report states, "The Inspector General found that many Athletic Commission practices, policies and procedures were either nonexistent or deficient, specifically those relating to post-bout medical care, tactical emergency plans and communication, and training. The Inspector General also found a lack of appropriate engagement and oversight by Athletic Commission commissioners and its chair."

The report further stated, "During the pendency of this investigation, the Inspector General received information that Melvina Lathan, the Athletic Commission chair at the time of the bout, and other Athletic Commission staff had received improper gifts from promoters. The Inspector General subsequently received allegations that current Athletic Commission Chair Thomas Hoover engaged in improper conduct in obtaining benefits for a relative and friends."

After concluding that the allegations against Lathan and Hoover were substantially true, the inspector general's report declared, "It is imperative that all Athletic Commission commissioners and staff adhere to the highest standards of ethics and professionalism. The Inspector General is referring this matter to the Department of State to take whatever action it deems appropriate against the employees identified in this investigation. The Inspector General is also referring this matter to the Joint Commission on Public Ethics for whatever action the commission deems appropriate."

The inspector general's report has flaws. But overall, it was an excellent piece of work that reflected the diligent efforts of staff members involved in the investigation. On the day the report was released, the New York State Athletic Commission announced that Hoover had resigned as chairperson.

But the NYSAC remains in turmoil. It didn't have to be that way.

On March 26, 2014, with the inspector general's investigation of the NYSAC underway and Melvina Lathan still serving as chairperson, Governor Cuomo announced the appointment of David Berlin as executive director of the commission. Berlin assumed his position on May 1, 2014. There was a transition period ending on June 7, 2014, after which he assumed the day-to-day duties of running the office and overseeing fight cards, responsibilities that had previously been assigned to Lathan. Before long, Berlin was implementing changes that were essential to the proper functioning of the commission. These initiatives included:

* Updating medical protocols for ring physicians.

* Instituting programs to educate fighters on how to apply for Obamacare, Medicaid, and other services.

* Updating NYSAC protocols with regard to illegal performance-enhancing drugs, including the thorny process of dealing with the United States Anti-Doping Agency.

* Urging a serious study of the effect that cutting weight and the timing of weigh-ins have on the health and safety of fighters.

* Instituting programs in an effort to ensure that activity in gyms is consistent with the health and safety of fighters and that gyms are properly licensed (only seven of the many gyms in New York were licensed when Berlin took office).

* Updating the standard New York State Athletic Commission bout contract and other NYSAC forms.

* Instructing that boxer information sheets be translated into Spanish and Russian.

* Holding regularly scheduled staff meetings to ensure that NYSAC personnel would know what was happening and could support one another.

* Overseeing four educational seminars for NYSAC inspectors, two for referees, and two for ring judges.

★ Effectuating pay raises for commission inspectors from $52 a day to $100 a day and for deputy commissioners from $104 a day to $150 a day. These were the first increases in their pay in twenty-five years.

★ Updating the commission's inadequate computerized record-keeping system.

"My philosophy for running the commission was simple," Berlin says. "I believed that the commission should be run in a way that's professional, open, and transparent. I also believed that integrity, ability, and knowledge of boxing should take precedence over political considerations in the hiring and assignment of employees."

Tom Hoover was greeted with high expectations when he succeeded Melvina Lathan as New York State Athletic Commission chairperson on June 16, 2015. Many people (this writer included) respected Hoover and thought he would partner well with Berlin in making a stand for what was right. But things went wrong from the start. "Hoover's way of doing things is to shoot from the hip without thinking things through," Berlin later said. "I'm not even sure he's capable of thinking things through."

By way of example, Hoover unilaterally issued an edict that corner-men were not allowed to give instructions to their fighter while a round was in progress. The time-honored tradition in boxing is that a fighter's seconds are allowed to shout instructions as long as they remain seated, stay under control, and refrain from berating the opposing fighter or referee. Hoover's view, as expressed to Berlin, was, "If a boxer needs to be coached during a round, he should find another job."

Hoover's edict led to an outpouring of anger from cornermen and confusion among inspectors, who were unsure what was and wasn't allowed as Hoover vacillated back and forth on the policy, sometimes changing his position during the course of a single fight card.

Hoover also decreed that new gloves must be worn by both boxers in every fight, which added substantially to the costs incurred by promoters on small club shows. "If a promoter can't afford new gloves," Hoover told Berlin, "he shouldn't be in the business." Eventually, that edict (like the no coaching from the corner rule) was rescinded. But Berlin recalls, "So much time and energy were spent internally to counteract Hoover's wrong decisions that it cut into our ability to work productively on behalf of the commission and the boxing world."

"Some of the idiocies," Berlin continues, "were almost comical." On October 16, 2015, Gennady Golovkin and David Lemieux weighed in for their fight that was scheduled for the following night at Madison Square Garden. Hoover was overseeing the glove selection process and tried to weigh the fighters' ten-ounce gloves on the same scale that was used to weigh the fighters.

Berlin also believed that Hoover was exercising poor judgment in the assignment of officials. One of those officials—an inspector named Dorothea Perry—was the godmother of WBA middleweight champion Danny Jacobs.

Prior to Jacobs's December 5, 2015, fight against Peter Quillin at Barclays Center, Berlin sent a list of inspectors who were to be assigned to each fighter to Hoover for his approval. Joe Shaffer (one of the NYSAC's better inspectors) was assigned to Jacobs. Hoover replaced Shaffer with Perry. That occasioned a flurry of objections from commission personnel, including Eric Bentley (NYSAC director of boxing at the time), who was incredulous that Hoover was replacing a highly regarded inspector with a fighter's godmother. Eventually, Jim Leary (counsel for the Department of State, which oversees the NYSAC) was brought into the deliberations and Shaffer's assignment was restored.

Perry was already on the inspector general's radar by then. A June 19, 2014, memorandum written by Kenneth Michaels (investigative counsel for the inspector general's office) recounts that Perry had asked to speak with him that day. The Michaels memorandum then states, "Perry told me that she had worked as an inspector the bout before the Abdusalamov fight and had not seen it but had a few comments . . . After the fight, she saw the doctors who examined Abdusalamov at the Golovkin fight [which followed Abdusalamov-Perez] and speculated that they might not have taken sufficient care of Abdusalamov because they wanted to see the last fight of the night. I asked her if she had any other basis for this speculation. She said she did not."

More significantly, in June 2014, the inspector general's office was in the process of investigating whether one or more NYSAC employees had sought to orchestrate an illegal work stoppage. There was no suggestion that Perry played a role in organizing the stoppage. But after the inspector general's office began investigating the matter, she sent an e-mail to Ralph

Petrillo (who had been dismissed as NYSAC director of boxing) with a copy to forty-eight commission personnel. That e-mail had language in it that could have been construed as part of an effort to defuse the inspector general's investigation.

Berlin wanted to dismiss Perry from her position as an inspector because he believed she had failed to properly carry out her duties on multiple occasions. Perry, in turn, filed a complaint against Berlin, accusing him of discriminating against her on the basis of age and race. Previously, she had filed similar complaints against Ron Scott Stevens (a former NYSAC chairman) and Felix Figueroa (a former NYSAC chief inspector). A Google search reveals that Perry also filed at least two lawsuits alleging racial discrimination against a private-sector employer.

Berlin says he was later told by Executive Deputy Secretary of State Anthony Giardina that there was a finding of "no probable cause" with regard to Perry's complaint against him.

Perry was retained as an inspector. Hoover later advocated for her appointment as a deputy commissioner. That effort appears to have ended with his resignation as NYSAC chairman.

Meanwhile, Hoover had created an environment in which some employees no longer felt comfortable in properly performing their job. On one occasion, he issued contradictory directives at a pre-fight meeting of commission personnel and openly mocked an inspector who asked for clarification.

A commission judge felt Hoover's wrath at an October 29, 2015, fight card at Aviator Hall in Brooklyn. The judge was wearing loose-fitting pants because of a medical condition. Hoover ordered him into the women's restroom (to the consternation of a woman who was there at the time) and berated the judge for his appearance. According to one witness, Hoover was wearing black jeans and work boots at the time.

Female employees accepted Hoover addressing the staff at commission meetings as "you guys." It was more problematic when he told his inspectors that they should "grow some balls." Three inspectors were assigned to the menial task of covering the entrance to restricted hallways at an August 1, 2015, fight card at Barclays Center. All three were women.

Other employees complained that, after a year on the job, Hoover still didn't know their name.

Berlin felt that Hoover went out of his way to undermine his author-ity and embarrass him in front of commission personnel. On one such occasion (Gennady Golovkin vs. David Lemieux at Madison Square Garden on October 17, 2015), Hoover changed the seating arrangements in the ringside commission area about twenty minutes before the fight card began. Berlin and two other employees were removed from their customary location at the front-row workstation. According to Berlin, he asked Hoover why the change had been made (since it separated him from the table where many of his tasks were to be performed). Hoover answered, "That's the way it is." Berlin told him he was being "childish." And Hoover responded, "Okay, so I'm a child."

"He's a bully who yells at people who can't yell back," Berlin says of Hoover. "But bullying and shouting aren't a substitute for competence."

But there was a more serious matter to be addressed. Berlin also believed that Hoover was violating the law. On December 1, 2015, he met with Special Deputy Inspector General Philip Foglia and Investigative Counsel Kenneth Michaels to outline his concerns. On December 23, Michaels advised him that the inspector general's office would further investi-gate the matter. Berlin returned to give sworn testimony on January 7, 2016. Eric Bentley testified the following day. Tom Hoover was ques-tioned on February 16.

Some of Hoover's alleged misconduct was at worst a minor abuse of power. For example, prior to a July 24, 2015, fight card at the Brooklyn Masonic Temple, Hoover parked his car (with a state placard in the win-dow) in a restricted area where the on-call ambulance was supposed to be. When told that the ambulance crew wanted to park there, Hoover said they should park in a nearby spot and left his car where it was.

More significantly, the inspector general's staff determined that Hoover had abused his position on multiple occasions by putting his son and others on lists of people authorized to receive credentials that enabled them to sit at ringside in the restricted commission area. The first time this is known to have occurred was at the August 1, 2015, fight card at Barclays Center, when Hoover arranged for a credential to be given to his son under a pseudonym and also to a family friend.

Ironically, shortly after that fight card (which featured Danny Garcia vs. Paulie Malignaggi), Hoover forced an inspector to resign because the inspector had asked for and received a free T-shirt from the Malignaggi camp.

"How does that fit with Hoover's handling of credentials for his son and friends?" Berlin asks. "Everyone knows that taking the T-shirt was wrong. But Hoover also knew that what he was doing with the credentials was wrong, which is why he put his son on the list under a fake name."

There was more.

On November 13, 2015, Berlin was reviewing a list of licensed judges preparatory to assigning officials for a December 5, 2015, fight card at Barclays Center when he saw an unfamiliar name: "Ron Abraham."

Checking NYSAC records, Berlin saw that Abraham had been issued a judge's license on October 29. But after communicating with amateur officials and looking at BoxRec.com, he determined that Abraham had never judged a fight in the professional or amateur ranks.

That day, Berlin sent an e-mail to Hoover asking if Hoover had licensed Abraham.

There was no response.

A second e-mail to Hoover sent five days later also went unanswered.

Finally, on November 20, Berlin e-mailed Hoover a third time, sending copies of the e-mail to multiple NYSAC and Department of State personnel, including Anthony Giardina.

Giardina suggested a conference call to resolve the matter. Hoover told the group that Abraham had been applying to become an inspector, not a judge, and "I gave him the wrong application."

That same day, Glenn Alleyne (the NYSAC community coordinator) sent a letter to Abraham advising him that his license was "deemed null and void ab initio" because "various necessary statutory prerequisites for licensure such as experiential requirements, training requirements, and the certification of passage of a written exam have not been met."

But that's not the whole story. Evidence gathered by the inspector general's staff supports the proposition that this wasn't an inadvertent error.

Hoover had personally handed Abraham's application to Glenn Alleyne and told him to license Abraham. Alleyne was responsible for processing applications from people seeking positions as referees, judges, and timekeepers. Athletic activities assistant Ana Rivas was responsible for processing the inspector applications.

Also, Abraham had filled out a five-page application. At the top of each page, the application stated in solid capital letters and large type that it was an "APPLICATION FOR PROFESSIONAL BOXING JUDGE." On page three, the application asked, "Do you now or have you ever held a license as a professional boxing judge in any state, jurisdiction, or territory?" Abraham checked the "no" box. On page four, the application asked, "Do you have experience judging sanctioned amateur boxing matches?" Again, Abraham checked the "no" box.

On page four, the application read, "State your qualifications as a boxing judge." Abraham answered, "At an early age, I became a student of the sport of boxing courtesy of my father, a lifelong follower of the sport. I have watched hundreds of amateur and professional matches over the past 35 years, both live and televised. I have also studied and followed the careers of many great boxers. I believe the knowledge I have acquired regarding the sport of boxing through my years of watching and studying the sport make me a good candidate for a boxing judge."

Abraham (according to the application he submitted to the NYSAC) is an experienced attorney admitted to practice in New York and New Jersey. It strains credibility to suggest that he (or anyone else) thought he was applying to be an inspector.

It should also be noted that the cover letter Abraham sent to Hoover with his completed application suggests a personal relationship between them in that it asks Hoover to give Abraham's regards to Hoover's wife and is signed "Ron."

Millions of dollars and a fighter's career can turn on a judge's scorecard. The Abraham incident raised questions regarding Hoover's credibility and also his attitude toward judges.

Meanwhile, the tug of war between Hoover and Berlin continued.

On February 16, 2016, Anthony Giardina called Hoover, Berlin, and Eric Bentley into a meeting and told them that, henceforth, they'd be reporting to Deputy Secretary of State Charles Fields instead of Giardina. Initially, Berlin was pleased. Recalling his early interaction with Fields, he says, "Charles clearly defined our roles. I was to be in charge of the day-to-day operation of the commission, while the commissioners would be the ultimate policy-makers."

But Berlin's optimism was short lived. On Friday, May 13, 2016, he was summoned to a meeting by Giardina. Fields was present but didn't speak. According to Berlin, Giardina told him, "We no longer have confidence in your ability to run the commission." Giardina then said that Berlin was to have nothing more to do with the NYSAC and instructed him to report on Monday morning to the twentieth floor at 123 William Street, where a desk and a position in the Department of State's legal department would be waiting for him.

Berlin says he asked Giardina why he was being terminated and was told there had been "too much turmoil" during his tenure. Berlin then asked, "What makes you think I'm qualified to work in the legal department?" and was told, "Well, you're a lawyer, aren't you?"

Berlin declined to take the new job that was offered to him. Instead, on May 16, 2016, he sent a four-page letter to Governor Andrew Cuomo in which he referenced wrongdoing at the commission (including acts which he believed to be criminal) and the politicization of the NYSAC to the detriment of its mission. He never received a response. No one from the governor's office reached out to him for further information or said, "Tell us what else we should know."

Hoover and Fields declined to be interviewed for this article.

For a while, it looked as though the storm would blow over. Then, on June 23, the *New York Times* published an article by Dan Barry headlined "Hired to Clean Up Boxing, but Pushed Out of His Role." The article referenced some of Berlin's allegations and noted with regard to the NYSAC, "Mismanagement, patronage and piecemeal corruption pepper its history."

Next, on July 25, the report of the inspector general's office on its investigation of the New York State Athletic Commission was released. That same day, it was announced that Hoover had resigned as NYSAC chairperson.

A source at the NYSAC says that chief medical officer Dr. Barry Jordan also offered to resign but that his offer was declined, in part because no succession plan is yet in place.

Potential witnesses are now being contacted and asked if they will testify before a federal grand jury in the Eastern District of New York. The ongoing investigation in the Southern District of New York could have more significant implications.

"Look under a rock," says an insider familiar with the situation. "Then look under the rock next to that one and the rock after that. There's a lot of bad things now, crawling around under the rocks at the New York State Athletic Commission."

PART TWO

As I wrote earlier this year, the administration of New York governor Andrew Cuomo has in some ways been a model of effective governance. Other times, it has fallen short of the mark.

The most notable failure of the Cuomo administration has been in the area of government ethics and the need for reform. On July 2, 2013, the governor announced the creation of a "Commission to Investigate Public Corruption" in New York. Less than a year later, he shut the commission down. At that point, the United States Attorney's Office for the Southern District of New York intervened.

The three most powerful men in Albany were Cuomo, speaker of the New York State Assembly Sheldon Silver, and majority leader of the New York State Senate Dean Skelos. Silver and Skelos were each indicted by a federal grand jury and found guilty at trial (Silver on seven counts of abusing his office for more than $4,000,000 in personal gain; Skelos, along with his son, on eight counts of bribery, extortion, and conspiracy).

In each instance, the prosecution was spearheaded by Preet Bharara (the United States attorney for the Southern District of New York). Now there are indications that Bharara has his sights set on the Cuomo administration.

A federal investigation over ring credentials?

No. A federal investigation into the possibility that the Office of the Inspector General of the State of New York was improperly influenced by the governor's office.

The inspector general was asked by the secretary of state to investigate the New York State Athletic Commission on November 11, 2013. As noted in Part One of this report, a staff member in the inspector general's office made courtesy calls to several people in December 2014 (more than a year later), telling them that release of the report was "imminent."

But the report wasn't released.

Eighteen months after that, on June 15, 2016, Paul Edelstein (the attorney for the family of Magomed Abdusalamov) brought an Article 78 proceeding in New York State Supreme Court against the inspector general's office, asking the court to order the inspector general to turn over "all reports, whether draft or final versions, pertaining to the Inspector General's investigation [of Abdusalamov vs. Mike Perez]."

Then, on June 24, 2016, Edelstein wrote to Preet Bharara. In part, his letter stated, "It is particularly concerning to this office that an independent commission such as the Inspector General's office is perhaps being influenced or pressured by the very state government it is charged with investigating. As such, we believe it would be appropriate for your office to investigate the matter further to determine if the report is being wrongfully and unlawfully suppressed."

On July 5, 2016, the New York State inspector general's office filed a motion to dismiss Edelstein's Article 78 proceeding, arguing, "The Inspector General's decision whether to release a final report regarding her findings is purely discretionary and not subject to judicial review." The motion to dismiss further maintained that draft reports are "exempt from disclosure."

Then word began to spread that several people had been approached by federal authorities and asked about the failure of the inspector general's office to release its report. There are indications that federal authorities might also have raised the issue with one or more persons at the inspector general's office. That could have been the catalyst for the July 25, 2016, release of the inspector general's report.

One day after the report was released, at least one potential witness received an inquiry from federal authorities asking if he would accept e-mail service of a subpoena to testify before a grand jury.

The inspector general's report was highly critical of Melvina Lathan (Tom Hoover's predecessor as chairperson of the New York State Athletic Commission). In part, the report stated, "Having served as chairperson of the Athletic Commission for over five years and as the sole commissioner receiving a full-time salary, Lathan was responsible for the daily operation of the Athletic Commission and for its leadership. Thus, she was primarily responsible for the deficient procedures and policies identified in this investigation and for deficient operation and oversight. Testimony revealed that the [other] commissioners did not engage in the kind of analysis of policies and procedures or management that is required to operate a commission properly."

And the report savaged Hoover for abusing his position to benefit family and friends, sometimes mocking Hoover's attempts to justify his conduct.

For example, Hoover had told the inspector general's staff that he added his son and a friend to the NYSAC credentials list because they were "prospective inspectors." The inspector general's report said the following about that: "Hoover testified that a background in boxing is a prerequisite for becoming a boxing inspector, but said that his son and his son's friend's only qualifications for becoming inspectors was that they were 'big guys.' Hoover's use of his son's middle name rather than their shared last name further suggests that Hoover knew his conduct was problematic."

But Hoover's ethical issues were minor compared to the larger problems that beset the New York State Athletic Commission. And there, in some respects, the inspector general's report fell short. It correctly devoted dozens of pages to the inadequate nature of the NYSAC's medical protocols and procedures in conjunction with Magomed Abdusalamov. But it ignored an instance when proper medical protocols and procedures appear to have been ripped asunder by the governor's office.

As noted earlier, a study of tapes, transcripts, and other material developed during the inspector general's investigation shows that evidence was gathered in a diligent and conscientious manner. As part of that effort, the staff compiled extensive testimony regarding political pressure that was brought to bear upon the NYSAC to license Antonio Margarito for a fight against Miguel Cotto at Madison Square Garden in 2011 despite overwhelming evidence of an eye injury that rendered Margarito unfit to fight.

The inspector general's report makes no mention of Antonio Margarito, which is a shocking omission that has upset several ring doctors. And concern among some commission medical personnel has grown since the most recent fight card at Barclays Center.

On July 30, 2016, Showtime televised a triple-header from Barclays promoted by DiBella Entertainment and headlined by Leo Santa

Cruz vs. Carl Frampton. The opening TV bout was Tony Harrison vs. Sergey Rabchenko. Dr. Avery Browne of the New York State Athletic Commission conducted a routine physical examination of Harrison in the dressing room before the fight. In response to a question from Dr. Browne, Harrison said that he'd taken Advil several hours earlier for a sore shoulder.

The New York State Athletic Commission "Drug Notice and Boxer Acknowledgment Form" states, "Boxers participating in a boxing match should avoid the use of non-topical non-steroidal anti-inflammatories (NSAIDS) within one week of a boxing match because of a potential increased risk of bleeding. Use of NSAIDS within one week of a boxing match may result in cancellation of the match."

Advil is one of the prohibited medications.

Dr. Browne is a defendant in a lawsuit brought by the family of Magomed Abdusalamov in conjunction with the injuries Abdusalamov suffered at Madison Square Garden on November 2, 2013. Browne was the ringside physician assigned to Perez's corner that night. He had nothing to do with the decisions regarding Abdusalamov's medical care. Piecing the story together from multiple sources, it would seem that Dr. Browne wasn't the decision maker with regard to what transpired next with Tony Harrison either.

Dr. Barry Jordan (the current NYSAC chief medical officer) wasn't at Barclays Center on July 30. Reached by telephone, Dr. Jordan said that Harrison-Rabchenko should be called off. There was extensive back-and-forth, during which promoter Lou DiBella and Alex Dombroff (an attorney for DiBella Entertainment) advised Charles Fields, John Signorile (the only NYSAC commissioner on site), and Eric Bentley that Harrison had mispoken to Browne and might have taken Tylenol instead of Advil.

Pressed to make a decision, Fields and Signorile ruled that Harrison-Rabchenko could go forward provided that Harrison agreed to sign a written declaration (drafted by Dombroff and NYSAC deputy commissioner Keith Sullivan with input from Department of State attorney Jim Leary) that he hadn't taken Advil and also agreed to go to a hospital after the fight for a toxicology test to determine if Advil was, in fact, in his system.

Al Haymon (Harrison's manager) approved the resolution. The declaration signed by Harrison read, "I certify and affirm under penalty of perjury that the only over-the-counter drug I have taken in the last 24 hours (from [*sic*] 8:00 PM on Saturday, July 30) is Tylenol in which the only active ingredient is acetaminophen. I misspoke during the pre-fight physical in stating that I took Advil. For purposes of clarification, I did not take any medication containing Ibuprofen in the last 24 hours."

Harrison's declaration was witnessed by Henry Hill and Amir Salaam from Team Harrison as well as Dorothea Perry (one of two NYSAC inspectors assigned to Harrison's dressing room) and Eric Bentley.

Haymon later told a third party that a sample was taken from Harrison for toxicology purposes after the fight. The result of that toxicology test is not publicly known.

Either way, testing Tony Harrison after the fight did nothing to protect him from a potential brain bleed.

One participant in the deliberations at Barclays Center says, "It would be unfair to punish a fighter because he doesn't know the difference between over-the-counter drugs." But this is an instance when, as with Cotto-Margarito, the New York State Athletic Commission changed the initial ruling of its own medical staff and appears to have been more interested in protecting itself with a hastily drafted statement than in protecting the fighter.

By way of comparison, on April 9, 2016, Alicia Napolean was scheduled to fight in the main event at 5 Star Banquet Hall in New York. During her pre-fight physical examination in the dressing room, she told the doctor that she had taken Advil that day. David Berlin (then the NYSAC executive director) and Dr. Jordon caucused. Napolean had sold thousands of dollars' worth of tickets. On Jordan's recommendation, the fight was canceled.

"It was a hard moment," Berlin said afterward. "But the decision was easy. A fighter is at risk every time he or she steps into the ring. We can't knowingly add to those risks."

Right now, the New York State Athletic Commission is in turmoil.

On July 9, 2016, the *New York Post* published an article that read in part, "At a time when the NYSAC needs to be working as a cohesive unit, there appears to be chaos. Several boxing promoters have complained about disarray within the NYSAC, with one prominent figure in the New York boxing industry charging, 'They just don't care.'"

On July 25, 2016 (the day the inspector general's report was released), Rick Karlin's "Capitol Confidential" column in the *Albany Times Union* ran beneath the headline "IG Issues Blistering Report on State Athletic Commission." In his column, Karlin declared, "The findings also appear to vindicate David Berlin, who recently left the Commission under pressure for what he said was his blowing the whistle on problems at the organization."

Barry McGuigan is widely respected throughout the boxing community as a former world champion and also for his work as a manager, newspaper columnist, and TV commentator. McGuigan was in New York with Belfast native Carl Frampton, who fought Leo Santa Cruz at Barclays Center on July 30.

"The commission in New York is horrible," McGuigan told this writer. "I've never experienced anything like it. I understand the need to protect fighters. But these people have made things unbelievably difficult for us at every turn. And half the time, it seems like they don't know what they're doing. It's like they don't want fights in New York."

Whether or not the NYSAC wants fights in New York—and one assumes that it does—the odds are that there will be fewer of them in the near future.

On April 14, 2016, Andrew Cuomo signed a bill passed by the state legislature lifting the ban on mixed martial arts competitions that had been in place since 1997.

The new law also addressed several medical issues. Ring physicians were reclassified as state employees rather than independent contractors, thereby halting an exodus of qualified ring doctors who were concerned that their own liability insurance wouldn't protect them against claims of medical malpractice lodged against them by fighters. In addition, the cost of fighter medical examinations (previously paid for by the state) was shifted to fighters and promoters.

But there was more.

The Muhammad Ali Boxing Reform Act mandates that promoters purchase medical insurance on a card-by-card basis to pay a fighter's medical expenses in conjunction with injuries suffered during a bout. However, the Ali Act doesn't specify a coverage minimum. That decision is left to the individual states.

Medical costs in New York are among the highest in the nation. But New York only required that promoters maintain a $10,000 medical insurance policy for each fighter (significantly below the $50,000 minimum required by Nevada, California, and Texas).

Berlin had advocated for raising the $10,000 medical insurance minimum to $50,000. At the same time, he proposed lowering a statutorily required $100,000 death benefit to $50,000.

"I did some research," Berlin says. "The cost of the insurance would go up with the new numbers, but cutting the death benefit would limit the increase. Ring deaths are rare, so the $100,000 was a less important number. We had to strike a balance between protecting boxers and not imposing excessive costs on promoters."

So far, so good. But there was a problem.

Governor Cuomo supported the proposed legislation, the centerpiece of which was the legalization of mixed martial arts. There were enough votes in the state senate and state assembly to enact the legislation if it came up for a vote. But there weren't enough votes in committee to bring the legislation to the assembly floor. So to gather support, Cuomo agreed to the last-minute insertion of a provision that requires all promoters of boxing matches and other martial arts competitions to provide medical insurance or another form of financial guarantee acceptable to the NYSAC with a minimum limit of one million dollars. This million dollars would be used to cover medical, surgical, and hospital care for the treatment of life-threatening brain injuries in situations where an identifiable causal link exists between the fighter's participation in a fight and the life-threatening brain injury.

The $1,000,000 insurance requirement is scheduled to take effect on September 1. It might have been well intended, but it's not practical. The cost of the premiums will make it impossible to promote most fight cards on a cost-efficient basis in New York.

Berlin first became aware of the $1,000,000 proposal in early 2015 and voiced his reservations to Executive Deputy Secretary of State Anthony Giardina and Brendan Fitzgerald (deputy secretary for General Government and Financial Services). In spring 2015, he was asked about the matter by state senator Joseph Griffo and expressed his concern that the requirement could put small promoters out of business while encouraging the flight of large promoters to other states.

The New York State Athletic Commission has now posted a set of proposed rules and regulations that, among other things, are designed to fine-tune the $1,000,000 insurance requirement. Public comments will be accepted by the NYSAC until August 27, after which the rules and regulations will be finalized.

In relevant part, the proposed rules and regulations state:

★ "'Identifiable, causal link' shall mean that the injuries sustained by the licensed professional during his or her participation in the authorized covered combative sports program were the direct and proximate cause of the life-threatening brain injury."

★ "'Life-threatening brain injury' shall mean an acute brain injury that, in the opinion of the professional licensee's treating physician, would result in the death of the professional licensee if left untreated."

★ "'Sustained in a program operated under the control of such licensed promoter' shall mean that the symptoms of the life-threatening brain injury must first manifest themselves during, or within twenty-four hours after the end of, the licensed professional's participation in the covered program, and the injury must be diagnosed by a physician during or within forty-eight hours after the end of the licensed professional's participation in the covered program."

Under the NYSAC's proposed rules and regulations, a brain bleed that is serious but not considered likely to "result in death if left untreated" would not be covered. Nor would a "slow" brain bleed that doesn't manifest itself within twenty-four hours.

New York has always been an expensive place to promote boxing. Hotel, food, and labor costs are higher in New York than elsewhere. New York's million-dollar insurance requirement might be the straw that breaks the camel's back.

NYSAC representatives have told several promoters that they've found an insurance company that will underwrite the required insurance policies for a premium cost of roughly $7,500 per fight card. That would be significantly more than the current premium cost. And more troubling, the $7,500 estimate seems too good to be true.

A study of medical insurance premiums paid by one promoter reveals that the promoter paid $87,820 in premiums during a recent one-year period for insurance covering fight cards in New York. And the insurance company paid out $169,000 to settle claims for medical treatment under those policies.

That's a 192 percent loss ratio. And the pay-outs were capped at $10,000 per fighter. The new law requires a policy minimum of $50,000 plus a $1,000,000 balloon for life-threatening brain injuries.

Michael Dean is the head of Francis L. Dean and Associates (the insurance underwriters identified by the NYSAC as being likely to underwrite million-dollar medical insurance policies for combat sports in New York). The company has offices in five states and brings in more than $60 million in insurance premiums annually.

"At this time," Dean said during a July 29 telephone interview, "we haven't finished our pricing model. It's being worked on by our actuaries. We hope to resolve this at our end within thirty to forty-five days. Then any policy we propose would be subject to the New York State Department of Financial Services (which regulates insurance in New York). We have some risks that are profitable and others that aren't. We want to be profitable, and we make adjustments to our rating structure accordingly."

Dean also acknowledged the possibility that Francis L. Dean and Associates might choose to not underwrite the policies. Moreover, because of the twenty-four- and forty-eight-hour windows in the proposed regulations, fighters might be sent for unnecessary, and costly, tests to avoid complications that would arise if symptoms became more obvious after the time-window had closed. The cost of these tests would be set against the $50,000 policy limit, and policy premiums would rise accordingly.

"I'm glad that the commission clarified the policy requirements with its new proposed regulations," Dean added. "But 'life-threatening brain injury' is still an ambiguous term."

Plans for fights are often made months in advance by promoters. The longer it takes to resolve the insurance issue, the fewer fights there will be in New York this autumn. Promoters might be able to pay a five-figure insurance premium for a major show at Madison Square Garden or Barclays Center. For a small club card, that wouldn't be practical. And even major events are in jeopardy.

Pat English (the attorney for Main Events, which is scheduled to co-promote Sergey Kovalev vs. Andre Ward with Roc Nation on November 19)

says, "The million-dollar insurance requirement was a factor in Kovalev–
Ward going to Las Vegas. I'm not saying that the fight would have wound
up in New York without it. But Roc Nation wanted the fight at Madison
Square Garden. And the million dollars made that impossible."

Boxing in Brooklyn appeared to be hitting its stride in recent months
when Lou DiBella promoted back-to-back fight cards headlined by Keith
Thurman vs. Shawn Porter and Leo Santa Cruz vs. Carl Frampton at
Barclays Center. That progress is now on hold. WBA middleweight champion Danny Jacobs fought his two most recent fights at Barclays under
the DiBella banner. His September 9 title defense against Sergio Mora
will be contested in Pennsylvania.

This is a situation where the New York State Athletic Commission
has to act. The new law states, "The commission may from time to time
promulgate regulations to adjust the amount of such minimum [medical
insurance] limits."

That's construed by some as meaning the commission may only
adjust the insurance minimums upward. Others believe that the NYSAC
can adjust the minimums up or down.

Who will be the decision makers regarding the insurance minimum?

The legislation that legalized mixed martial arts and was signed by
Andrew Cuomo on April 14, 2016, also increased the number of commissioners on the New York State Athletic Commission from three to five.

Tom Hoover was serving as a holdover in a term that expired on
January 1, 2016. One day after his resignation was announced, the NYSAC
revealed that Ndidi Massay had been named interim chairperson.

Massay was one of more than a dozen nominees for a variety of positions who were confirmed pursuant to a single voice vote by the New
York State Senate Standing Committee on Finance on June 17, 2016,
without their having appeared before the committee. No press release
was issued after her confirmation.

On July 26, 2016, in response to an inquiry from this writer, Laz
Benitez (a press officer for the New York State Department of State)
wrote, "Massey will serve in a part time capacity on an interim basis until
a permanent Chair is designated by the Governor."

One day later, the Department of State press office issued a clar-
ifying statement that read, "The 'interim Chair' title is being used as

a functional title to denote that Commissioner Massay will manage the agenda and lead Commission meetings until a new Chairperson is formally designated by the Governor. Use of this functional title for Commissioner Massay does not denote and should not be confused with the formal designation of a full-time Chairperson of the State Athletic Commission."

Ms. Massay is a businesswoman and attorney with no known experience in the sport or business of boxing. She did not attend the July 30 fight card at Barclays Center, the first of her tenure as interim chairperson.

John Signorile is serving as an NYSAC commissioner pursuant to a term that expired on January 1, 2015. He and Edwin Torres (an eighty-five-year-old retired New York State Supreme Court judge now serving on the NYSAC pursuant to a term that expired on January 1, 2014) were commissioners during the events described in the recent inspector general's report.

A cynic might note that the New York State Athletic Commission is starting to resemble a world sanctioning organization. It now has an interim chairperson, an acting executive director, two commissioners with terms that have expired, and two empty seats.

That might be amusing but for the fact that boxing is a dangerous sport. Each little mistake has the potential to undermine the safety and fairness of the competition and increase the chances that a fighter will die.

Writing in *Moneyball* about the failure of baseball to understand and embrace the sabermetric revolution in a timely fashion, Michael Lewis declared, "The game itself is a ruthless competition. But in the space just off the field of play, there really is no level of incompetence that won't be tolerated."

The same is often said of government and politics.

The New York State Athletic Commission isn't charged with overseeing human resources, mass transit, or some other public sector where problems sometimes seem insoluble. It's a small commission charged with regulating several dozen fight cards each year. It's not hard to do the job right if conscientious knowledgable people are put in charge. But if political expediency takes precedence over good government, it creates a mess.

Right now, the New York State Athletic Commission is a mess.

If Andrew Cuomo really wants to begin the process of solving the problems at the New York State Athletic Commission, he'll bring back David Berlin.

It's rare to find someone in boxing who genuinely cares about the sweet science, understands the sport and business, is ethical and smart, and is a good administrator. Berlin exemplified all of these qualities as executive director.

All Governor Cuomo would have to do is say, "This matter has now landed on my desk; not the desk of some subordinate. I've studied the matter. And while I don't agree with everything that Mr. Berlin has said and done, I think he's the right person for the job."

But that won't happen.

So let's close for now with the thoughts of Teddy Atlas, who has been in boxing as an amateur fighter, trainer, and television commentator for more than four decades.

"I've fought for this sport my whole life," Atlas said recently. "I thought David Berlin was the right guy and he would help the commission and help boxing. And he did make the commission better while he was there. But it's a political position. Politics has always been the shadow that looms over the commission. And the politics came in and ruined it."

In early 2016, I wrote, "The New York State Athletic Commission is at a crossroads. Things could get better or they could get worse. Much worse."

Turmoil Grows at the New York State Athletic Commission

On October 29, 1975, with New York City on the verge of bankruptcy, President Gerald Ford announced that he opposed federal financial assistance to ease the city's fiscal crisis. The following day, a banner headline on page one of the *New York Daily News* blared, "Ford to City: Drop Dead."

On August 31, 2016, the New York State Athletic Commission told small boxing promoters in New York to drop dead.

The commission's monthly meeting (which was open to the public) began at 11:16 a.m. and lasted for eleven minutes. All three commissioners (Ndidi Massay, Edwin Torres, and John Signorile) were in attendance, as were Anthony Giardina (the newly appointed interim executive director), Eric Bentley (demoted earlier in the week from the position of acting executive director to director of boxing), and Kim Sumbler (who was formally installed in the newly created position of MMA project coordinator).

The meeting was a dog-and-pony show. The commissioners had already decided what to do behind closed doors. A motion was made to adopt a set of proposed rules and regulations governing combat sports in New York that had been posted in July on the NYSAC website. Despite strong opposition from the boxing community and clear indications that the rules and regulations will undermine the ability of boxing promoters to do business in New York, the motion passed by a 3-to-0 vote. On September 1, the rules and regulations became law.

The seeds of boxing's latest dilemma can be found in an April 14, 2016, press release issued by the office of New York governor Andrew Cuomo headlined "Governor Cuomo Signs Legislation Legalizing Mixed Martial Arts in New York State." The headline could just as easily have read "Governor Cuomo Signs Legislation that Threatens to Destroy a Class of Small Businesses in New York."

The new law requires all promoters of boxing matches and other martial arts competitions to provide medical insurance or another form of financial guarantee acceptable to the New York State Athletic Commission with a minimum coverage of one million dollars. This million dollars would be used to cover medical, surgical, and hospital care for the treatment of life-threatening brain injuries in situations where an identifiable causal link exists between the fighter's participation in a fight and the life-threatening brain injury.

For all other fight-related medical costs, a $50,000 insurance policy is required.

The $1,000,000 insurance requirement is not economically viable. The cost of the premiums (currently estimated to be in excess of $15,000; more than triple the current premium cost) will make it impossible to promote most fight cards on a cost-efficient basis in New York. David Berlin (then executive director of the NYSAC) warned legislators and Department of State officials of the problem as far back as June 2015 when the proposal was first discussed. Multiple promoters and others in the boxing industry voiced similar concerns when the law was enacted in April of this year and again when the NYSAC posted its proposed rules and regulations in July.

An August 27, 2016, letter from Joe DeGuardia and Lou DiBella (two leading New York promoters) to the Department of State (which oversees the NYSAC) warned, "All boxing in the state of New York—marquee events and club shows alike—are under an immediate danger of extinction."

The DeGuardia-DiBella letter then elaborated, "To date, we are not aware of any insurance carrier approved to provide $1 million in insurance coverage for life-threatening traumatic brain injuries in New York and, to the extent there is such a carrier, we believe the cost may be higher than the amount currently projected by the NYSAC. Even if the cost of the coverage is consistent with the amount projected by the NYSAC, the cost will increase the cost to promoters in New York—both MMA and boxing—and will make promoting smaller shows cost-prohibitive."

The political powers that be in New York have sought to justify the million-dollar insurance requirement on grounds that it's designed to protect the health and safety of fighters.

But the insurance requirement isn't about protecting fighters. A state athletic commission protects fighters by refusing to license fighters who shouldn't be allowed to fight. A state athletic commission protects fighters by instituting proper medical procedures and protocols and hiring competent doctors to implement them. A state athletic commission protects fighters by hiring referees who know when to stop a fight and inspectors who recognize signs of trouble.

The million-dollar insurance requirement has nothing to do with that. It's about who pays for a fighter's medical care after the system has failed to safeguard the fighter. The fighter's family? The hospital where the fighter is treated? The state? That's a legitimate issue. But let's be honest about the fact that the million-dollar-insurance requirement will undermine every small promoter in New York and clears the way for UFC to be the only promoter of any professional combat sport competition in New York in the immediate future.

Let's also acknowledge that, while the proposed insurance requirements will make boxing cost-prohibitive for small promoters, the requisite policy coverage has more holes in it than a piece of Swiss cheese.

For example, the rules and regulations approved by the NYSAC on August 31 state that, even in cases of "acute brain injury," the policy need only apply in the event that the condition would, in the opinion of a fighter's treating physician, "result in the death of the [fighter] if left untreated."

In other words, the prospect of a fighter being paralyzed and unable to speak for life because of an acute brain injury wouldn't necessarily be covered. Nor, because of timing limitations contained in the rules and regulations, would a "slow" brain bleed that doesn't manifest itself within twenty-four hours.

Moreover, as the August 27 DeGuardia-DiBella letter warns, "The proposed insurance requirement undermines the very purpose of the statute that brought about its existence. The primary reason MMA was legalized in New York (which led to the proposed regulations and the increased minimum insurance requirements) was the projected economic activity that legal MMA would bring to New York. However, the

anticipated additional insurance requirements will make it cost prohibi-
tive for boxing promoters to do business in New York, thereby decreasing
economic activity in New York."

That prophesy is now coming true.

UFC was sold recently for $4 billion. UFC's new owners can afford to
self-insure or pay high insurance premiums. Bellator (another MMA promoter) is a subsidiary of Viacom and is expected to get insurance under
a Viacom umbrella policy. UFC fight cards are currently scheduled for
Madison Square Garden on November 12 and the Times Union Center
in Albany on December 10.

Boxing promoters have been left out in the cold. To date, no insurance carrier has been willing to underwrite a million-dollar medical
insurance policy for boxing, let alone a million-dollar policy that makes
economic sense for a small show.

There were eleven fight cards in New York during the last four
months of 2014 and eleven during the last four months of 2015. There are
no boxing matches presently scheduled in New York for the remainder
of this year. DiBella Entertainment had been holding September 24 for a
fight card at Barclays Center to be headlined by Danny Garcia. That's now
off, and DiBella has moved his "Broadway Boxing" series to Foxwoods
Resort Casino in Connecticut for the foreseeable future.

And it's not just boxing people who will lose money. It's also hotels
and restaurants near New York fight venues, their service staff and kitchen
workers. It's the ticket takers and other "little people" who work on site.
And don't forget the taxes that are generated when there's a big fight in
New York.

NYSAC personnel were aware of this problem long before the legislation passed. Yet except for David Berlin, there's no record of anyone at
the NYSAC (including commissioners John Signorile and Edwin Torres)
voicing concern. Then, when the legislation passed in April of this year,
the commission failed to make realistic plans that could be put in place
on September 1 (either finding an insurance carrier that would underwrite the policies for an affordable premium or taking steps to lower the
insurance minimum).

The commission fiddled while boxing in New York burned.

"They don't know what the fuck they're doing," DiBella says. "It's a
total mess."

An August 5, 2016, e-mail sent to all deputy commissioners and inspectors by Eric Bentley (who served briefly as acting executive director) supports DiBella's point. This e-mail, sent in the wake of the July 30 Leo Santa Cruz vs. Carl Frampton card at Barclays Center in Brooklyn, read in part, "There are some instances that occurred this past weekend that are very concerning and will need to be addressed immediately. Hopefully, by sending this written communication to all, we can help prevent future mistakes and continually improve our operations."

Among other things, Bentley's e-mail declared (partly in solid capital letters and bold type), "NEVER LEAVE A FIGHTER ALONE FOR ANY REASON AFTER A PRE-FIGHT URINE HAS BEEN COLLECTED. This is one of the most basic and important rules to follow."

That was followed by another declaration in solid capital letters and bold type: "NEVER TELL A BOXER OR CORNER THAT YOU ARE NEW OR YOU DON'T KNOW THE RULES. In any situation where you may be confused or where clarification is necessary, you should always remain calm and collected, and simply explain to the fighter and their corner that you need to discuss the matter with a supervisor."

There was more.

"Everyone needs to understand the proper way to wrap a hand, as well as any incorrect methods that a corner may try to sneak past you. We only allow 6 inches of tape on the hand before wrapping; not on the wrists, not on the elbows, not on the fingers, not on the forearms. We also do not allow the knuckle pads to be rolled on the knuckles. They are to remain flat (if necessary, they can be folded in half)."

Bentley further admonished, "As an inspector, if you notice something that you think is being done incorrectly by another inspector, ask your colleague to step to the side and have a private conversation to discuss your concerns. You may be wrong, so to call a matter to the attention of a fighter or their camp (or even the opponent and their camp) is completely unprofessional and is equivalent to shouting 'FIRE!' in a crowded room."

Problems like this arise when inspectors are poorly trained and assigned to fights on the basis of political priorities and personal favoritism rather than competence.

Meanwhile, the NYSAC is currently engaged in a round of personnel changes that resembles a game of musical chairs.

The Department of State has oversight responsibilities with regard to the commission. For several years, the person primarily responsible for this oversight was Executive Deputy Secretary of State Anthony Giardina, an attorney who worked for former New York governor Mario Cuomo (Andrew's father) earlier in his career and has been with the Department of State since 2012.

In February 2016, Deputy Secretary of State Charles Fields assumed Giardina's oversight role with regard to the NYSAC. When Fields addressed the commission staff for the first time, he told them that he knew nothing about boxing but was a big fan of Mike Tyson.

By and large, Fields sided with Tom Hoover in the chairman's ongoing conflict with David Berlin. In May 2016, Berlin was dismissed and Eric Bentley became acting executive director. Two months after that, Hoover resigned under fire after the inspector general's office concluded that he'd abused his position for personal gain. Ndidi Massay was named interim chairperson after Hoover's departure.

Then, on August 31, it was announced that Fields had been stripped of his responsibilities vis-à-vis the New York State Athletic Commission and that Giardina had resigned as executive deputy secretary of state to become the NYSAC's interim executive director. Eric Bentley was relegated to his old role as director of boxing, and Kim Sumbler was formally installed as MMA project coordinator.

Other personnel changes included the departure of longtime athletic activities assistant Ana Rivas, who, on August 22, sent an e-mail to dozens of commission personnel, promoters, and others advising them that she would leave the NYSAC on September 9.

The commission has also interviewed a half dozen candidates for newly created deputy commissioner slots. Some of the candidates are qualified. Others are basing their hope of appointment on political priorities rather than competence.

That same balancing of competence and politics will be part of the decision-making process when Governor Cuomo fills four of the NYSAC's five commissioner seats during the next few months.

The statute that legalized professional mixed martial arts competition in New York also expanded the NYSAC from three to five commissioners.

That's two open positions to begin with. Additionally, Edwin Torres and John Signorile (each of whom was criticized in the July 2016 inspector general's report for "a lack of appropriate engagement and oversight" following the inspector general's investigation into the tragedy of Magomed Abdusalamov) are serving as holdover commissioners on expired terms. Ndidi Massay's term runs until 2019.

Political observers—not just the boxing community—should watch very closely to see who Governor Cuomo appoints to the commission. This isn't just a combat sports issue. It's a good government issue.

Several boxing insiders who've met Massay (the recently appointed interim chairperson) say that she acknowledges knowing next to nothing about the sport and business of boxing. Let's assume that Massay is a smart, conscientious, well-intentioned attorney and businesswoman. The fact remains that state athletic commission commissioners (and particularly the chairperson) should have a working knowledge of the sport they regulate.

Would Andrew Cuomo appoint a bright capable attorney with no experience in politics to run his reelection campaign? Obviously not. Why not? Because as bright and capable as that person might be, he or she wouldn't have the requisite experience to run a political campaign. And Andrew Cuomo's reelection campaign matters to Andrew Cuomo.

Meanwhile, events at the New York State Athletic Commission are taking place against the backdrop of two investigations by federal law enforcement authorities.

One of these investigations is centered in the United States Attorney's Office for the Southern District of New York and, among other things, is exploring whether the Cuomo administration improperly influenced the inspector general of the State of New York in conjunction with its inquiry into the life-changing injuries suffered by Magomed Abdusalamov. The other investigation is being conducted by the Public Integrity Section of United States Attorney's Office for the Eastern District of New York and is believed to be focusing on wrongdoing by NYSAC officials.

These investigations began separately, but some information gathering is now being coordinated by the FBI. One potential witness who was interviewed in August says he was asked about the process by which the legislation legalizing mixed martial arts and instituting the million-dollar insurance requirement was enacted and whether there might have been an intention to favor UFC to the detriment of boxing.

That's not to say that the answer is yes; only that questions are being asked.

Governor Cuomo signed the legislation on April 14, 2016, in a ceremony at Madison Square Garden. UFC chairman and CEO Lorenzo Fertitta was there for the signing.

Under the law and subsequently adopted NYSAC rules and regulations, many of the guidelines applicable to the oversight of combat sports apply only to boxing. In that regard, the aforementioned August 27, 2016, letter from Joe DeGuardia and Lou DiBella to the Department of State declares, "The proposed regulations dealing with contract oversight contain an unexplained anomaly. Provisions that should apply equally to boxing and MMA have arbitrarily only been written to apply to boxing."

The DeGuardia-DiBella letter then elaborates, "[The proposed regulations] contain essentially the same rule that has been in effect for some time in New York. Contracts between boxers and promoters are limited to an initial duration of three years. We recognize that this is the regulatory framework within which we currently promote. However, we take issue with the fact that [this provision] only applies to the promoter-boxer contractual relationship and does not apply to contracts entered into between MMA promoters and fighters. The exclusion of MMA from the proposed regulations is arbitrary and unfairly singles out boxing. This same disparity exists in the required disclosure for boxing promoters. This regulation sets forth the numerous disclosures a boxing promoter must make to the NYSAC. Again, while these disclosures would be applicable in the context of MMA as well, the regulations only govern boxing promoters. MMA should not be exempt from regulations that are designed in theory to avoid exploitation of fighters in New York."

"We do not believe the disparities pointed out in this section are a case of mere oversight," the DeGuardia-DiBella letter states in closing. "Both sports are under the authority of the NYSAC, and it makes no sense that only certain provisions of the law apply to MMA. Such cherry-picking is unfair to boxing and arbitrary."

One might add that the million-dollar insurance requirement is specifically aimed at acute brain damage, which is less likely to occur in mixed martial arts competition than in boxing. Spinal cord injuries are more common in MMA, and the long-term cost of treating a spinal cord injury is often greater than the cost of treating a brain injury. But the recently enacted New York law makes no special provision for spinal cord injuries.

All of this leads to the question: "Why have the political power brokers in New York done this?" The insurance debacle wasn't just predictable. It was predicted and should have been dealt with months ago.

As noted above, UFC was sold recently for a reported $4 billion. That's $4,000,000,000. Numbers like this engender a feeding frenzy where politicians seeking campaign contributions and other amenities are concerned.

On September 1, 2016 (one day after the NYSAC adopted the new rules and regulations), the *Wall Street Journal* reported that UFC executives acknowledge having spent $2.2 million over the past eight years on lobbying efforts leading to passage of the new law. This total doesn't include campaign contributions that might have been made directly to Governor Cuomo or state legislators.

Right now, Governor Cuomo and the NYSAC are helping one big business (UFC) and hurting a lot of little ones.

Earlier this summer, NYSAC officials told several promoters that the commission had arranged for the requisite million-dollar insurance policy to be made available to promoters for a premium of roughly $7,500. That struck Pat English (the attorney for Main Events) as unlikely. English wrote to the commission on August 6 asking to see a sample policy. Three days later, he was advised that his letter was being treated as a request for information under New York's Freedom of Information law.

That's known as stalling for time.

"To have an inquiry of this nature treated as an Open Public Records Request is off-putting and not what I expected," English responded in a letter to the Department of State. "It is important for promoters and their representatives to have an honest dialogue with the representatives of the commission. A routine inquiry should not be treated as an Open Public Records Request."

NYSAC officials now concede that promises of a million-dollar medical insurance policy at an affordable premium were "premature."

Meanwhile, at least one commission employee was told that personal cell phone records might be sought in an effort to find out who has been discussing NYSAC matters with the media without authorization from the secretary of state's office.

Instead of trying to find out who's talking about problems at the New York State Athletic Commission, the people in charge should put their energy into solving the problems.

The point person in the effort to rehabilitate the NYSAC will be Anthony Giardina. He appears to have been brought in both to transform the commission and also to represent Governor Cuomo's interests as the federal investigations unfold.

One person who has worked with Giardina says, "He's smart. He's personable. He has good administrative skills. He's politically savvy and knows how to operate within a political environment. I like him. But he has no real background in boxing, so the question is whether he'll surround himself with people who know boxing and do what's right or implement a narrow political agenda."

Giardina is aware that there are problems at the commission that go far beyond the million-dollar-medical-insurance controversy. Yes, he'll watch Andrew Cuomo's back. But he also has the governor's ear. One hopes that he'll press for the appointment of competent personnel in key positions, including the four open commissioner slots.

The NYSAC is broken. It can be fixed if Governor Cuomo is more interested in getting it to function properly than in using it as a vehicle for granting political favors and repaying political debts. It's not hard to do the job right if conscientious, hard-working men and women who understand the sport and business of boxing are pressed into service at every level.

Political observers should watch the New York State Athletic Commission closely. Not because they care about combat sports; most of them don't. But because it offers an easily understood case study on how Andrew Cuomo governs.

And by the way . . .

Two months after announcing that he opposed federal financial assistance for New York, Gerald Ford signed legislation that provided low-interest loans to the city.

New York survived. Boxing in New York will too.

2016 ended on a dismal note for the New York State Athletic Commission.

Andrew Cuomo and the New York State Athletic Commission

When the powers that be at UFC wake up on Christmas morning, they'll revel in a sleigh laden with gifts from New York governor Andrew Cuomo and the New York State Athletic Commission. Boxing fans and New York's boxing promoters will find a lump of coal beneath the Christmas tree.

Previous articles by this writer have catalogued shortcomings at the New York State Athletic Commission. It's a matter of record that an investigation by the inspector general of the State of New York found that the commission has been plagued by incompetence and corruption for years. Tom Hoover (the most recent NYSAC chairperson) and Melvina Lathan (his predecessor) were both forced out of office as the inspector general's investigation progressed. The inspector general's report also noted "a lack of appropriate engagement and oversight" by NYSAC commissioners John Signorile and Edwin Torres.

Meanwhile, David Berlin (the NYSAC's highly respected executive director who had been brought in to clean up the mess) was dismissed on May 13, 2016, in part because he refused to put a political agenda ahead of properly doing his job. Berlin's termination came one month after Governor Cuomo signed a bill passed by the state legislature that lifted a 1997 ban on mixed martial arts competitions in New York. The new law also imposes insurance requirements on the promoters of professional combat sports events that are so out of line with economic reality that they threaten the existence of most fight cards in New York.

All of this has drawn the attention of federal law enforcement officials. The United States Attorney's Office for the Southern District of New York is exploring whether the inspector general's office failed to release its report on the New York State Athletic Commission in a timely manner and also whether the Cuomo administration improperly influenced the inspector general's office in conjunction with the content of the report.

In addition, several witnesses who were interviewed by federal prosecutors in the Southern and Eastern Districts of New York say that they were asked about the process by which the legislation legalizing mixed martial arts and instituting the insurance requirement was enacted and whether there might have been an intention to favor UFC to the detriment of boxing.

The past few years have seen a series of high-profile criminal prosecutions aimed at some of New York's most influential political power brokers. Most recently, on November 22, 2016, Joseph Percoco (a close friend and former top aide to Governor Cuomo) was indicted by a grand jury on federal corruption charges in conjunction with a bribery and bid-rigging scandal for which he is alleged to have received at least $315,000 in bribes. The federal investigations as they relate to Governor Cuomo's office and the New York State Athletic Commission are likely to continue.

The point person in the effort to rehabilitate the NYSAC is Tony Giardina. The New York Department of State has oversight responsibilities with regard to the commission. Giardina was executive deputy secretary of state until August of this year, when he resigned to become the NYSAC's interim executive director (a step down on the organizational chart).

Giardina is a competent, politically savvy Cuomo loyalist with good administrative skills, who seems sincere is his efforts to strengthen the NYSAC. In recent months, he has orchestrated expanded training seminars for the commission staff and worked with the medical advisory board to update medical protocols. In November, Nitin Sethi succeeded Barry Jordan as the NYSAC's chief medical officer, which is widely regarded as a step in the right direction.

But there's a learning curve to becoming an effective government regulator of boxing and mixed martial arts. Giardina, by his own admission, is not knowledgable with regard to combat sports. And in too many instances, he appears to be operating within a politics-first environment. He's trying to stop the bleeding, improve performance, and clean things up at the New York State Athletic Commission. But he has to do it within the boundaries of Andrew Cuomo's political agenda.

And he has to do it at a time when the legalization of professional mixed martial arts in New York is placing new responsibilities on a commission that was having trouble handling what it was already charged to do.

Professional mixed martial arts made its long-awaited return to New York on November 12, when more than 20,000 fans packed Madison Square Garden for an eleven-bout card headlined by Conor McGregor vs. Eddie Alvarez. UFC 205 (as the event was called) generated a live gate of $17.7 million, a record for both UFC and the Garden.

The New York State Athletic Commission ceded much of the control over UFC 205 to UFC. State officials appeared at times to be little more than cheerleaders for the promotion. Four on-site Department of State communications personnel retweeted UFC and Madison Square Garden tweets on the New York State Department of State Twitter account throughout the night. There were twenty-three such retweets.

"I feel like we're working for UFC," one on-site New York State Athletic Commission employee said.

Mixed martial arts is now getting special treatment from the NYSAC. Under rules and regulations adopted by the commission in August, many restrictions that should be applicable to the oversight of all combat sports apply only to boxing, not MMA.

Moreover, UFC (which acknowledges having spent millions of dollars on lobbying and having made millions of dollars in campaign contributions to New York political interests) seems to be getting favorable treatment vis-à-vis its direct competitors.

One of things that made UFC's November 12 fight card at Madison Square Garden special and generated a great deal of publicity was the fact that UFC 205 was the first professional mixed martial arts event in New York in two decades.

But here's the rub. On September 1 (the first day that mixed martial arts promoters could be licensed under the new law and the first day that they could apply for mixed martial arts dates), Bellator MMA told the New York State Athletic Commission that it wanted to promote an MMA fight card at Barclays Center on October 29. The commission refused to approve the date.

Why the refusal?

Laz Benitez (a spokesperson for the Department of State) says the request was denied pursuant to Section 207.15(a) of the NYSAC's rules and regulations, which states that licensed promoters must apply to the commission for the approval of a date on which a professional boxing or mixed martial arts event is scheduled at least sixty days prior to the date unless otherwise authorized by the commission.

Bellator's request was made fifty-eight days prior to the proposed date.

But here's the catch. Bellator couldn't apply for an MMA promotional license before September 1. And more to the point, the sixty-day requirement is waived as a matter of course for most promotions. It exists so the commission has time to properly assign NYSAC personnel to fight cards in the event of multiple shows on the same night (which wasn't the case here) and also to ensure that low-level promoters have time to put the puzzle pieces together to properly promote a show. Bellator is a major promoter.

A more credible reason for Bellator being denied the October 29 date is that UFC wanted to be the first company to promote an MMA card in New York under the new law, and the political power brokers who control the NYSAC from above wanted UFC to have its way. That, according to sources, is what Bellator's lobbyists were told when they went to the powers that be. Meanwhile, whatever angst Barclays Center might have felt over losing the proposed October 29 Bellator show evaporated when UFC announced in early November that UFC 209 will be contested at Barclays on February 11, 2017.

And there's another, more serious problem percolating just beneath the surface with regard to MMA.

On April 14, 2016, Governor Cuomo's office issued a press release heralding the return of mixed martial arts to New York. In part, the press release read, "Mixed martial arts contests will be supervised either directly by the New York State Athletic Commission or by a sanctioning entity approved by the Commission." On August 31, Jim Leary (counsel for the NYSAC) elaborated on this third-party supervision of MMA, saying that it would apply only to certain amateur cards.

But . . . As asserted by promoter Lou DiBella, "Right now, you have a situation where some small promoters are putting on MMA shows using unknown fighters, paying them under the table, and calling them amateur shows. That way, they can get around the state insurance regulations and a whole lot more. You couldn't do that with boxing because amateur boxing is more closely regulated than amateur MMA and amateur boxing is so obviously different from professional boxing."

This relates to an issue that has shut down boxing in New York since September 1 and is threatening to wipe out club fights in New York for the foreseeable future: Insurance.

The law legalizing mixed martial arts that was passed earlier this year contained a trade-off. In order to appeal to legislators who opposed the expansion of combat sports, Governor Cuomo engineered the insertion of a provision in the bill that requires all promoters of boxing matches and other martial arts competitions to provide medical insurance or another form of financial guarantee acceptable to the NYSAC with a minimum coverage of one million dollars per fighter. This million dollars would be used to cover medical, surgical, and hospital care for the treatment of life-threatening brain injuries in situations where an identifiable causal link exists between the fighter's participation in a fight and the life-threatening brain injury. For all other fight-related medical costs, a $50,000 insurance policy is required. This insurance requirement took effect on September 1.

The million-dollar insurance requirement is not practical. It was a classic case of leap before you look. The cost of premiums will make it impossible to promote most fight cards in New York on a cost-efficient basis.

UFC was able to secure a state-approved policy for UFC 205 through AIG (its regular insurance carrier in Nevada). But the cost of the policy exceeded $40,000; more than eight times the amount that boxing promoters are accustomed to paying for medical insurance in New York.

Moreover, as autumn passed, no insurance carrier had submitted a proposed policy satisfactory to the State of New York insofar as the million-dollar minimum coverage for boxing was concerned. That led Lou DiBella to declare, "It's unthinkable that this law was passed when no policy was available. How do you enact a law where there is no legal way for an industry to abide by it? Something incomprehensible went on here."

Meanwhile, boxing disappeared from New York.

On October 3, Star Boxing (Joe DeGuardia's promotional company) announced that it was canceling fight cards previously slated to take place in New York for the rest of the year. "Currently there isn't any insurance policy approved by the State," DeGuardia's statement read. "Therefore, the cost is currently irrelevant as there is no legal way to hold a professional boxing match in New York as the insurance required by the new regulation cannot be purchased at the present time. Star Boxing plans to move its events to venues outside of the State of New York until, when, and if this situation is corrected."

Golden Boy and Roc Nation also abandoned plans to promote fight cards in New York.

Lou DiBella weighed in further as follows: "I have been extremely active promoting shows in New York. But at this time, I have moved all of my shows to other states for the foreseeable future. I couldn't do a show in New York if I wanted to, as no insurance required by the new law and regulations currently exists. The State of New York has, at least temporarily, crippled the boxing industry. They are depriving young New York athletes, as well as managers and promoters, of their livelihoods. This is doing nothing to improve the health and safety of fighters. In fact, the reverse is true. Local fighters are forced to leave the state to fight in other jurisdictions. None of them have the insurance requirements in a law, supposedly written to allow MMA in our state, that disproportionately affects and hurts boxers and the boxing business. More importantly, the majority of these states require minimal medical safeguards and testing. The State of New York has actually detrimentally affected fighter safety."

Then, on October 28, DiBella issued a press release that read, "DiBella Entertainment has released its dates on hold with the New York State Athletic Commission through the end of the year, effectively ending the boxing program in New York until at least 2017. This announcement is a direct result of New York's new insurance requirements, which have made it impossible for promoters to purchase the coverage necessary to do an event in the state, and the New York State Athletic Commission's failure to use its authority to alter the requirements."

Fans of the sweet science have now gone four months without a professional boxing card in New York.

DiBella hopes to end this drought. He's now planning to co-promote a card at Barclays Center with Mayweather Promotions on January 14, 2017, and believes that, because Mayweather Promotions is a Nevada-based corporation, it can get a policy from a Nevada insurer approved by the State of Nevada that will be acceptable to New York. DiBella estimates that the premium for this policy would exceed $40,000 and expects that Barclays would defray half the cost.

As an alternative, the New York Department of Financial Services recently approved the basics of a policy with United States Fire Insurance Company as the carrier that, if finalized, would address the million-dollar insurance minimum, carry a deductible of $500 per fighter, and cost $830 per fighter. This policy grew out of an insurance program created by The Wellington Group and SportsInsurance.com.

The Wellington Group is a small New York City insurance broker that was founded in 2015. Its online description reads in part, "The Wellington Group is leading the industry in offering insurance services for our clients who are in the cannabis business." Joe Charles is its principal and CEO.

SportsInsurance.com facilitated Wellington's dealings with Crum & Forster (the parent company of United States Fire Insurance Company). On December 15, Mark DiPerno (president of SportsInsurance.com) told this writer, "The surprise factor made this more difficult. The New York State legislature went ahead and produced this million-dollar requirement but neglected to inform the insurers that it was coming, so everyone was left flat-footed. No one was working toward resolution of the issue. The first problem we had when it came to our attention was finding an insurer who was even willing to go down this road."

To that, Laurence Cole (whose company brokers insurance policies for combat sports throughout the country) adds, "I can broker a medical insurance policy with $50,000 coverage per fighter with a $500 deductible per fighter and a $100,000 death benefit per fighter and it will cost the promoter about $4,100 for a ten bout card. Add on New York's million-dollar requirement for life-threatening brain injuries and you're looking at a minimum of four times that amount. We told the commission in 2015 when the matter was first discussed that this would be cost-prohibitive for most boxing cards in New York; that it would end all the small fight cards and put most small promoters out of business in New York."

There will be other costs as well.

"Certain things still have to be established," Mark DiPerno acknowledges. "We'll need complete baseline testing before every fight to ascertain whether a pre-existing condition contributed to a problem."

That would add to the promoter's costs since, under the recently passed New York legislation, the promoter rather than the state now pays for fighter medical examinations. The promoter will also be responsible for all medical costs that fall within the deductible.

Thus, Lou DiBella says, "The January 14 fight card [at Barclays Center] will happen. The bigger problem is that the issue isn't solved. Broadway Boxing [DiBella's New York City club fight series] is out of business. Joe DeGuardia's shows are out of business. Local fighters who would normally be developed in New York are out of business and have nowhere to go for fights. Dmitry Salita [Star of David Promotions] has taken his shows out of New York. I want to know how this happens; a law that, in effect, stops boxing in the state. Why and how? Who did this? Something's not right."

Other promoters are in accord:

★ Joe DeGuardia: "It is ridiculous that our elected officials have not corrected this absurdity. It is a travesty that deprives New York boxers, as well as managers, trainers, promoters, and venue employees of their livelihoods."

★ Eric Gomez (president of Golden Boy Promotions): "It's a huge concern. I hope it changes."

★ Bob Arum: "Boxing is in a crisis position in the State of New York, and we must find a way to resolve the insurance issue before we can go back to presenting boxing events to the fans in New York."

★ Richard Schaefer: "I think anybody in boxing would agree that it's a bit of a mess there."

On November 16, Brooklyn borough president Eric Adams joined the fray, declaring, "Too many people pass legislation and are focused on the paper it's written on instead of the people who are impacted by it. New York State is the Empire State, where we build empires instead of destroying them, and we are destroying the empire of boxing in New

York. That cannot happen. We are going to mobilize and move in the right direction."

But there's no guarantee that a solution will be forthcoming. On December 16, Tony Giardina told this writer, "I'm working with what we have. I've heard that the smaller cards will have a difficult time or that it will be impossible to promote them. But institutions adapt, and the end result is often less bad than the most dire predictions. I don't see any change in the million-dollar requirement until there is a solid factual basis for making a change. We're not there yet on the data."

New York State Assembly leader Joseph Morelle (who co-sponsored the bill to legalize professional MMA in New York) told Amy Dash of BloodyElbow.com that he would face an uphill battle in the state legislature if he tried to lower the insurance requirement. Instead, he pointed to a provision in the law that provides, "The commission may from time to time, promulgate regulations to adjust the amount of such minimum [insurance] limits."

In Morelle's words, "The state athletic commission could now say, 'Well, this is not affordable for small promoters, and so we are going to make an adjustment to the coverage.' That is allowed in the law, and hopefully they will begin to have that conversation."

But Jim Leary (counsel for the NYSAC) points to the last section of the law, which states, "Within twelve months of the effective date of this section, the state athletic commission shall make any recommendations to the governor, temporary president of the senate, and speaker of the assembly regarding legislative changes which may be necessary to effectuate the purpose and intent of this chapter, including, but not limited to, appropriate adjustments to the insurance requirements contained therein."

In Leary's view, this indicates that the NYSAC can't unilaterally adjust the million-dollar insurance minimum.

Meanwhile, DiBella declares, "Andrew Cuomo and legislators from both parties in Albany got the campaign contributions from UFC that they wanted. I don't think there's a coincidence that a law to enable UFC to be legal in New York passed and that in effect killed boxing. I don't believe in accidents. I don't hate on MMA and UFC, and I don't begrudge what they're trying to do. But in effect, they put an entire sport out of business. Apparently 2.2 million dollars of lobbying money and countless campaign contributions can cripple small businesses to the advantage of one multi-billion dollar company. Apparently, alleged health and safety concerns can mask the desire to minimize competition and a fair marketplace. I hope that this becomes evident to United States attorney Preet Bharara."

DiBella's reference to the health and safety concerns of the powers that be as "alleged" is not entirely without merit.

The statute passed by the state legislature requires the promoters of professional combat sports in New York to provide insurance for medical, surgical, and hospital care with a minimum limit of one million dollars "for the treatment of a life-threatening brain injury sustained in a program operated under the control of such licensed promoter, where an identifiable causal link exists between the professional licensee's participation in such program and the life-threatening brain injury."

However, the rules and regulations recently enacted by the New York State Athletic Commission appear to contravene the statute. More specifically, the commission has chosen to define "life-threatening brain injury" as "an acute brain injury that, in the opinion of the professional licensee's treating physician, WOULD result in the death of the professional licensee if left untreated" (emphasis added).

Again, the statute says "life-threatening." The rules and regulations promulgated by the NYSAC define "life-threatening" in a manner that, on its face, is inconsistent with the statute. And the insurance policy recently approved by the New York State Department of Financial Services tracks the language of the rules and regulations, not the statute.

Paul Edelstein is the lead attorney for the family of Magomed Abdusalamov, who suffered horrifying brain damage as a consequence of his participation in a November 2, 2013, fight at Madison Square Garden. The Abdusalamov tragedy set in motion the inspector general's investigation of the NYSAC, which in turn led to a report by the inspector general that detailed incompetence and corruption at the commission.

Edelstein makes it clear just how much of a con the million-dollar insurance minimum is.

"One million dollars is a nice big round number," Edelstein says. "But it's illusory. The chances of a policy being triggered to pay off above the

$50,000-limit are slim. What you're going to have in most instances is, the carrier will deny coverage. If there are $90,000 worth of tests and no surgery, it won't be covered above $50,000 under the rules and regulations because the fighter survived without surgery. And if surgery is necessary, the carrier will say, 'Well, you don't know that the patient would have died without the surgery.' There have been instances of a serious subdural hemotoma where the patient has survived without surgery. So suppose the doctor says, 'He might live without surgery; he might die without surgery. I just don't know.' The million-dollar requirement we're talking about now is close to useless."

Tony Giardina characterizes Edelstein's statement as "inflammatory." When asked, "What should have been done differently with regard to the insurance issue?" Giardina answers, "The state athletic commission is responsible for carrying out the mandate of the state legislature, and we're doing that in the best possible way. The commission is part of an administration. I don't see anything else that the commission should have done."

But let's get real. If someone has lung cancer, the doctors can't say with certainty that the patient will die from it. But they treat the cancer. Can any sane person fathom a medical insurance policy that only covers treatment for lung cancer if the doctors say that, without treatment, the patient will die as a consequence of the cancer?

To make the point again: The recently enacted New York statute does not give the NYSAC the right to weaken the insurance requirement by disingenuously narrowing the definition of "life-threatening" to the point where many life-threatening situations aren't covered. Whether or not the commission can unilaterally lower the million-dollar insurance minimum itself is an open issue.

The justification often cited by Governor Cuomo, state legislators, and NYSAC personnel for their decisions with regard to these issues is twofold: (1) the advent of MMA will boost the economy of the State of New York, and (2) we're doing this for the health and safety of the fighters. But given the havoc wreaked, one has to consider the possibility that their real motivation hasn't been how much money MMA will contribute to the economy of the State of New York but rather how much money UFC has contributed to campaign committees working on behalf of Andrew Cuomo and various New York State legislators.

On December 16, Giardina was asked, "To what extent is Governor Cuomo aware of the insurance issue?"

"He's very aware of it as far as we know," Giardina answered.

And regarding the health and safety of fighters, one might consider the thoughts of UFC cover girl Ronda Rousey (one of the most proficient and famous mixed martial artists in the world).

Talking about her trademark armbar maneuver in her autobiography—*My Fight, Your Fight*—Rousey explained, "When you do the armbar, the aim is to put so much pressure on the person's arm that you pop the joint out of the socket. You can feel it when it pops. It's like ripping the leg off a Thanksgiving turkey. You hear it pop-pop-pop, then squish."

Then, describing her use of an armbar against Miesha Tate, Rousey recounted, "Pulling her arm straight, I arched back until I felt the squish, her ligaments snapping between my legs. She was still trying to escape. I grabbed her hand and pushed it over the side of my hip, forcing her elbow to go more than ninety degrees in the wrong direction. I ripped off muscles from her bone and tendons. With a vice on her injured arm, I sat up to punch her in the face with my other hand. With her elbow fully dislocated, there was nothing holding her in that position anymore except the pain and her fear of me."

So much for the health and safety of fighters.

And on top of that, Lou DiBella states, "The last two catastrophic head injuries that occurred in New York boxing matches were directly related to mistakes by state-appointed officials and failures by political appointees and their personnel to abide by their already existing protocols and directives. Fix yourselves. Don't scapegoat athletes and a sport that is ingrained in the history and fabric of your state."

In theory, policy decisions at the NYSAC are made by its commissioners and then implemented by the commission staff. Traditionally, the NYSAC had three commissioners (one of whom was designated as chairperson). The April 2016 legislation that legalized professional mixed martial arts competition in New York increased the number of NYSAC commissioners from three to five.

NYSAC commissioners are appointed by the governor subject to approval by the state senate.

Eight months after they were created, the two new commissioner slots have yet to be filled, which says something about Andrew Cuomo's priorities as they relate to the NYSAC. Two of the commissioners—John Signorile and Edwin Torres—are serving pursuant to terms that expired one and two years ago respectively. The third sitting commissioner—Ndidi Massay—was appointed in June of this year and is currently serving as interim chairperson.

The New York State Athletic Commission says that everyone at the commission cares deeply about the health and safety of fighters. On Saturday, October 8, the commission held a seminar on medical issues that was attended by a dozen ring physicians. The seminar began at 9:30 a.m. and ran until 5:00 p.m.

How many of the three commissioners sat in for the entire seminar? None.

One of the doctors in attendance says that Ndidi Massay was there "for the last hour or two," while John Signorile and Edwin Torres weren't there at all.

On Saturday, October 15, the NYSAC conducted a seminar for inspectors that ran from 10:30 a.m. to 3:30 p.m. Massay and Torres did not attend.

On the evening of Wednesday, November 2, the NYSAC held a preparation session at the Renzo Gracie Gym for deputy commissioners and inspectors who had been assigned to the November 12 UFC event at Madison Square Garden. The session lasted approximately ninety minutes. None of the three commissioners was there.

On fight night, Massay and Signorile arrived at Madison Square Garden after UFC 205 had begun. Torres didn't attend the show at all.

A review of the November 9, 2016, meeting of the NYSAC is instructive.

Kim Sumbler (the commission's MMA project coordinator) proposed implementing a multi-tiered pay scale for referees and judges on MMA fights based on purse amount. At present, some jurisdictions have a pay scale keyed to the size of the venue. Others pay a flat rate.

Massay responded, "I'm a little concerned about creating policy like this. No one else does it on purses. Are we gonna be, you know, what's the public gonna think? Let's take the haters out there. How are we gonna get criticized on this? What are they gonna say? I wanna be prepared for any negative backlash."

At that point, Massay was reminded that there was a live video stream of the meeting.

Then Tony Giardina observed, "If you think about the parties who are going to be interested here, it's pretty much the promoters because they have to pay the fees and you have the officials themselves. The general public isn't going to be even necessarily aware. I guess it's public information because of open meetings and so on, but I don't think it's something that they're going to be concerned about. We've reached out to the promoters and we've reached out to the officials, and they're comfortable with using purse size."

The proposal was approved.

Also at the November 9, 2016, NYSAC meeting, Edwin Torres (1) complained that a sample MMA glove didn't fit properly (he had it on the wrong hand); and (2) listened to a discussion of guidelines for suturing a fighter's cuts and asked, "Why would anybody allow the application of sutures in the middle of a fight?"

The suture guidelines attracted public notice after UFC's second show in New York (a December 10 fight card in Albany). As reported by Marc Raimondi of MMAFighting.com, multiple UFC fighters and coaches complained that, in a departure from past protocol, NYSAC officials would not let doctors stitch fighters up in the arena and required that they be transported by ambulance to a nearby hospital where they had to wait as long as four hours for the procedure to be completed.

In mid-September of this year, Ndidi Massay told George Willis of the *New York Post*, "I'm confident boxing and MMA will thrive in the State of New York with the team we have."

The team they have?

The interim executive director is just that. Interim. Four of the five commissioner seats are open for appointment. The state needs to train a whole new generation of referees and judges. The commission has some highly qualified inspectors and others you wouldn't send out to buy coffee because they'd bring back tea.

It's not surprising that Lou DiBella states, "The people in charge at the commission now are a bad joke. They're puppets; that's all. Do you think that Ndidi Massay, John Signorile, and Edwin Torres actually sat down and had an intelligent discussion about the million-dollar insurance requirement before they approved a set of rules and regulations that are destroying boxing in New York? Because if you do, you're a fucking moron. And if any of the commissioners disagrees with what I just said, let them sit down in a public forum for a question and answer session on the record with the promoters they're putting out of business. I'm not talking about a press release from the commission or a statement that someone gives to a shill reporter saying how much Ndidi Massay cares about the health and safety of fighters. I'm talking about honest answers to questions about the mess that Andrew Cuomo and his puppets at the commission have made. But you know that none of the commissioners will do it. Because if they did, they'd be exposed as a bunch of know-nothing political hacks."

In the past—at least in theory—key NYSAC staff employees were appointed by the commissioners. Now, under recently enacted guidelines, the Department of State (not the commissioners) appoints the NYSAC executive director, all deputy commissioners, and other staff personnel.

Taking the power of appointment away from the commissioners and giving it to the secretary of state was an acknowledgment that the commissioners were failing to carry out that portion of their responsibilities in an appropriate manner. A rational solution to this problem would have been to appoint competent knowledgable commissioners. Instead, the power of appointment has been given to a highly politicized department of government whose leaders know virtually nothing about combat sports.

Eric Bentley is currently serving well as the NYSAC's director of boxing. Kim Sumbler is knowledgable regarding mixed martial arts. But multiple sources say that Ndidi Massay has been sniping at Sumbler and that Sumbler has complained to them that the commission is letting politics interfere with the appointment of inspectors for MMA.

The appointment of deputy commissioners has, in at least one instance, also raised eyebrows. In May of this year, Bentley sent an e-mail to all inspectors saying that the NYSAC was looking for "qualified deputy commissioners" and enclosing a link that inspectors could click on if they were interested in applying for the job. Individuals from outside the commission were also encouraged to apply.

Some very capable people were passed over for the open deputy commissioner positions. One person who was hired was Mario Mercado.

Mercado is well spoken and personable. He was first hired by the NYSAC in April 2014 as an athletic activities assistant. A February 4, 2015, memorandum written by David Berlin (then NYSAC executive director) details concerns that Berlin had regarding Mercado's job performance and what Berlin viewed as Mercado's tendency to play fast and loose with the truth. The memorandum also references the claim (corroborated by a source still at the NYSAC) that Mercado had used his state-issued credit card for personal expenses, most notably a charge of approximately $500 incurred at a Manhattan restaurant.

Mercado resigned from the commission on February 17, 2015, which, according to a person familiar with the proceedings, was one day before he was going to be dismissed.

On October 15, 2016, Mercado was rehired by the Department of State as a NYSAC deputy commissioner.

It might be that there's an innocent explanation for Mercado's previous conduct. But the NYSAC declined to make him available to be interviewed for this article.

Tony Giardina was interviewed by telephone on December 16. Jim Leahy (counsel for the NYSAC) and Department of State spokesperson Laz Benitez were teleconferenced into the call.

Giardina was asked, "What is the official policy with regard to state athletic commission personnel who use their state credit card for personal expenses?"

"You can't do that," Giardina answered. "No commission employee who has a state credit card can use that credit card for anything other than commission purposes."

There was a follow-up question: "Has the New York State Athletic Commission had to deal with this issue in the past two years?"

At that point, there was a conversation between Giardina, Benitez, and Leary that this writer wasn't privy to. Then Giardina came back on the telephone.

"I'm not comfortable going down this line of questioning," he said.

Meanwhile, on November 17, 2016, New York State inspector general Catherine Leahy Scott issued a press release trumpeting the fact that former NYSAC chairman Tom Hoover had entered into an agreement with the state pursuant to which he had agreed to pay a $2,000 fine for admitted ethics violations.

In part, the press release declared, "The former Athletic Commission chairman's use of his government appointment to reward family and friends with free event tickets and inappropriate job opportunities helped illustrate his skewed priorities and the clear dysfunction previously at the Commission's top levels. Today's settlement, with its included admission of wrongdoing, helps emphasize how imperative it is that all commissioners and staff adhere to only the highest standards of professionalism and ethical conduct."

Perhaps Catherine Leahy Scott's next press release regarding the New York State Athletic Commission can explain the hows and whys of Mario Mercado's appointment as a deputy commissioner. A representative of the inspector general's office has already contacted the NYSAC to inquire about the matter.

The new leadership at the New York State Athletic Commission is entitled to a grace period within which it fixes the many problems that plague the commission. It's not entitled to a grace period during which it makes things worse. Meanwhile, a crucial test is fast approaching. Andrew Cuomo is expected to designate four NYSAC commissioners shortly after the first of the year.

Governor Cuomo has been on the right side of many issues. If he's truly concerned about good government and the health and safety of fighters, he'll appoint smart, hardworking, conscientious, ethical men and women who have an understanding of combat sports and a record of excellence in their past professional endeavors to the commission. These appointees should not be beholden in any way to the people they regulate, nor should they be advocates for a particular interest group (such as UFC).

The governor can no longer claim ignorance of the issues involved and the problems currently facing the New York State Athletic Commission. They've been too widely reported upon for that. Nor will a flurry of press releases extolling the virtues of the governor's nominees cover up the nature of his appointments if the appointees are mediocre.

Either Andrew Cuomo is serious about good government or he isn't. The people he appoints as NYSAC commissioners will tell us whether he cares more about political gamesmanship or doing the job right.

2016 marked the passing of three men who defined their sport: Muhammad Ali, Gordie Howe, and Arnold Palmer.

A Note on Arnold Palmer

All great athletes are physically gifted, work hard at their craft, and are fierce competitors. But great athletes are not necessarily great sportsmen. Arnold Palmer, who died on September 25, 2016, at age eighty-seven, was both.

Palmer was one of the greatest golfers of all time. More significantly, he brought golf to the masses. And with the guidance of sports marketing entrepreneur Mark McCormack, he redefined the economics of sports.

Before Palmer, off-the-field income for an athlete generally meant opening a steakhouse in his hometown. If an athlete landed a footwear endorsement, he might be paid $500 and receive a dozen pairs of shoes. McCormack sold corporate America on the idea that companies could build product brands around Palmer as a symbol of excellence. For thirty consecutive years (1961 through 1990), Arnold was the highest-grossing athlete in the world in endorsement income.

I met Palmer in December 1992 when I was asked by his representatives at IMG if I wanted to write a book about him. I'd previously authored *Muhammad Ali: His Life and Times*, which was on the *New York Times* bestseller list. That had led to a flurry of offers from other athletes.

Palmer was special. I wanted to tell his story.

Arnold was "everyman" in an elitist sport. From corporate boardrooms to the steel towns of Pennsylvania, people saw what they wanted to see in him.

As I wrote in the preface to *Arnold Palmer: A Personal Journey*, "Palmer epitomizes The American Dream and mirrors what Americans like to think of themselves. He's bold, charismatic, a bit impatient, a winner; a man who identifies with his home town, has been married to the same woman for 39 years, succeeds at everything he has ever done, and still seems like a regular guy. Palmer is every mother's loving son and every man's best friend. He's the boy next door with the all-American smile, confident but not arrogant, reassuring and fun."

"In the early 1960s," I continued, "Palmer seemed to blend with images of John F. Kennedy, excitement, and youth. Then the decade turned violent. America was torn apart by political assassinations, urban riots, and Vietnam. But 'Arnie' remained 'Arnie' and resisted the tide. Athletes like Bill Russell, Jim Brown, and Arthur Ashe challenged what they believed was wrong with the prevailing American orthodoxy. Palmer continued to personify everything that he and middle America thought was right. At a time when Muhammad Ali refused induction into the United States Army, and John Carlos and Tommie Smith marked the 1968 Olympics with upraised fists, Palmer continued to evoke images of America the way Dwight Eisenhower, Norman Rockwell, and John Wayne wanted it to be. And the qualities that led millions of people to think of him as 'The Quintessential American' endure to this day. Very few athletes hold onto their humility when they become great and retain their magic when they grow old. Palmer has done both."

Arthur Klebanoff was the head of IMG's literary agency in the early 1990s.

"I should warn you," Klebanoff told me before my first meeting with Palmer. "Arnold can't stand Muhammad Ali."

Palmer hadn't met Ali at that time although they shared many traits. Each man had been an elite athlete who transformed his sport. Each man was remarkably charismatic. Arnold, like Muhammad, was a people person. I can't imagine Arnold being rude to a waiter, a cab driver, or a fan.

But Palmer had issues of principle with Ali. Arnold had served in the United States Coast Guard from 1950 to 1953 and didn't like Muhammad's refusal to be inducted into the United States Army. He was also at odds with the segregationalist teachings of the Nation of Islam that Ali adhered to in the 1960s.

But what aggravated Palmer most about Ali was Muhammad's mouth as it related to the field of play. Ali's bragging about how great he was and the way he demeaned some of his opponents offended Arnold's sense of sportsmanship.

Fast forward to June 1993. The Smithsonian Institution was honoring five great athletes who had helped shape modern America: Ali, Palmer,

Kareem Abdul-Jabbar, Chris Evert, and Ted Williams. The celebration extended over a long weekend and included a White House reception, a formal dinner, and an awards ceremony attended by Bill Clinton.

Palmer was an accomplished pilot and fascinated by aviation. He'd taken his first flying lesson in 1956 and began soloing two years later. On the Saturday afternoon that we were in Washington, DC, for the Smithsonian celebration, Arnold asked if I'd like to visit the Smithsonian Air and Space Museum with him.

There was no entourage. Just the two of us. We walked into the museum like any other visitors. Most of our conversation that afternoon revolved around aviation. Among its many treasures, the museum houses the *Wright Flyer* from Wilbur and Orville Wright's 1903 flight at Kitty Hawk; the *Spirit of St. Louis*, which Charles Lindbergh flew in the first solo trans-Atlantic crossing in 1927; and the command module *Columbia* from the 1969 Apollo 11 moon landing.

I asked Palmer, if he could have been part of any one of those three missions, which would he choose. His answer surprised me. Given Arnold's swashbuckling nature, I thought he'd opt for Lindbergh's solo flight. Instead, he told me, "Definitely, the moon landing. The technology behind it fascinates me."

We also talked about Ali. Arnold was particularly interested in knowing whether Muhammad's Parkinson's syndrome affected his cognitive abilities. I assured him that, at the time, there were no intellectual deficits. When we got back to the hotel, Palmer told me that he'd like to meet Ali. I made the introduction. They chatted briefly and were together again later that day in a meeting with Bill Clinton at the White House.

"Muhammad Ali seems like a nice man," Arnold told me afterward. "I like him."

Arnold Palmer loved his life. And he loved being Arnold Palmer. With the possible exception of Babe Ruth, no athlete ever did as much for a sport as Palmer did for golf. He had a reverence for the game, a remarkable camaraderie with his fellow golfers, and a generous spirit toward the public. He was the perfect representative for golf in his time.

Every death is of significance to those who are directly affected by it. The enor-
mity of Muhammad Ali's life was reflected in the fact that the entire world
mourned his passing.

A Letter from Angelo Dundee

Dear Tom,

I thought I'd write and bring you up to date on what's been happening here in heaven.

Things are good and, usually, peaceful and serene. After all, this is
heaven. Then Ali got here.

What a scene. Fifty-two years ago, Ali shook up the world. Now he's
shaking up paradise.

The first person Ali saw was his mother. Years ago, Muhammad told a
group of students, "My mother was a Baptist. She believed Jesus was the
son of God, and I don't believe that. But even though my mother had a
religion different from me, I believe that, on Judgment Day, my mother
will be in heaven."

Ali's mother was laughing and crying when she saw him and saying
over and over, "My baby! My baby!" He hugged her for a long time.

Most people get here and, after seeing their family, they want to
meet Abraham Lincoln, Winston Churchill, Nelson Mandela, Gandhi,
Michelangelo, Shakespeare, or some great religious leader. After Ali finished hugging his mother, he started signing autographs and posing for
selfies with fans. He did that for hours. I think he set a record for most
autographs signed by a person on his first day in heaven.

"It's just like on earth," Ali said.

The first famous person Ali asked to see was Malcolm X. When
Malcolm broke with Elijah Muhammad in 1964, Ali sided with Elijah.
He believed that Malcolm was wrong and Elijah was God's Messenger.

"I didn't do right by you," Ali told Malcolm when they reunited in
a grove of olive trees. "What you saw was right. Color don't make a man
a devil. It's the heart, soul, and mind that count."

"I'm proud of what you accomplished," Malcolm said as he and
Muhammad embraced. "You're still my little brother."

Later in the day, Ali got together with Joe Louis. Right away, Ali asked Joe, "Did Sonny Liston get here?"

"He had some trouble," Joe said. "But they finally let him in."

Ali and Sonny had dinner together that night.

"You scared me bad," Ali told him.

At one point, Joe Frazier came over to the table to say hello.

"I forgive you," Joe told Ali. "But I still want to fight you again."

Ali told Joe that he'd done enough fighting on earth and wanted to lead a more peaceful life in paradise.

That night, Ali and I talked about the outpouring of love that swept the world when he passed. Ali's eyes got wide and he blurted out, "Man! That was big! It was bigger than for Elvis."

Twenty years ago, Ali proclaimed, "I believe, if you're a good Muslim, if you're a good Christian, if you're a good Jew; it doesn't matter what religion you are, if you're a good person you'll receive God's blessing. Muslims, Christians, and Jews all serve the same God. We just serve him in different ways. Anyone who believes in One God should also believe that all people are part of one family. God created us all."

Ali told me he's happy to see that people of all races, religions, and creeds are in paradise. If you see a particularly pretty star in the sky tonight, that's the twinkle in Ali's eye.

Meanwhile, yesterday, Ali walked into a gym where some kids were training. These are boys who died young and never had the chance to box on earth. Ali taught them some moves, did the Ali shuffle, hit the heavy bag for a while. They loved him. And there was a gleam in his eye.

I knew what was coming.

"Does Joe Frazier really want to fight me?"

"I think he does," I said.

"Doesn't Joe know this ain't the Ali he fought before? This ain't the Ali he fought at Madison Square Garden. This ain't the Ali he fought in Manila. I got my legs back. My reflexes are sharp. I'm prettier and faster than ever. Slow-movin' Joe Frazier wants to fight me? Let me think about it."

This should be fun.

Best always,
Angelo

For more than fifty years, Howard Bingham and Muhammad Ali were inseparable.

Howard Bingham: A Remembrance

Howard Bingham, who died on December 15, 2016, was Muhammad
Ali's truest, most trusted, loyal friend.

Bingham was born in Jackson, Mississippi, on May 29, 1939. For most
of his life, he was a freelance photographer. Over the decades, he took
more than five hundred thousand photos of Ali. If Muhammad was Don
Quixote, then Howard was his Sancho Panza.

Years ago, Bingham told me how his relationship with Ali began.

"I was with a black newspaper in Los Angeles called *The Sentinel*,"
Howard reminisced. "My assignment that day was to cover Ali at a news
conference to announce an [April 23, 1962] fight at the Los Angeles
Sports Arena against George Logan. I'd never heard of Cassius Clay, which
was his name at the time. But I went to the news conference, introduced
myself, took a couple of photos, and left. Then, that afternoon, I was
driving downtown and saw these two guys on the corner of Fifth and
Broadway, Cassius Clay and his brother Rudolph. I asked if they wanted
a ride someplace because it looked like they were waiting for a bus, and
they said no. They were just watching the girls go by. So I asked if they'd
like to take a ride with me. They got in the car, and I had some errands
to do. Then I took them by a bowling alley, to my mother's house, and a
couple of other places, and we hit it off good."

"That was in the spring," Bingham continued. "Ali came back to Los
Angeles a couple of months later to fight Alejandro Lavorante, and then
again at the end of the year for Archie Moore. Both times, I showed him
around. He and Angelo offered me money to be a press secretary or guide
and I did all that stuff, but I never took the money. It wasn't something I
wanted to get paid for. As far as I was concerned, we were friends. Then,
on New Year's Day 1963, Ali called me up and asked if I wanted to come
to Miami and hang out with him for a while. I said yeah. I'd never been
on an airplane before. I arrived in Miami on a Sunday night. Ali met me
at the airport, and the next morning we drove to Louisville to his parents'

home. After that, we went to Pittsburgh, where he had a fight against Charlie Powell. I'd never been in cold weather before, so he bought me earmuffs, an overcoat, and long underwear."

I met Howard Bingham in 1988. Muhammad had married Lonnie Williams two years earlier. There was talk of a new biography that would update Ali's life story and correct errors propagated by a faux autobiography—*The Greatest: My Own Story*—that had been ghost-written by Richard Durham and published in 1976. My name had come up as a prospective biographer. I was in Los Angeles on a business trip. Howard met me at the Beverly Wilshire Hotel to check me out. Apparently, I passed the test because, in October 1988, I was called to a meeting in New York with Muhammad and Lonnie.

Muhammad Ali: His Life and Times followed. Howard was crucial to the researching and writing of the book. He set up interviews, educated me on the nuances of Ali's life, and defended me against attacks from Herbert Muhammad (Ali's former manager, who was trying to torpedo the project because he didn't have a financial interest in the book or control over it). Howard was my guardian angel.

When the first draft of manuscript was complete, Muhammad, Lonnie, Howard, and I gathered at the Alis' home in Berrien Springs, Michigan, to read every word aloud. By agreement, there was to be no censorship. The purpose of our reading was to ensure that the book was factually accurate. Lonnie and I did all the reading with one exception.

I had told Muhammad that I wanted to dedicate the book to Howard.

Ali was pleased. "I'm glad you understand how good Howard is," he said.

On day one of our reading, I asked Muhammad to read the dedication.

Ali stood up, cleared his throat, and very clearly read, "For Howard Bingham, there's no one like him."

"That's a joke, right?" Howard said.

Muhammad shook his head and showed Howard the dedication page. Howard began to cry.

Later that day, we came to a quote in the manuscript that put the dedication in context.

"Everybody says I love people," Muhammad's tribute to his friend read. "So it's only fair that I have the best friend in the world, and that's Howard Bingham. He never asks for anything. He's always there when

someone needs him. There's no one like him. He's the best there is. And
if you write that, I don't want Howard to think I'm getting soft, so write
down that he's lucky I'm his friend too. And tell him I said I'm the only
person in the world who likes him."

The end game for Howard wasn't pretty. His final years were spent
in an assisted living facility because of cognitive issues. Doctors removed
a brain tumor and most of his colon. In April of this year, his oldest son,
Damon, died. On June 3, Ali left this world to join the immortals.

Howard's bottom line was always what was best for Muhammad.
Wherever they are now, I hope they're together. ·

★ ★ ★

A word about the photograph on the back cover of this book . . .

When Howard Bingham died, the remembrance above was published
with that photograph. Since then, I've received a number of comments
regarding the photo, including one from Lonnie Ali, who wrote, "Oh my!
This photograph makes me cry."

The photo came about by accident rather than design.

While researching and writing *Muhammad Ali: His Life and Times*,
I spent considerable time in 1988, 1989, and 1990 at the Alis' home in
Berrien Springs, Michigan. Howard always joined us.

I realized early on that straightforward Q&A sessions wouldn't elicit
much new information from Muhammad. The best way to research was
to hang out with him, carry pen and paper at all times, and write down
whatever came my way. That might happen while we were watching
old Ali fights on television, talking about interviews I'd conducted for
the book, or simply conversing in the course of Muhammad's everyday
routine.

Muhammad was in his late forties then and healthier than he would
ever be again. He was having trouble coordinating the muscles he used in
speech, but was able to communicate well on most occasions. His physical
tremors were becoming more pronounced, but he was still stronger than
most men his age. He'd decided to get into better shape. That led to his
losing twenty pounds, in part by taking long walks each day.

I'm not a gifted photographer. Never was; never will be. But I thought
it would be nice to have some photos that memorialized my trips to

Berrien Springs. And I wanted a photo of Howard, who had become a friend. So I brought a disposable Kodak Instamatic camera with me on one of my visits.

On the day in question, Muhammad, Howard, and I went for a walk that lasted well over two hours. From time to time, I stopped to take notes. Muhammad and Howard would keep walking. When I finished writing, I'd run to catch up with them. In one of those moments, I liked the way that Muhammad and Howard looked together. So I snapped a photo from behind. More than a quarter-century later, the image still speaks to me.

Muhammad and Howard aren't touching, but there's a closeness between them. They're relaxed and comfortable with each other.

Howard is carrying two cameras. He always had cameras when he was with Muhammad, and most other times as well. Like the rest of us, Howard liked freebies. Thus, the jacket from the Mirage. He's physically strong and striding forward.

Muhammad had reached what was an ideal weight for him at that time in his life. But he no longer floated like a butterfly. His feet are close together and not well balanced as he walks. The phrase "Ali shuffle" has taken on new meaning. His shoulders are a bit stooped. Howard has become his protector.

Then as now, they're walking together into the unknown. In the words of Lonnie Ali, "The picture says it all. Best friends forever. I can see them in Heaven, walking together in the same way. Howard always at Muhammad's side, never leaving him to make the journey alone. Some pictures of Muhammad, I can't look at without becoming very emotional. This is one of them. I wish I could move time back to when this picture was taken and enjoy their company once more. I'd probably kiss Muhammad's cheeks raw and hug Howard so tight he couldn't breathe. My two best friends are gone."

Some additional thoughts on "The Greatest" . . .

Thoughts on the Passing of Muhammad Ali

January 17, 1942–June 3, 2016

> *Come on, death*
> *Bring it to me*
> *Take your best shot*
> *You ain't nothin'*
> *Come on, death*
> *How long you been tryin'?*
> *You can't beat me*
> *I'm immortal*

★ ★ ★

"They Look Like They're Happy Together"

In 1996, Muhammad Ali and I co-authored a short book about bigotry and prejudice that was keyed to religious and racial divisions. To spread the message, we visited schools in a half dozen cities across the country, talking with students about the need for tolerance and understanding. In February 1997, our journey brought us to Boston.

Muhammad and I had talked on several occasions about gay rights. I don't know how his views evolved in later years. In the mid-1990s, he believed that a gay lifestyle was at odds with the Qu'ran.

Ali and I were staying at the Ritz-Carlton Hotel in Boston. As we got out of the limousine that had taken us around the city, the customary crowd gathered around Muhammad. Then I heard the unexpected.

"Omigod! It's Tom Hauser."

The person who blurted out those words was Elizabeth Swados, a gifted playwright, director, and author whom I'd known in the early 1980s. Liz was with a friend, a woman named Roz Lichter. Muhammad signed autographs outside the hotel for a while. Then we invited Liz and Roz to join us inside.

I don't remember much about the conversation that the four of us had. I remember the aftermath clearly. It was obvious that Liz and Roz were coupled. After they left, Muhammad turned to me and asked, "They're lesbians, aren't they?"

"I assume so," I said.

A smile crossed Muhammad's face, the smile that the whole world fell in love with.

"They look like they're happy together," he told me.

The thought that Liz and Roz (whom he'd never met before and would never meet again) were happy pleased Muhammad. Ali wanted people to be happy. It was one of the reasons he gave as much of himself as he did. He loved the idea that, by giving someone a few seconds of his time, he could make that person happy.

I thought about that afternoon in Boston earlier this year when I read that Elizabeth Swados had died of complications stemming from esophageal cancer. The tributes were led by her wife, Roz Lichter.

Her wife!

That couldn't have happened two decades ago when Muhammad and Liz met.

I thought about it again on the morning of June 12, 2016, when, two days after Muhammad Ali was buried, I awoke to news of the horrifying mass murder at a gay nightclub in Orlando.

"They look like they're happy together."

What is it about that idea that the haters don't understand?

★ ★ ★

Twenty-five years have passed since *Muhammad Ali: His Life and Times* (my first writing about Ali) was published. Someone told me recently that the book has stood the test of time. My response was, "No! It was Ali who stood the test of time, and did so more successfully than any popular icon ever."

The world is a far different place now than it was a quarter-century ago. In sports, superstars have come and gone. Michael Jordan was replaced by Kobe Bryant, who was followed by LeBron James. Tiger Woods no longer sits upon his throne.

Ali himself receded from the spotlight after lighting the Olympic flame at the 1996 Olympics in Atlanta. New generations don't know the heady nature of what it once meant to be heavyweight champion of the world. Nor do they understand the social and political climate of the 1960s, when Ali was at his best as a fighter and his influence outside the ring was at its peak.

To fully appreciate Ali, one had to have lived through his time.

Yet Ali remained adored throughout the world. A real-life superhero, the champion of champions. And his legacy is vibrant. It can be seen in self-pride among oppressed people around the globe . . . In the belief that, unless there's a very good reason for killing, war is wrong . . . One can posit—and I believe it's true—that the acceptance by America of a black man with a Muslim name in the 1960s and 1970s paved the way for the election of Barack Obama in 2008.

The cornerstone of Ali's emergence onto the world stage was violence. But he was a warrior who became a messenger of peace. The measure of his life isn't in the massive number of celebrities and dignitaries who marked his passing. It's in the outpouring of love from hundreds of millions of common men and women who celebrated his having walked among us.

Very few people from the beginning of time have had a farewell like Ali.

Several years ago, I collaborated with a young author named Bart Barry on a project designed to introduce Ali to a new generation of Americans. I lived through Muhammad's glory years, traveled with him during and after the writing of *Muhammad Ali: His Life and Times*, and sat beside him on a sofa watching tapes of "The Rumble in the Jungle" and "The Thrilla in Manila." Bart had a different perspective. His appreciation of Ali was from a historical point of view. Yet we arrived at the same conclusion.

"Other fighters since Ali," we wrote, "have graced the sweet science of boxing and been great. More great fighters will follow. Someday, as surely as autumn leaves change color and fall to the ground, a young man will step in a boxing ring and be greater than Ali. But Muhammad Ali will always be The Greatest."

So let us turn to the literature of the ages in closing.

To Charles Dickens: "Man is but mortal. There is a point beyond which human courage cannot extend."

Muhammad Ali challenged that notion.

To Shakespeare.

"I saw him once," Horatio says of Hamlet's father. "He was a goodly King."

To which Hamlet responds, "He was a man. Take him for all in all. I shall not look upon his like again."

And to Peter Pan, when Captain Hook demands, "Who are you?"

"I am youth," the eternal boy answers. "I am joy. I am freedom."